UNDER THE
RED
FLAG

UNDER THE
RED
FLAG

A HISTORY OF COMMUNISM
IN BRITAIN, C. 1849–1991

KEITH LAYBOURN AND DYLAN MURPHY

SUTTON PUBLISHING

First published in 1999 by
Sutton Publishing Limited · Phoenix Mill
Thrupp · Stroud · Gloucestershire · GL5 2BU

British Library Cataloguing in Publication Data
A catalogue record for this book is available from the British Library

ISBN 0 7509 1485 8

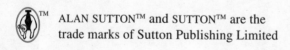
ALAN SUTTON™ and SUTTON™ are the
trade marks of Sutton Publishing Limited

Typeset in 10/14 pt Times.
Typesetting and origination by
Sutton Publishing Limited.
Printed in Great Britain by
Redwood Books, Trowbridge, Wiltshire.

To Julia Mary Laybourn and Jo Haley

CONTENTS

List of Plates

Between pp. 108 and 109

ACKNOWLEDGEMENTS

Many people have helped us in the development of the research and reading that led to the publication of this book. The formative influences of Jack Reynolds (1915–88), David Wright (1937–95) and David James (1944–95) have contributed to this volume. In addition, we must recognize Martin Crick and Martin White who have made many constructive suggestions on the history of Marxism in Britain over many years. We would also like to thank Steven Bird, Archivist at the National Museum of Labour History, Manchester, who allowed us access to the records of the Communist Party of Great Britain and Andrew Flynn, his assistant, whose knowledge of that archive was of immense help. We would also like to acknowledge the assistance of Philip Dunn, of the National Museum of Labour History, for access to and help with the Communist Party of Great Britain photographic archive, from which most of the images included in this book have been drawn. We would also like to acknowledge the help and advice given by staff at Sutton Publishing, most obviously the guidance of Christopher Feeney and Sarah Moore. The Crown copyright material is published by permission of the Controller of Her Majesty's Stationery Office. The authors and the publisher wish to apologize for any inadvertent infringement of copyright. Finally, we would also like to thank those veteran Party members, such as Geoff Hodgson, for their time and help in supplying local source materials.

ABBREVIATIONS

BSP	British Socialist Party
BUF	British Union of Fascists
CC	Central Committee (of the CPGB)
CI	Communist International (or Comintern)
CND	Campaign for Nuclear Disarmament
Cominform	Communist Information Bureau
Comintern	Communist (Third) International
CPB	Communist Party of Britain
CPGB	Communist Party of Great Britain
CPSU	Communist Party of the Soviet Union
CUG	Communist Unity Group
EC	Executive Committee (of the CPGB)
ECCI	Executive Committee of the Communist International
ETU	Electrical Trade Union
FSL	Fife Socialist League
ILP	Independent Labour Party
IS	International Socialists
IWMA	International Working Men's Association
JPC	Joint Production Committee
LCDTU	Liaison Committee for the Defence of Trade Unions
LRC	Labour Representation Committee
LWC	London Workers' Committee
NAC	National Administrative Committee (of the ILP)
NATO	North Atlantic Treaty Organization
NEC	National Executive Committee (of the Labour Party)
NLWM	National Left-Wing Movement
NMM	National Minority Movement
NSP	National Socialist Party
NUM	National Union of Mineworkers
NUWM	National Unemployed Workers' Movement
NUWCM	National Unemployed Workers' Committee Movement
PB	Political Bureau (of the CPGB)
PCE	Spanish Communist Party
POUM	Spanish Workers' Party of Marxist Unity
PPPS	People's Press Printing Society
Profintern	British Bureau of the Red International of Labour Unions
RCP	Revolutionary Communist Party
RILU	Red International of Labour Union (or Profintern)

SDC	Scottish District Council of the SDF
SDF	Social Democratic Federation
SDP	Social Democratic Party
SL	Socialist League
SLL	Socialist Labour League
SLP	Socialist Labour Party
SPGB	Socialist Party of Great Britain
SWMF	South Wales Miners' Federation
SWSS	South Wales Socialist Society
TGWU	Transport and General Workers' Union
TUC	Trades Union Congress
UMS	United Mineworkers of Scotland
USSR	Union of Soviet Socialist Republics
WSF	Workers' Socialist Federation
YCL	Young Communist League

INTRODUCTION

The Communist Party of Great Britain (CPGB) never captured the centre stage of British politics. It was formed in 1920 with about 3,000 members, peaked in the early 1940s with a membership of around 56,000 and expired in 1991 with just over 4,700 members.[1] It seems ironic, then, that the Party should still claim, at least up to the 1960s, that its principal objective was to form itself into a party of the masses when its chances of doing so were very poor. Whether as a revolutionary party up to the 1950s or as a party which believed over the last forty years of its existence that change could come through parliamentary action – as suggested in its *The British Road to Socialism* – it is clear that the CPGB had little more than a toe-hold on working-class support. That support was largely the preserve of the Labour Party through the trade unions until the mid-twentieth century. Even when the Labour Party relinquished some of its working-class membership in the 1970s the latter drifted over to the Conservatives, not the CPGB. Indeed, the Party was never able to attract working-class people away from its political competitors in any significant numbers. The main purpose of this book is to examine, in detail, the contours of the CPGB's history in order to explain why it was never able to secure a significant political presence.

The Historiography of Debate

There are two central questions in the history of the CPGB. The first is – why was the Party formed? In this debate there are those, such as Martin Crick, who point to the growth and development of Marxism in Britain from the arrival of both Marx and Engels in the country in 1849 through to the formation of the Social Democratic Federation (SDF) in 1883, and who suggest that many of the policies of earlier British Marxism were called upon when the CPGB was formed in 1920.[2] Crick and others maintain CPGB was the product of an indigenous revolutionary movement, if somewhat encouraged by events in Russia. However, this view is rejected by the many historians, including Raymond Challinor and Walter Kendall, who have written that it was Lenin who insisted upon British revolutionary socialist parties uniting together as the CPGB and that it was this factor alone which forced many organizations to overcome their differences.[3] Whether Lenin's influence was a good or bad thing is open to debate but it seems to have unified revolutionary socialist groups in a way that had not been accomplished before.

The second, and central question, is why did the CPGB not become the mass party of the working class which it sought to be? Indeed, if this were to be a wider study the question would be – why did the CPGB do so badly in comparison with other communist parties throughout the world? Many reasons have been put forward for the CPGB's disappointing performance, ranging from the poor economic conditions of the interwar years and the Stalinist degeneration of the Party to the suggestion that communism was alien to the British social and political system since it was dominated by Moscow. There is probably some truth in all these explanations but of much more importance may be the fact that the CPGB was formed too late to exert much influence on the trade union movement and to make good the connection that previous Marxist organizations had often neglected. Without the trade union movement the CPGB was unlikely to win the support of the working classes, and it is patently obvious that it gained few members from the working classes when compared with the Labour Party. Not surprisingly the CPGB was an immensely sectarian organization until near the end of its existence and it attempted to impose what many would now see as inappropriate policies on the British political tradition of compromise and radicalism.

The five main chapters in this book examine these two questions and investigate various themes and debates that have dominated the history of communism in Britain. The generic question they ask is – why was communism not more successful in Britain? This was the issue that dictated the twists and turns of the movement in Britain and inspired its various debates.

Marxist activity began in Britain in the mid-nineteenth century with the arrival of both Marx and Engels in 1849 but was not organized until the formation of the SDF and, to a lesser extent, the Socialist League in 1884. These developments are examined in Chapter One, where the difficulties of the SDF are analysed in relation to the limiting policies of Henry Mayers Hyndman, its leading figure, who eschewed trade union support and upset international socialists with his nationalistic policies. It has been suggested that his neglect of the institutions of the working class ensured that Marxism in Britain would falter while the 'independent' Labour Party attracted the support of some of the radical sections of the working class. However, despite the pre-First World War growth of the SDF (which became the Social Democratic Party and then the British Socialist Party), it is clear that its membership was still small when compared with other socialist parties, such as the Independent Labour Party (ILP), not to mention the Labour Party itself. Indeed, after the failure of the Socialist Unity campaign of 1911 to 1914 the British Socialist Party (BSP) (the old SDF) was forced to apply for affiliation to the Labour Party despite the opposition of Harry Quelch and other leading figures; affiliation was granted in 1916.

It was the First World War that changed the fortunes of the revolutionary Marxist groups in Britain and led to the formation of the CPGB. Lenin defined a new way forward for revolutionary socialists at the Zimmerwald anti-war conference in 1915, criticizing the social chauvinism of official socialism, 'the labour lieutenants of capitalism'. Lenin also saw the First World War as an imperialist war which signalled the end of world capitalism. The international social revolution was thus an immediate possibility and Lenin felt that the priority was to 'turn the imperialist war into civil war' and to hasten the military defeat of the revolutionaries' own state.[4] This was achieved in Russia in 1917 with the February and October revolutions, which paved the way for the formation of the Comintern and the creation of new communist parties in other countries. Whether these events led to the formation of the CPGB is not really open to question, although historians are divided about the extent to which it was either the British experience of the revolutions or Lenin that dictated its formation.

Chapter Two examines the above events. It also looks at the Class Against Class policies that attacked all social democratic parties including the reformist Labour Party; these policies were generated between 1928 and 1932 when Harry Pollitt was finally able to secure their relaxation in relation to trade unionism. What is evident throughout this period is that the Party was only able to secure limited support, even during the General Strike of 1926. The introduction of the Class Against Class policy by the Comintern in 1928 proved a disastrous development for the CPGB, which, as a result, had to break its connections with the Labour Party and the trade unions, and was forced to offer the rather amorphous and inconsequential Workers' Charter as its means of appealing directly to the British workers.

It was Hitler's rise to power in Germany in 1933 that led the Comintern to gradually abandon its Class Against Class policy and begin its United Front and Popular Front policies against fascism. Yet, unlike in France and other countries, the introduction of these new policies carried little influence in Britain. The Labour Party was simply not prepared to forget its differences and unite with the CPGB to oppose fascism, and the reaction was pretty much the same when the Seventh Congress of the Comintern (1935) pressed forward with the Popular Front, aiming again to unite all opponents of fascism. Chapter Three examines these events and makes it quite clear that the United and Popular Fronts failed in Britain despite the fact that the CPGB had abandoned its revolutionary objectives, was prepared to compromise with capitalist politicians and had supported Sir Stafford Cripps' Unity Campaign in 1937. Why was this the case? Why did such obviously less sectarian policies fail to elicit support? Was it because of the intransigence of the Labour Party, the suspicion that the CPGB was operated by Moscow or the sheer irrelevance of Communist politics and tactics to British politics? There has been some dispute about the precise extent of Communist influence, particularly among trade unionists, during the 1930s and early 1940s. John Callaghan has suggested that the

CPGB's failure to extend its support owed a great deal to its inability to capture the support of the trade unions. This contrasts with the views of both Nina Fishman and Richard Stevens, who argue that the CPGB was becoming a growing force within the trade union movement at this time.[5] If this was the case, of course, then its failure to exert more influence upon the Labour Party has to be explained.

The United Front, the Popular Front and the trade union policy of the CPGB in the 1930s form the basis of Chapter Three but it also examines the controversial issue of the 'about turn' from a pro-war to an anti-war policy in September and October 1939, which isolated the CPGB from the rest of British politics at the beginning of the Second World War. By any standards this change of heart was a traumatic event which threatened what little influence the CPGB exerted throughout the country. The point was emphasized by the Labour Party's pamphlet *Stalin's men: about turn*, which dubbed the CPGB 'not only the slaves of Moscow but the allies of Hitler'.[6] Not surprisingly, the U-turn on the war has produced a debate between those who feel that the Party's decisions were determined by Stalin and those who feel that they were a natural development of a policy commitment to peace which had operated in the late 1930s.[7] To some, however, it seemed as though the CPGB was not prepared to follow through its opposition to fascism, which it had fought so purposefully since 1933. Indeed, Harry Pollitt was forced to resign from his position as General Secretary of the Party because he could not reconcile himself to opposing Britain in her fight against Nazi Germany. Only Operation Barbarossa released the CPGB from its anti-war stance, although the Party had been drifting towards a pro-war position since the summer of 1940 following the fall of France.

Chapter Four focuses upon the highpoint of CPGB success in Britain: following the German invasion of the Soviet Union and the Soviet Union's entry into the war there was no more determinedly patriotic organization than the CPGB. It demanded the maximum effort from all workers to boost arms production. It opposed wartime strikes and argued for the opening of the Second Front in Europe in order to relieve the German military pressure upon the Soviet Union. However, success in attracting support was short-lived and with the onset of the Cold War the Party's membership began its inexorable decline.

The fall in the Party's already limited influence, undoubtedly the dominant theme of its last forty years, is examined in Chapter Five. During the years 1951 to 1991 the CPGB attempted to adapt to the political conditions of British society. It abandoned revolutionary action and accepted in its new policy statement *The British Road to Socialism* (1951) that change could come through the parliamentary route. It gradually began to detach itself from too close an association with the USSR after the Soviet invasion of Hungary in 1956. By the late 1960s, following the invasion of Czechoslovakia, Party support for the Soviet Union began to diminish. In the late

1970s and throughout the 1980s the Party leadership adopted a commitment to Eurocommunism which led it into conflict with many of those who supported the Soviet Union and the Soviet political model. Eventually the Party abandoned even this stance and what survived of Marxist–Leninist ideas gave way to an individualist type of 'pick-and-mix' socialism that bore little resemblance to the ideology it had supported in the 1920s. Nevertheless, the CPGB continued to decline. Why was this? Was it because it could never penetrate the mainstream of British political tradition, or because of British hostility to the Soviet Union engendered by the Cold War or because it did too little too late? Alternatively, was the problem of longer standing? Had history crept up on a party that had never been able to establish a niche in British politics and society? Perhaps E.P. Thompson was correct in his suggestion that the CPGB was attempting to grow 'Winter Wheat in Omsk', to use the title of an article he wrote in 1956 suggesting that Stalinist ideas were never likely to thrive in the inappropriate conditions experienced in Britain.[8] There were changes in the Party but they came too late.

The Argument

This book will argue that the answers to questions about the CPGB's failure have much to do with the realignment of British politics in the early twentieth century and the close association of the Party with the Soviet Union. At first the link with the USSR benefited the CPGB in terms of providing policies that appealed to some British workers and in financial support. But the Moscow Show Trials of the mid- and late 1930s turned the association with the USSR into a negative factor. Also, even though the SDF had opportunities to grow within Britain it refused to participate in the development of the trade union movement and so missed the opportunity to capture the political support of the working classes, which was then increasingly won by the emerging Labour Party. Indeed, Frederick Engels criticized the SDF for the sectarian attitude it adopted[9] but his efforts were to no avail since the SDF even withdrew from the Labour Representation Committee in 1901 after failing to get it to adopt a socialist clause in its constitution. Without this base of support within the labour movement the CPGB lost out to the ILP as the main left force in Britain, operated within a small niche in the British political system and was heavily dependent upon the Communist Party in the Soviet Union for financial support and, thus, policies. As Moscow dictated, the CPGB adopted the Class Against Class, the United Front, the Popular Front, and anti-war and pro-war positions over the seventy-one years of its existence. It did assert its independence, both organizational and political, from the Soviet Union in 1968 over Czechoslovakia, and during the late 1970s and throughout the 1980s, but the collapse of communism in Eastern Europe, and its decline and eventual collapse in the Soviet Union meant that it was unrealistic for the CPGB to continue. In any case, its last fifteen or so years were spent moving the Party into policies which would have been disowned by its founders of 1920 but which moved into other agendas, including feminism and green politics, and took it even beyond the compromises evident in the acceptance of the Popular Front and abandonment of revolutionary politics in 1935. The Party did become more adaptable and pragmatic as time went on but it was still too closely associated with the Stalinist leadership of the Soviet Union and the USSR's imminent collapse clearly triggered the end of the CPGB in November 1991.

I

Beginnings: the Emergence of Marxism in Britain, c. 1849–1914

Socialism existed in Britain, in various forms, about seventy years before the formation of the CPGB in 1920. Yet it was not until the 1880s that socialists established themselves in viable organizations concerned with the class struggle. Even then, few socialist organizations had grasped the basic tenets of Marxist economic analysis.

Marxism is a political and philosophical account of social development worked out by Karl Marx and Frederick Engels, and is based upon the premise that the history of mankind has been the history of class struggle. It assumes that there is a dialectical process to history which has taken it through different stages, each characterized by the fact that the nature of the economic base – the mode of production (the 'base') – determined the 'superstructure' of society, that is, its ideas and government. Marx argued that in each epoch the nature of the 'base' threw up class antagonisms based upon the relationship of people to the 'mode of production'. For an industrial Britain in the nineteenth century this meant that there was tension between the bourgeoisie (the owners of industry) and the proletariat which took the form of class conflict that would ultimately lead on to communism. The conflict was based upon the exploitation of the workers by the expropriation of surplus value, which, as Marx explained, is the unpaid labour of the working class.[1] The proletariat would end its exploitation, Marx said, by overthrowing the capitalist state, abolishing private property and instituting a transitional state of society that he and Engels described as the dictatorship of the proletariat.[2] During this transitional phase of society, class antagonisms would disappear and society would move into a higher phase of development based upon the principles of communism – 'from each according to his ability, to each according to his needs'.[3] Marxist ideology accepted that different societies would develop at different rates towards a communist state since they had different vestiges of old systems, although it was assumed that Britain, as an advanced industrial state, would be among the first communist states to emerge. In addition, Engels, who worked

1

closely with Marx, emphasized that the economic determinism which was implicit in this system did not prevent politics, religious ideas and philosophical theories exerting an influence. In other words, the superstructure could influence events.[4]

Until the 1880s Marxist economics were almost ignored. There were very few groups and individuals who had rejected reformism and taken the path of struggle, and who were attempting to understand the need for a revolutionary change in society or to study the science of Marxism and the movement towards the abolition of class society. Perhaps this was not surprising since up to the 1890s there was a limited literature that would appeal to the masses. In addition the sectarian nature of some of the so-called Marxist organizations, most particularly the SDF, meant that Marxist appeal was confined to the few rather than the masses which Marx and Engels sought. This was a source of contention since both Marx and Engels felt that the SDF had turned Marxism into a sterile dogma.[5] Indeed, it is quite clear that there were only two significant figures in British Marxism in the 1880s, Henry Mayers Hyndman and William Morris, and both would be better described as quasi-Marxists than Marxists as such. Hyndman, in particular, failed to acknowledge the hopes that Marx and Engels were prepared to place in trade unionism in order to develop a mass movement; other Marxists, such as Eleanor Marx and Engels, were prepared to work with and through some trade unions to promote the movement.[6]

Yet there were some threads of Marxist influence beginning to penetrate British society for some years before the emergence of the Social Democratic Federation in the 1880s and Marxist ideas had been discussed in the London working men's clubs on a regular basis in the 1860s. This had much to do with the direct influence of Marx and Engels, the founders of British Marxism. They had first met in Cologne in November 1842. Engels had subsequently been converted to communism in 1843 while working in his father's factory in Manchester. He wrote two articles on his newly acquired communist outlook – 'The situation in England' and 'Outlines of a Critique of Political Economy' – the second of which criticized the existence of private property and the spirit of competition.[7] At this stage he began a long correspondence with Marx and they met in Paris in September 1844, declaring their mutual agreement by collaborating on *The Holy Family*. They thus formed a political partnership that continued until Marx's death in 1883. Though Engels had lived in Britain before, both men came to the country in 1849 as exiles having co-written the *Communist Manifesto* in 1848. The *Manifesto*, along with Marx's *Critique of Political Economy* (1859) and *Capital* (1867), set out the essential basis of Marxism – Historical Materialism and the Theory of Surplus Value (later more accurately named The Labour Theory of Value).

In 1864 Marx formed the International Working Men's Association (IWMA), which later became known as the First International. His inaugural address to the IWMA marked the beginning of international Marxism: it stated that 'the misery of the working man had not diminished from 1848 to 1864' even though industry and commerce had expanded enormously.[8] The IWMA made the first significant attempts to put into practice the famous slogan set forth in the *Communist Manifesto*, 'Workers of all lands unite'. Among the IWMA's achievements was success in drawing international attention to the poor treatment of Fenian prisoners in British gaols during the mid-1860s. On behalf of the General Council of the IWMA, Marx also wrote to Abraham Lincoln supporting the Union States in their struggle with the Southern slaveholders. Marx's writings for the IWMA – particularly his pamphlet on the Paris Commune, *The Civil War in France*, where he supported the Communards' execution of their hostages including the Archbishop of Paris – projected him to the British press as a dangerous radical.

However, the IWMA was never to become as centralized as Marx wished. There was a protracted struggle between Marx and Michael Bakunin (a leader of European anarchism) lasting several years. Sections of the IWMA already existed as national affiliated organizations when the dispute broke out, whereupon Bakunin set up a secret committee to align those influenced by anarchism under his leadership, thus creating an International within the International. This debilitated the IWMA and Marx had Bakunin and his supporters expelled in 1872, thus effectively winding up the International rather than letting the name (and its authority) fall into anarchist hands.[9]

These events were allied to other important, though often contending, forces, perhaps more Republican than Marxist, which were emerging around the activities of the Chartist leader James Bronterre O'Brien, most particularly his journal the *Red Republican* and the O'Brien clubs in Soho. These began to form an oppositional culture to the existing social and political systems of capitalism in the 1850s and 1860s. The survivors of Owenite agitation were also active at this time. Many of these forces came together in London in the late 1850s and early 1860s when socialists, Marxists and Republicans began to mingle with foreign exiles from Poland and Italy, such as Garibaldi, in a period of reformist zeal which Royden Harrison has so brilliantly recaptured in his book *Before the Socialists*.[10]

Nevertheless, the IWMA had attracted the affiliation of a large number of British trade unions as a result of its ability to prevent blacklegging by foreign workers during strikes, and its Central Provisional Committee contained such well-known trade unionists such as George Howell, George Odger and J.B. Leno. This association with trade unions alienated some socialist activists who left to form the Land and Labour League in 1869, a body of which Karl Marx claimed paternity and which, influenced by O'Brienites, demanded land nationalization, the abolition of the national debt, equal electoral rights, the payment of MPs, the reduction of working hours and a variety of other measures. The movement was further divided by the creation of the new French Republic which gave a stimulus to Republicanism in the early 1870s and encouraged the formation of Republican clubs in more than fifty towns throughout Britain. Disintegration occurred further as a result of the formation of the Paris Commune, fighting for its existence between March and May 1871, which brought about a split between the meritocratic goals of middle-class republicans and the social republican ideas of the working-class left. Many labour aristocrats preferred the former, believing that communism 'would make the skilful and thrifty workmen suffer for those who were neither'.[11] Marx himself, while eventually viewing the Commune as a form of 'proletarian dictatorship', gave his support to it from the outset,[12] although on 12 April 1871 he wrote, 'What resilient vigour, what historical initiative and what self-sacrifice these Parisians are showing.'[13] Indeed, Marx was at pains to offer his support to the Commune on 28 May 1871, two days after its fall. When he presented his Address on the Civil War in France to the General Council of the IWMA 'It was written to defend the honour of the Commune and to justify it against the vilification and injustice of its enemies, and it did so brilliantly.'[14]

From the summer of 1871 the British and European left splintered into numerous sectarian groups and the First International soon disintegrated in the circumstances already mentioned. By 1872 the support of the British trade union movement had been lost and Marx transferred the headquarters of the International to New York where it was in less danger of being captured by Bakunin and the anarchists. Obviously, Marxism in Britain was in disarray in the 1870s.

At the beginning of the early 1880s socialism and Marxism in Britain was to be found in small groups of activists scattered through a variety of different organizations and lacking a sense of unity and coordination. There were a few hundred socialists at most in 1880. Marxism as a movement began in earnest with the formation in 1881 of the Democratic Federation, a body which spawned the Social Democratic Federation in 1884.

The Social Democratic Federation in the 1880s

The Democratic Federation was formed following a meeting of London radicals at the Rose Street Club, Soho, on 2 March 1881. It became the Social Democratic Federation in 1884, although it was committed to socialism by 1883. It began as a Radical organization on the fringes of the Liberal Party, despite Henry Mayers Hyndman's Conservative credentials, and pursued an eclectic body of policies and campaigns ranging from Home Rule for Ireland to land reform and the democratic reorganization of the Empire. Hyndman steered the organization towards socialism after reading Marx's *Capital* and – in chapter three of his *England for All* (1881) – plagiarized the theory of surplus value, which explained how workers were robbed by their employer of the value of the work they produced and were provided merely with the minimum wage necessary for subsistence. With *England for All* as his programme, Hyndman reduced Marxist theory of development to a rigid orthodoxy rather than 'making the workers raise themselves to its level by dint of their own class instinct'.[15]

Despite Hyndman's move towards Marxism, the publication of *England for All* led to a split between Marx and Hyndman, which Walter Kendall feels may have been a major factor in Marxism's failure to take root in the British labour movement.[16] Marx felt that his ideas had been misrepresented and broke off all relations with Hyndman, whom he regarded as a well-meaning petty bourgeois writer but not a Marxist. The acrimony between the men was later to flow over into a running feud between Engels and Hyndman. Engels wrote that the leader of the Democratic Federation, Hyndman, is an ex-Conservative and an arrantly chauvinistic but not stupid careerist, who behaved pretty shabbily towards Marx . . . and for this reason was dropped by us personally'.[17] Indeed, the hostility developed to such an extent that Engels encouraged Eleanor Marx, Dr Aveling (Eleanor Marx's husband) and William Morris to split from the SDF and form the Socialist League in December 1884. Eleanor Marx wrote in a letter that 'our majority was too small to make it possible for us to really get rid of the Jingo faction and so, after due consideration with Engels, we decided to go out, and form a new organization. This is to be called the Socialist League.'[18]

Nevertheless, despite these later developments and Hyndman's book, the original programme of the Democratic Federation had emphasized the need for political reforms such as triennial parliaments, payment for MPs, equal electoral districts, the abolition of the House of Lords and manhood suffrage for all parliamentary and municipal elections. It also favoured the eight-hour day, several years before Tom Mann wrote his famous pamphlet on the subject, and advocated the nationalization of land and railways, public housing and free education. It aimed to 'unite the great body of people, quite irrespective of party in favour of these principles of justice, freedom, and steady progress, which are now too often set aside to suit the convenience of factions.'[19] Its principal aim was to bring about a 'thorough reform of the present Electoral System . . . so that the working classes may be enabled to send their own representatives to Parliament'. It was also concerned to expose the injustices that were occurring in Ireland and Gladstone's policy of repression in response to the agitation of Davitt's Irish Land League, formed in 1879.

The Democratic Federation soon lost the support of the middle classes, who were quickly turned away by its hostility towards the British government's actions in Ireland. Thereafter, the movement became increasingly Marxist in orientation. Hyndman was influenced partly by the American Henry George's tour of Britain in 1882, during which land reform and the Single Tax became the focus of debate, and was joined in the Democratic Federation by H.H. Champion, E. Belfort Bax and William Morris, who all supported the demand for land reform. John Burns and Harry

Quelch, members of the working class who were active in labour organizations, were also attracted to the movement and by its second annual conference in 1883 the Democratic Federation had adopted nationalization of the means of production and exchange as its central aim. It produced *Socialism Made Plain* (1883) which emphasized the need for land reform and noted that 30,000 persons 'own the land of Great Britain' and that they had got it by robbery and confiscation.[20] This assessment was in fact drawn from the so-called New Doomsday Book, *The Return of Owners of Land* (1873), which was later publicized by J. Bateman in *Great Landowners of England and Wales* (1883). By 1883, supported by such evidence, the Democratic Federation had come to accept that land reforms were 'stepping stones' to the ultimate objective of the common ownership of the means of production.

As already suggested, there were numerous factions gathered together within the emerging SDF, based partly upon the German Social Democratic Party and partly upon a tradition of British Conservative paternalism. The influence of the German Social Democratic Party appeared in the way in which Hyndman emphasized political, rather than economic, action and state socialism. Under Hyndman's leadership, the SDF was to be quasi-Marxist in approach. Acting as a propaganda organization based in London, it aspired to be a committee of public safety awaiting a spontaneous revolution of which it would take charge, offering palliative measures in the meantime to further the cause of Marxism. As a result of its mechanical one-sided understanding of Marx's ideas, the SDF leadership treated Marxism as a rigid dogmatic formula to be regurgitated parrot fashion. Consequently, the Hyndmanite initiative failed and its policies often swung from the ultra-revolutionary to the purely reformist.

There were also O'Brienite radicals, trade unionists, anarchists and intellectuals attracted to socialism. In addition, Andreas Scheu's Scottish Land and Labour League wanted affiliation with the SDF, rather than fusion and central control which Hyndman favoured, and was anti-parliamentarian in approach. Then, immediately before and during the First World War there were those, such as Zelda Kahan and John Maclean (later to be appointed Soviet Consul in Scotland), who favoured a more international approach. The diversity of these groupings guaranteed that there would be constant conflict within the SDF and little semblance of unity. Indeed, there were to be many political breakaways from the parent organization, including the Socialist League formed in 1884 and the Socialist Labour Party and the Socialist Party of Great Britain, created in 1902 and 1903 respectively. In the end, the international and peace section of the SDF, by that time known as the British Socialist Party, forced Hyndman and his supporters out of the movement in 1916.

The SDF has been presented as a failing organization that offered a rather weak foundation for the Communist Party of Great Britain when it was formed in 1920. This view of the SDF is not surprising given that it has been, until recently, ill-served by historians. An official history was written by H.W. Lee and E. Archbold but this was a blatant apologia which argued that the party disappeared because it was successful, its principles having been accepted by the labour movement at large and the Labour Party in particular.[21] Walter Kendall also provided a valuable study of its activities in the early twentieth century and C. Tsuzuki offered some narrative details of its activities in his biography of Hyndman.[22] None of these books provided a comprehensive and balanced view of the SDF's history. However, their shortcomings have been largely overcome by Martin Crick's recent detailed account of the SDF's national and local movements, which has challenged the accepted views of the Federation's development and failures.[23]

It used to be argued that the SDF failed to make much of a political impression because of the obstacle presented to its growth and unity by Hyndman's domineering and self-publicizing character, his nationalism, his anti-Semitism, his hostility to women's suffrage, and his fawning regard for the royal family – an obsequious message from the SDF to Edward VII spurred the Scottish SDF to attack the party leadership through its new paper the *Socialist*.[24] The prominent communist R. Page Arnot referred to Hyndman as 'the evil genius of the Socialist Movement'[25] and C. Tsuzuki tended to portray him in a similar light.[26] Eric Hobsbawm was less harsh but suggested that 'Hyndman's personality made it difficult for him to collaborate except with inferiors', that he was quirky and drove many gifted socialists out of the SDF:

> Especially, he cannot escape blame for the failure of the SDF to exploit its unique position as the pioneer socialist organization in Britain. Engels' bitterness had good reasons. He saw the SDF throw away opportunity after opportunity in the 1880s when it had the field virtually to itself, he saw Hyndman alienate valuable supporters, and the major advances of the movement left either to Marxists forced to act independently of it, or to theoretically far more confused and undesirable elements. The 'new unionism' of 1889–90 and the triumph of independent working-class candidates in 1892 demonstrate what could have been achieved: but it was not the SDF who achieved it. Rather it hindered these achievements and in turn never fully recovered from its loss of initiative.[27]

Apparently, from Hyndman's domination sprang the SDF's hostility towards trade unionism as a means of bringing about change, and the party's intensely nationalistic, patriotic and imperialistic policies. As a result the SDF became immensely sectarian, effectively a small élite of middle-class and working-class men out of the mainstream of trade unionism in Britain and incapable of adapting itself to the changing political situation. Indeed, Henry Collins suggested that it was dominated by a narrow dogmatism due to the lack of Marxist literature in Britain and the contaminating influence of the

German Social Democratic Party's Gotha programme, inspired by Ferdinand Lassalle, which displayed a distinct dislike of trade unionism.[28] Stanley Pierson made a similar point. He argued that three strands formed the basis of British Marxism – organized religion, the writings of Thomas Carlyle and John Ruskin, and the republicanism of Tom Paine flowing through to the utilitarianism of Jeremy Bentham and J.S. Mill and the secularism of Charles Bradlaugh. He maintained that the problems of the SDF stemmed from the fact that Hyndman was influenced by Lassalle's national socialism, which ran counter to these three streams.[29] Willard Wolfe, in his study of Fabian socialism, has also argued that Hyndman was largely out of step with the rest of the membership of the SDF in his advocacy of Lassallean state socialism.[30]

Such views have come under intense scrutiny. Mark Bevir has suggested that Hyndman was neither a straightforward revolutionary nor an uncomplicated parliamentary reformer but reflected both contemporary Marxism and the sentiments of the old Soho, O'Brienite section of the SDF.[31] The O'Brien supporters were the dominant force in the London district and provided the silent majority for the SDF. In two recent articles, Bevir has rejected Pierson's 'three streams' idea. In a piece focused upon Hyndman, Bevir charts the history of radical conservatism as a distinctive intellectual tradition and the influence it exerted upon Hyndman and the SDF. In a second article, which examines the early years of the SDF, he maps out the influence of Bronterre O'Brien on the Federation. The two pieces together help to dispel the impression that Hyndman simply applied the German scheme of socialism. Indeed, Bevir is at pains to present Hyndman's theories not as private ideas but as one facet of an existing political tradition. He represents Hyndman's radical conservatism as the next step in a lineal succession of ideas which originated with Edmund Burke's diatribe against the French Revolution, and progressed through the work of Samuel Taylor Coleridge, Robert Southey and the ideas of both Thomas Carlyle and Benjamin Disraeli. Bevir claims that radical conservatism had much in common with its Liberal counterpart but, unlike the Liberals, Hyndman felt that the Industrial Revolution had destroyed the old society without establishing a new direction. He suggests that the rationale of radical conservatism was to renew the paternal position, to alleviate the condition of the working class and to stave off anarchy. To Bevir, Hyndman linked his belief in radical conservatism with his belief in the inevitability of the collapse of capitalism. Bevir also suggests that the O'Brienites were the silent majority within the SDF, whom supported Hyndman throughout the Socialist League split in the mid-1880s. He notes that Bronterre O'Brien believed that social problems had political solutions and could be dealt with through Parliament. O'Brien also believed that since land was owned by the few, capitalist exploitation was inevitable. He felt that the way to rectify this situation was to introduce the political reforms of the Charter, particularly manhood suffrage, which would get rid of unrepresentative government and enable the people to eradicate poverty through legislation. The first piece of legislation would have been a Land Nationalization Act to free the people from the tyranny of the landlord and the capitalist.

To Bevir, it was these views that dominated London clubland between the 1860s and 1880s. Such views were supported by Charles and James Murray at the Rose Street Club and by Edward Dunn, secretary of the Marylebone Democratic Association. These ideas, in placing the emphasis upon political reform, were supportive of the views that Hyndman was developing. Gradually, the O'Brienites began to go one step further and accepted the collectivization of the means of production, noting that social change also needed social solutions. Indeed, at a special meeting at the Anderton Hotel in January 1884 it was James Murray who proposed the resolution 'that this meeting of Socialists demands universal suffrage, proportional representation and the payment of members as a means of obtaining reduction of the hours of labour, socialization of the means of production, and the organization of Society'.[32] This extension into socialism cemented the relationship with Hyndman, and Bevir explains the transition of the O'Brienites from radicals to socialists in terms of the general economic conditions of the time which saw Britain facing deep depression.[33] When it came to the splits in the SDF, and most particularly to the one that led to the formation of the Socialist League, it is clear that the majority of SDF members, dominated by the O'Brienites, stayed with Hyndman; Bevir concludes that 'in my opinion the bulk of the membership stuck by Hyndman because, like them, but unlike the founders of the Socialist League, he wanted political reforms to create a democratic state as a preliminary to ending capitalist exploitation'.[34] In other words, Bevir feels that the split was not, as Tsuzuki would have it, between those who would or would not support electoral action or parliamentarianism, but between those who believed in political action as the basis of bringing about social reform and those who did not. The O'Brienites supported Hyndman because his political strategies were like their own. Hyndman was in tune with his movement.

Crick is also critical of the stereotyped images of Hyndman and the SDF: he argues that Hyndman was never as dominant as has been suggested, that the SDF was far less dogmatic and sectarian than is often supposed, and that it acted as an important training ground for socialists and carried more local influence, particularly in Lancashire, than is usually acknowledged. The 'SDF was not the highly centralised body it is often portrayed as being. Its branches were autonomous, its debates democratic and, as Hobsbawm points out, the party often ignored Hyndman where he conflicted with its fundamental orientation and eventually abandoned him altogether.'[35] Yet one should still remember that Hyndman, and his friends, controlled *Justice*.[36]

There is much that rings true in the revisionism offered by Bevir and Crick although much of the assessment still remains open to debate. However, the debate about the origins of Hyndman's ideas hardly affects the conclusion that he espoused the seeking of state socialism through political action and rejected trade unionism, even if there is uncertainty about the reasons for this approach. There is also no doubt that some of the old charges about Hyndman – that he was autocratic, intensely nationalistic, and anti-Semitic – are still valid. Hyndman's character was certainly central to many of the problems of the SDF.

William Morris said that 'Hyndman can accept only one position in such a body as the SDF – that of master: some may think that position on his part desirable; I don't and I cannot stand it.'[37] Eleanor Marx, writing to Karl Liebknecht in January 1885 stated of the Socialist League that 'One of our chief points of conflict with Hyndman is that whereas we work to make this a really international movement . . . Mr Hyndman, whenever he could do so with impunity, has endeavoured to set English workmen against "foreigners".'[38] These views were echoed by many other members of the SDF who left to form the Socialist League in December 1884. The fact is that for the majority of the years between 1881 and 1916 Hyndman, supported by Harry Quelch and H.W. Lee, dominated the proceedings and actions of the SDF, even though there were several occasions when his political dominance was challenged and overthrown. It was his attitudes that dominated the actions of the SDF and this was most apparent in the case of trade unionism.

Hyndman's one-sided mechanical interpretation of Marxism meant that he believed that socialism was to be preached to the working class and he did not understand, as Engels did, that the working class would be won to socialism only through a party based on its own mass organizations, and particularly trade unions. This lack of confidence in the ability of the working class to take control of its own destiny led the SDF to adopt a sectarian approach to the emerging labour movement. As a result of its belief in the inevitable collapse of capitalism, the SDF adopted a policy of 'waiting for socialism'.

From the start, Hyndman saw 'the trade union fetish' as the 'chief drawback to progress'.[39] He was willing to support the demands of the trade union leaders for immediate reforms, such as an eight-hour working day, but was formally opposed to the alliance between Social Democrats and the trade unions for political purposes. Hyndman felt that an alliance here would be disastrous because the trade unionists were 'an aristocracy of labour, who in view of the bitter struggle now drawing nearer' represented a 'hindrance to the complete organization of the workers which can alone obtain for the workers their proper control over their own labour'.[40] Not surprisingly, the SDF followed the Hyndman line of reasoning in the manifesto it published in *Justice* (6 September 1884), accusing the trade unions, not entirely unreasonably, of concluding an alliance with capitalism, forgetting the existence of the class struggle, and catering to the needs of a few favoured workers rather than the masses who lived in misery. The trade unions were urged to understand that it was revolution, not reform, that was required. Also, accepting the 'iron law of wages', Hyndman and the SDF suggested that trade unions could not influence the level of wages in the existing capitalist system. It followed that strikes were ineffective and pointless, 'a lowering of the flag, a departure from active propaganda, and a waste of energy'. SDF members were encouraged to explain to their fellow members that strike pay would be better spent on socialist propaganda. This was the official line of the SDF throughout the 1880s and was reiterated at the 1889 Birmingham conference where there was no reference to trade unions in the nine points of the outlined SDF programme. With the emergence of new unionism Hyndman and the SDF changed their views on the 'iron law of wages'; however, the position with regard to trade unions remained the same. They were seen in a good light if they supported socialism and in a bad light if they focused upon industrial action alone.[41]

This lack of a positive policy towards unions was a fatal flaw in the SDF's political programme. Engels recognized this in 1891 when he suggested that the SDF was becoming a 'mere sect because they cannot conceive that living theory of action, of working with the working classes at every possible stage of its development'.[42] Tom Mann was similarly critical: 'I am convinced, however, that Hyndman's bourgeois mentality made it impossible for him to estimate the worth of industrial organization correctly',[43] a fact that led Mann to leave the SDF. The lack of a positive policy towards trade unions and industrial action was to undermine constantly the position of the SDF in relation to other socialist and Marxist groups. Keir Hardie, deciding to form the Independent Labour Party in opposition to the SDF, reflected that the latter's methods were likely to antagonize rather than enlist working-class support and objected to the foolishness of one of Hyndman's favourite sayings – 'no slave class ever emancipated itself'. To this doctrine, which applied to the trade unions the badge of inferiority, Hardie 'could give no assent'.[44] Not surprisingly the issue of trade unionism and working-class action was a recurring theme throughout the history of the SDF and was evident in the case of the Socialist Unity debate before the First World War.

The SDF's attitude to trade unionism was partly conditioned by the extracts of Marx's writings that it published. *Wages, Labour and Capital*, which was translated by J.L. Joynes and serialized in *Justice* in 1884, the first volume of *Capital*, partially translated in *Justice* in October 1885, and the *Communist Manifesto*, serialized in *Justice*, made little reference to trade unionism and emphasized instead the political plane. The first two pieces suggested that trade unions could have no more than a marginal influence upon wages and working conditions, although the *Communist Manifesto* did briefly mention trade unions as defensive, but progressive, institutions used by workers to 'keep up the rate of wages'.[45] In a period of weak trade unionism when the collapse of capitalism seemed imminent it seemed foolish for Marx and Engels to assign much importance to trade unionism and SDF members, lacking access to the later writings of Marx and Engels, gained a mistaken impression that trade unionism lacked importance. Yet, as Engels was at pains to stress in the late 1880s and early 1890s, both he and Marx favoured the 'new' trade unionism that emerged in the mid- and late 1880s for it was different from the 'fossilized men' who led the old trade unions: 'not a trace of the old formalist spirit and the craft exclusiveness of the engineers, for example; on the contrary, a general call for the organisation of all Trade Unions into one brotherhood and for a direct struggle against capital'.[46]

Crick is quite right to suggest that there were many members of the SDF who disagreed with Hyndman over trade unionism. There was strong support for it among provincial members of the SDF: the organization did campaign for the unemployed and helped out during strikes in 1886 and 1887. Hyndman gave his support to the dockers involved in the famous London Dock Strike of 1889 but did not believe that their actions could bring about any permanent improvement. Yet one should not ignore the fact that Harry Quelch led a section of the SDF towards cooperating with the trade unions in the 1890s, which prompted the SDF's first official pronouncement in favour of them in 1897 and its involvement in the formation of the Labour Representation Committee (LRC), an alliance between trade unionists and socialists, in 1900. The LRC began to suggest that trade unions embodied socialist principles and therefore supported them.

There was clearly heated debate about trade unions within the SDF. Hyndman clashed with members at the SDF's 1894 conference, where he fought against allowing trade unions to attend the international congress to be held in London in 1896.[47] His views were rejected by J. Hunter Watts but he won the debate. However, despite Hyndman's victory, the 1896 SDF Conference heard Wilhelm Liebknecht praise British trade unionism, and this led to the delegates present at the 1897 conference advocating that SDF members should join trade unions and demand their political support. In any case, there was much trade union support for the SDF in important industrial areas such as Lancashire, where there were many more political opportunities. In spite of these variations, the SDF, in all its political forms, retained the image that it was dubious about the value of trade unionism. Indeed, the issues of trade unionism, syndicalism and industrial action were later to divide the British Socialist Party (dominated by the old SDF/SDP) on the eve of the First World War.

The dominance of Hyndman and the political and industrial attitudes which the SDF projected meant that, in the 1880s, it carried little political support. The SDF's main stronghold was London where it had significant influence upon London Trades Council, in the Gasworkers' Union through Will Thorne and on the local democratic institutions such as boards of guardians and school boards. Tom Mann, Will Thorne, Eleanor Marx and others participated in the struggles of unskilled workers. There was even a joint council of the ILP and the SDF to deal with unemployment.[48] Yet even here its impact was limited. The London Radicals reorganized as the Metropolitan

Radical Federation in 1885–6 and many of them gravitated towards offspring organizations, most notably the Socialist League.

Outside London, it was Lancashire that dominated SDF activities. However, in the 1880s, the Lancashire branches struggled to survive. The Blackburn branch was reduced to six members at one stage and the Oldham branch collapsed. Otherwise, only Nottingham, where John Burns obtained 598 votes in the Nottingham West constituency at the 1885 general election (5.4 per cent of the vote), provided any evidence of significant support for the SDF.

The real problem was that in the 1880s there were real tensions between the small group of London activists who dominated the SDF. Hyndman's patriotic concern about General Gordon's problems in Khartoum in 1884 worried many who had already noted Hyndman's nationalistic tendencies. Others were alarmed that Hyndman, with the support of H.H. Champion and John Burns, was anxious to put forward parliamentary candidates to allow the SDF to benefit from the popular agitation that took place in the mid-1880s. Certain members felt that the SDF would look ridiculous if its candidates were humiliated in such elections, while William Morris, and some, although not all, of his supporters, objected to the whole idea of parliamentary politics, which they saw as corrupt and an obstacle to social change. Morris, Eleanor Marx and others eventually left the SDF in 1884 as a result of Hyndman's excessive personal influence and the opportunism of parliamentary reformists in the SDF. Morris later wrote, in 1890, that 'No programme is worthy of acceptance by the working-classes that stops short of the abolition of private property in the means of production'.[49]

Faced with concerns about Hyndman's excessive personal control over party policy and fears of parliamentary failure the majority of the SDF's Executive Committee left to form the Socialist League on 30 December 1884. The leaders of the new party were Morris, Dr Aveling, Eleanor Marx, Ernest Belfort Bax and Andreas Scheu. They were joined by some anarchist groups. However, Joseph Lane's working-class Labour Emancipation League (formed in 1881, committed to the belief that labour was the foundation of all wealth and in favour of nationalization) remained a separate organization.

These departures left the SDF very much under Hyndman's control and allowed him to pursue his 'step-by-step' approach to socialism and his acceptance of palliatives, which involved obtaining £340 from the Conservative agent Maltman Barry, the infamous 'Tory Gold', to support the three SDF candidates in the 1885 general election.[50] The incident not only brought the SDF into ridicule but also produced no political advantage, for while Burns received 598 votes in Nottingham, John E. Williams received a mere 27 in Hampstead and John Fielding only 32 in Kensington. Morris and the Socialist League were appalled at this action and the SDF's political failures led to a decline in its already paltry support. As Lee wrote later: 'The effect of the disagreement arising out of the candidature was, in my opinion, worse than that of the split which led to the formation of the Socialist League, for added to the loss of members was the feeling of depression among those who remained.'[51]

The SDF recovered some ground in the winter of 1886–7 as a result of the demonstrations of the unemployed, its espousal of the 'right to work' fight and the subsequent campaign to establish popular control of the Metropolitan Police, which culminated in the famous Trafalgar Square Meeting of 13 November 1887 – 'Bloody Sunday' – when two demonstrators were killed by police and soldiers. This produced a temporary alliance between the SDF, the Radical Federation, the Socialist League and the Fabians within the compass of the Law and Liberty League. They held a mass demonstration of 40,000 people in Hyde Park on Sunday 20 November at which the mounted police charged the crowd. Alfred Linnell, a passer-by, was crushed by the police horses and died of his wounds twelve days later. His funeral cortege was followed by 120,000 people, including William Morris, John Burns and Cunninghame Graham.

Popular agitation was a useful platform upon which to build support for the SDF but the renewed interest in the Federation soon slipped away. There were several reasons for this. In particular, the antipathy of Hyndman towards trade unions meant that the SDF lost out to other socialist organizations in the north which worked with the unions before they eventually joined with the Independent Labour Party in January 1893. The international socialist credentials of the SDF were further undermined by its attitudes towards international conferences in 1888. In September 1887 the TUC had called for a meeting on the eight-hour day legislation. As a result, two meetings were held on the same day in 1888 – one dominated by the trade unionists and Paul Brusse, the French possibilist leader, and the other, which favoured the formation of the Socialist International, supported by Engels and the French Marxists, led by Jules Guesde. The SDF went to the former, associating with the trade unionists Hyndman had so much ignored, rather than to the latter to which the SDF ought to have been attracted.

By 1890 the membership of the SDF was in decline. Hyndman was largely discredited, other socialist organizations were emerging, the SDF's policy of palliatives alienated many would-be supporters and the northern parts of Britain were seeing the emergence of new trade unions and numerous small socialist groups which were not attached to the SDF. Despite the corrective work of both Bevir and Crick, it is still clear that the SDF was hamstrung by a leader with a domineering attitude, quirky views and an indolence towards organizing for change, due partly to his assumption that the SDF would act as some type of committee of public safety when the revolutionary moment arrived. The fact that Hyndman favoured political reforms as a means of bringing about social revolution might have endeared him to the O' Brienites but it must be remembered that this group represented only a small proportion of socialist opinion by the mid- and late 1880s. Other socialist groups had emerged and, for a short time, the Socialist League looked likely to challenge the SDF for primacy within the British socialist movement.

Marxist activity in Britain during the 1880s was evidently deeply rooted in the past. Recently, Bevir has examined the early years of the SDF and established that some of Bronterre O'Brien's supporters were the dominant force in the London district that provided the silent majority for the SDF.[52] He argues that this fact explains why the majority of the SDF stayed with Hyndman through the constant splits and fragmentation and supported his ambiguous attitudes towards trade unionism and palliatives. Generated in London clubland and the Manhood Suffrage League, the O'Brienite views supported the political approach to bringing about change which Hyndman had emphasized.[53] The fact that they were republican in politics did not seem to pose a problem since they had come to accept the need for collectivization, the eight-hour day and public works for the unemployed. Effectively, they had come to accept Hyndman's views by the mid-1880s.

Socialism in Britain re-emerged during the 1880s, albeit out of a deeply rooted radical tradition. This was the decade when the number of British socialists increased from a few hundred to about 2,000 active members as a result of the development of the SDF, the Socialist League and the Fabian Society, the first two of which were quasi-Marxist. Yet why did the socialist and Marxist movements as a whole not do better? The answer may have something to do with the dominating nature of Hyndman's leadership of the SDF. Arnot, Collins and Hobsbawm have focused upon Hyndman's ability to alienate fellow socialists with his anti-trade union sentiments, his intense nationalism and his narrow dogmatism.[54] More recently, such views have been challenged by both Bevir and Crick, who feel that Hyndman was much more a product of his time than is usually acknowledged and that he has been stereotyped into a myth. Apparently, Hyndman was never as dominant, and therefore as destructive, as is often supposed.[55] There is, however, sufficient evidence to suggest that Hyndman's policies, if not omnipotent within the SDF, were vitally important in forcing Morris and the Socialist League members out and in deflecting trade unionists, such as Mann, to other socialist organizations. The dominance of Hyndman is evident from the early days of the SDF.

William Morris and the Socialist League

William Morris was, like Hyndman, a vital figure in the emergence of socialism and Marxism in Britain in the late nineteenth century. Yet since his death in 1896 many books and commentaries have asked why he joined the socialist movement and have enquired about the precise nature of his contribution. Historians have speculated about whether he was a romantic, a utopian socialist or a revolutionary socialist in the true

Marxist tradition. Early writers often dismissed his socialism as an aberration but E.P. Thompson, in his seminal work *William Morris: Romantic to Revolutionary*, raised Morris to the level of the finest socialist and Marxist theorists of his day.[56] Morris's commitment to socialism was not an aberration but owed much to his youthful revolt and was reflected in his article 'How I became a Socialist' in 1894. He described his hatred of modern industry and the commercialization of art, and his frustration at the slowness of socialism to develop, although he felt that 'the seeds of a great change, what we others call Social-Revolution were beginning to germinate'.[57] Thompson presents Morris as a Marxist, much as Robin Page Arnot did in the 1930s,[58] and an inspirational figure for many who wished to become involved in the 'making of socialists' and the promotion of Socialist Unity in the 1890s. The fact that he left the Socialist League in 1890 and that his anti-parliamentary and anti-state socialist ideas were rejected by the majority of British socialists does not seem to have diminished his importance.

Fiona MacCarthy's more recent contribution is less forceful about Morris's socialist commitment but, by examining the forces that shaped his life, comes to the conclusion that his commitment to socialism was not a temporary madness.[59] In attempting to uncover Morris as a whole, MacCarthy lays great emphasis on his background and the importance of his family and childhood. She says his socialism emerged, like that of Hyndman, out of Tory morality, and particularly through Charles Kingsley and Christian socialism.[60] She argues that the balance of evidence suggests that Morris's life led him to socialism and that he was committed to revolutionary socialism of a Marxist kind.

These modern assessments seem fair and balanced in the light of the recent evidence. Morris, like Hyndman, came from the middle classes and drew partly upon the influences of conservative paternalism but the similarities between the men ended there since Hyndman's policies and opportunism contrasted sharply with the ideas that Morris developed through the mid-1880s. During his early years Morris railed against capitalism and 'Gradgrindism' and particularly objected to the exploitation of workmen and the loss of skill represented by the development of machine production. Influenced by John Ruskin, he also became involved in medievalism. He had long been interested in medieval poetry and in the 1850s, as a young architect, he became involved in the medieval revival and Gothic architecture. Heroism, beauty, high endeavour and love were now combined with a sense of nostalgia and loss at the removal of Gothic architecture and by its replacement with bogus or mock-Gothic machine-cut buildings. Leading the anti-scrape movement against Victorian rebuilding, Morris focused upon the revival of skill and design since he felt that the satisfaction which the medieval craftsmen got from their work must be restored to modern workers. In effect Morris was offering a solution to Marx's theory of alienated labour in capitalist society.

The 'savageness and rudeness' of Gothic architecture particularly appealed to Morris. He felt that every man had within him a slumbering creative power and he maintained that labour must be creative – demanding intellectual, moral, physical and mechanical powers. Where was the joy in making a cog? From this background and interest Morris, the poet, craftsman and designer, set up the Red House at Bexley in Kent, and associated with the Pre-Raphaelite Brotherhood, a small group of artists who were determined to raise the banner against the conservative art of their times.

Morris's political education began in the late 1870s when, convinced of the need for freedom and democracy, he helped form the Eastern Question Association when it became known that Disraeli had formed an alliance with the Turks, a sensitive decision since the Turks had committed atrocities against Christian Bulgarians. This was the first political commitment from Morris, who had become a very successful businessman. He set up Kelmscott Press at Kelmscott Manor, his Oxfordshire retreat, before moving to Kelmscott House in London, and established the Merton Abbey Works of Morris & Co., on the River Wandle in Surrey, where tapestries, chintzes, wallpapers and stained-glass windows were made. His financial successes were a source of embarrassment to him. Morris joined the Democratic Federation in January 1883 and remained an active socialist until his death in 1896. He carried many of his ideas into the SDF, the Socialist League and the Hammersmith Socialist Society.

Morris was a moral socialist, even though in 'How I became a Socialist' he described himself repeatedly as a 'practical socialist'.[61] His socialism came from a sense of moral injustice rather than any fine understanding of Marxist economic thinking. He believed in the need to revive medieval architecture and work skills as part of his vision of the future presented in his utopian work *News From Nowhere*. In this book Morris emphasized the satisfaction that medieval craftsmen got from their work in obvious contrast to the experience of the modern worker of the late nineteenth century, and advocated that the skill of the workman should replace the uniformity of modern machinery.[62] He was also committed to genuine democracy and workers' involvement in the running of society which he felt would be best represented through cooperation and brotherhood rather than state socialism. Above all, he did not believe in parliamentary socialism, which, to him, was both undemocratic and reactionary, and maintained that it was essential to support workers when they were on strike. Although he worked with anarchists, he himself was a believer in cooperation rather than individual anarchism, which he felt had no responsibilities to the community as a whole. His poetry and writings began to combine thoughts on medieval literature, society and craftsmanship with his new-found socialist ideas. This was evident in his *A Dream of John Ball* (1886), which took the form of a speech and discussion from prison by this medieval advocate of democratic rights.

Morris joined the Democratic Federation/SDF in 1883 but left in December 1884 and helped form the rival Socialist League, which was committed to the 'religion of socialism'. By late 1884 tensions were building within the SDF, particularly between Andreas Scheu's Scottish Land League and Hyndman and his supporters. Others became contemptuous of the activities of the SDF and, in Morris's words, it was felt by many that 'the old organisation was not worth having'.[63] As a result the dissidents met and announced, on 30 December 1884, the formation of the Socialist League. They explained in their manifesto issued on 13 January 1885 that there had been 'a tendency towards political opportunism . . . towards national assertion, the persistent foe of socialism . . . to attempts at arbitrary rule'.[64] The new organization took the Merton Abbey, Hammersmith, Woolwich and Leeds branches of the SDF, the Labour Emancipation League and the Scottish Land and Labour League with it and established a new branch at Norwich.

Morris became the editor and financial benefactor of *Commonweal*, where some of his writings, such as *A Dream of John Ball* and *News from Nowhere*, first appeared. These works provided the inspiration for many socialists who did not want to see the development of state socialism, although Morris's anti-state and anti-parliamentary attitudes became even more evident in *News from Nowhere*.[65] Published as a book in 1890, it offered a vision of a cooperative type of socialism in contrast to the state socialism put forward by some thinkers, including Edward Bellamy in *Looking Backwards*. Typically utopian, it envisaged London a century into the future where life and work were enjoyable, based upon good fellowship and cooperation, and where money was no longer required and medieval beauty was appreciated. As Guest, from whose perspective it was written, travels around London, he finds that he is not embarrassed because 'here I could enjoy everything without an afterthought of the injustice and miserable toil which made my leisure; the ignorance and dullness of life which went to make my keen appreciation of history; the tyranny and the struggle full of fear and mishap which went to make my romance'. Guest found that the transition from capitalism to socialism came through industrial conflict, and for this Morris drew heavily upon the disturbances in London in November 1887.

Despite this inspirational guidance the Socialist League was never a unified organization. It was always small, peaking at about 700 members at the end of 1886, and lacked unity for it had gathered together a disparate array of talents. There were anti-Hyndmanites, anti-parliamentarians, parliamentarians, educationalists and anarchists within its ranks. By the late 1880s it had become dominated by the anarchists. Their views went well beyond the collectivist, brotherhood and commonwealth attitudes that Morris was advocating.[66] Morris soon found that his control of *Commonweal* was being challenged and in 1889 he was forced to reassert that he was a communist and did not wish to qualify the term. He made it clear that the communistic life would be one of equality between men and one of brotherhood and not of 'an individual man doing what he pleases under all circumstances'.[67] Shortly after producing *News from Nowhere* as articles in *Commonweal*, Morris left the Socialist League, driven out by anarchist activities.[68]

Morris dominated the Socialist League until the late 1880s and offered policies that were distinctively his own. He and his colleagues had formed the Socialist League in order to overthrow the existing system by force and felt that it would be 'a body of able, high-minded competent men, who should act as instructors of the masses, and as their leaders during critical periods of the movement'.[69] The Socialist League members thought it might act as a form of committee of public safety, in the same way as the SDF saw itself acting once the revolution came about, but it saw itself as initiating that revolutionary situation and not simply idly awaiting the spontaneous revolution while in the meantime advocating palliatives and reforms.

This difference between the SDF and the Socialist League was reflected in the conflict over parliamentary action. The SDF, as already noted, put candidates forward to contest parliamentary seats and took 'Tory Gold' to do so in the 1885 general election with the object of splitting the Liberal vote. Such actions appalled Morris, who was most critical of the 'Tory Gold' scandal. Morris's attitude towards parliamentary action appeared strongly after the third annual conference of the Socialist League. In a letter to John Glasse he wrote:

> I believe that the Socialists will certainly send members to Parliament when they are strong enough to do so: in itself I see no harm in this, so long as it is understood that they go there as rebels, and not as members of the governing body, prepared by passing palliative measures to keep 'Society' alive. But I fear that many of them will be drawn into that error by the corrupting influence of a body professedly hostile to Socialism: & therefore I dread the parliamentary period (clearly a long way ahead at the present) of the progress of the party, and I think it will be necessary always to keep alive a body of Socialists of principle who will refuse responsibility for the actions of the parliamentary portion of the party.[70]

Later that year, Morris formulated his policy of abstention designed to prevent Parliament swallowing up all socialist effort and energy, and to encourage workers to organize their own industrial activities, as in the case of the strike of the Northumberland miners in 1887. He had already informed John Lincoln Mahon before the third annual conference of the Socialist League that 'finally, you must not forget that whatever open steps I might take, I personally would have nothing to do with politics properly so-called. The whole business is so revolting to a decent quiet body with an opinion of his own that if that were the road, I should not be able to help dropping off it.'[71]

This was an attitude most readily understood by many of those who formed Socialist League branches in 1885 and 1886 and was particularly strong in the case of the Leeds branch. It had been formed as the Leeds branch of the SDF in 1884 but on 8 February 1885 had decided to become the Leeds Socialist League after a speech in which Mahon stressed to members that 'such a revolution involved the termination of political opportunism and State Socialism of the SDF and a full endorsement of the purely revolutionary propaganda to which the Socialist League was pledged'.[72]

Morris naturally gave support to trade unionists and workers who were involved in strike activity and this policy seems to have gained wide support within the Socialist League, but he found himself in conflict over it with Mahon and many others who argued that the success of socialism would have to come through involvement in both parliamentary and municipal politics. There were many members of the Socialist League in the provinces who agreed with this view, including Fred Jowett, later to become the first Labour MP for Bradford in 1906, who was one of the leading members of the Bradford Socialist League between 1885 and 1887.

Morris left the Socialist League in 1890 and, with the 120 members of the Hammersmith branch, pursued his vision of socialism and 'the making of socialists' through their activities. He soon found that he had to compromise on his views and to contemplate attempts to bring about some form of Socialist Unity with the prospect of some type of accommodation with the SDF. He also had to consider working with the middle-class, bureaucratic, non-class-war and institutional approach to socialism offered by the Fabian Society – the third of the major socialist parties which had emerged in the early and mid-1880s – as his own brand of socialism moved from the particulars of policy to a general commitment to inspiring and making socialists. There is little evidence that he ever approved of what he had always considered to be a rather arid and gentle form of socialism which played down the importance of class conflict.

Despite the obvious failure of Morris's movement, Stephen Yeo has seen his work as vital to the development of the early socialist movement. Yeo has emphasized how Morris was responsible for the Socialist League's 'single-hearted devotion to the religion of Socialism, the only religion which the Socialist League professes'.[73] He maintains that the 'religion of socialism' that Morris generated was not a backwater in the early days of the movement but a vital part of the process of development of British socialism between 1883 and 1896, when the demands of party politics consumed the time, energy and resources of the socialist movement.[74] Indeed, Yeo argues that there was a sense of unity between socialist politicians and religion but that this disappeared in the mid-1890s without Morris's resolute hand as employers began to strike back at trade unions and as electoral politics became more important.

Yeo's views have been much criticized, not least because some of the agencies of the 'religion of socialism', such as socialist Sunday schools and the Clarion movement, survived until the First World War. Yet the core of his argument is valid since there was a rising concern for electoral success within the socialist movement, sparked by its disastrous performance in the 1895 general election.

The SDF, Fabians and Other Socialist Groups, *c*. 1890–1914

The SDF and the Socialist League had been the flagship organizations of British Marxism in the 1880s. Other groups had also dabbled with Marxist ideas with less impact and commitment. In particular the Fabian Society, formed on 4 January 1884, had emerged to consider the reconstruction of society on Marxist lines but had not got far along that track before re-forming itself into an organization whose essential activity was to propagandize for gradual social and economic change through the extension of municipal and state control. The Fabians certainly helped in the formation of bodies committed to the extension of socialism through electoral and democratic means. The most obvious and important of these was the Independent Labour Party, formed in 1893, which waxed and waned in the 1890s but grew rapidly before the First World War, claiming a membership of well over 20,000 in 1906 and of 30,000 in 1912 when it also had 1,070 representatives in local government.[75] Marxist organizations did not perform as well but did experience a revival of interest in the years immediately before the First World War.

The national membership of the SDF had fallen to 453 by 1890, organized in 34 branches, with 368 of these members being affiliated to 25 branches in London and 50 to 4 branches in Lancashire. The SDF grew steadily thereafter, reaching 3,259 members in 1897. By that time it was clear that the SDF was strong in two main areas – London and Lancashire. Indeed, Lancashire, with 1,021 members in 19 branches in 1894, had more members than London at that time although the London membership was normally the larger. SDF membership fell away fairly significantly at the end of the century and dipped further in 1902 and 1903 when the Socialist Labour Party (SLP) and the Socialist Party of Great Britain (SPGB) split away;[76] the SDF lost 80 members to the SLP in 1902 and 88 to the SPGB in 1903.[77]

There were numerous issues, in addition to the major concern of Socialist Unity, that were to dominate the SDF's activities between 1890 and 1914. Firstly, it was involved in the formation of the LRC in 1900 but was annoyed when James Ramsay MacDonald, rather than Hyndman, became secretary of that body. At its annual conference in August 1901 the SDF voted 54 to 14 in favour of secession from the LRC, as a result of an unlikely alliance between the Scottish 'impossibilists' – who later formed the Socialist Labour Party with its commitment to industrial action – and the Hyndmanites.[78]

Most historians agree with the view of H.W. Lee 'that the decision was a sad mistake' and that:

All the propaganda that we did afterwards, all the influence we were able to bring to bear in a Socialist direction, would have been much greater indeed had we carried it on and exercised it as an integral part of the LRC, and not as an outside body at which many supporters of Independent Labour Representation looked a trifle askance because of our withdrawal from the LRC.[79]

Hyndman also admitted at the 1914 British Socialist Party conference that it had been a mistake for the SDF to withdraw from the LRC.[80]

Many individual members of the SDF still attended LRC conferences, reflecting a concern by some that there should have been no withdrawal, but they often insisted that socialism should be accepted *per se* without attempting to explain the need for socialism in terms of the needs of working people. There was alarm at the split among some members of the SDF in Lancashire, who had always worked closely with the ILP and the LRC, and there was great pressure for Hyndman to rejoin the LRC. Indeed, A. Greenwood of Blackburn, at the annual conference of the SDF in 1905, said:

The LRC represents the beginning of the last and greatest struggle for the political machinery of the country by the most intelligent and best organized workers. This does not seem to be appreciated by the SDF. . . . the LRC movement is a semi-conscious recognition of the conflict of interests between the proletariat and the master class; it is better in character than its leader in the House of Commons. We want to make it a Socialist movement, and must establish sympathetic relations with it.[81]

Harry Quelch's reply for the SDF's Executive Committee, explaining its departure from the LRC, typified the rigid sectarian attitude of the SDF leadership:

Not a single new reason has been placed before us for adopting the course recommended. . . . If we rejoin the LRC we shall have no say in the selection of candidates but will be called on to support them no matter whom they are. . . . We cannot have Socialist unity under the LRC, which contains anti-Socialists.[82]

As previously stated, the SDF did gain some political success outside London, most particularly in Lancashire. Crick's main argument is that the SDF did well where it put its resources. The organizational work of J.J. Terrett, Tom Mann, Dan Irving and Herbert Burrows ensured that many of Lancashire's industrial towns, most particularly Blackburn, Burnley, Nelson and Rochdale, had well-developed SDF organizations. Terrett was in fact a paid organizer of the Federation in 1893 and delivered 363 lectures and established twenty-four new branches in the north in that year. Dan

Irving, a Bristol man who had lost a leg in an accident on the Midland railway, was a member of the Starnthwaite Labour Colony, a farming commune set up by the Revd H. Mills, a Fabian; Irving campaigned regularly in Burnley and Nelson and, in the course of 1893, accepted an invitation from the Burnley SDF to become its full-time secretary. All this groundwork resulted in the formation of the Lancashire District Council of the SDF, which comprised twenty-one branches, in August 1893. In the same month the Federation held its annual conference in Burnley, where the local branch claimed a membership of 600; this had risen to 1,000 by the end of the year. The branch appointed a committee of thirty-six members who invited Hyndman to stand as their prospective parliamentary candidate.[83]

A small number of SDF town councillors were returned in Blackburn, Burnley and Rochdale in the 1890s and early twentieth century. Salford South was contested in the 1892 and 1895 general elections; Hyndman contested Burnley in 1895, 1906 and December 1910; and Irving contested Accrington in 1906, Manchester North West in 1908, Rochdale in 1900, 1908 and December 1910. He later fought Burnley in the 1922 and 1923 general elections. Despite the fact that all these parliamentary contestants were defeated some, including Hyndman and Irving, polled remarkably well. As Jeff Hill and Crick have suggested, their success was based partly upon the close collaboration between the trade unions, the ILP and the SDF and the decision of many Lancashire SDF branches not to leave the LRC at the end of 1901, although this in turn may have contributed to a lack of distinctiveness in the local policy of the SDF. Alan Kidd makes much the same point, stressing that the SDF was not dogmatic and inflexible and noting that in Manchester there was a 'diversity of political philosophy and practice' that sustains this view.[84]

Hill and Crick quite rightly suggest that there was a close relationship between the ILP, the SDF and the trades councils in some areas of Lancashire, but one cannot ignore the fact that there were also serious tensions; for example, in Rochdale in July 1901 the ILP feared that the SDF would 'steal a march' in the selection of a joint socialist candidate.[85] Such sentiments were not unusual among ILP branches in Lancashire.

Outside Lancashire and London, the major area for SDF success was Northampton, where a variety of SDF candidates contested parliamentary seats in 1895, twice in 1906 and twice in 1908.[86] Leicester saw an SDF/BSP challenge in the parliamentary by-election of 1913 but the city was never an established stronghold of SDF influence. Also, despite Harry Quelch's contest in the Dewsbury parliamentary by-election in 1902, there is little evidence that the SDF had much lasting influence there or in the rest of Yorkshire.

The third major development of this period was that the SDF continued to shed members as a result of the Boer War and the dominating policies of Hyndman. The SDF's policy towards foreign nations and colonialism was intensely nationalistic and any criticism it had of the famous Jameson raid of 1896 was tempered by its anti-Semitic and anti-German references. At the outbreak of the Boer War in 1899 the SDF became instinctively critical and aware of the class implications of the conflict. At first the Federation held anti-war demonstrations. Then Hyndman began to see the war as a product of the efforts of a few, mainly Jewish, capitalists. The longer it went on the greater was his inclination to praise the British troops and the less equivocal the SDF became in its hostility to the conflict. The SDF was clearly divided between those who were advocating a more internationalist approach to imperialism and the Boer War, and those, like Hyndman, who were instinctively nationalistic. This conflict, and the increasing feeling that the movement was 'dictated by the old man [Hyndman] and varied with his moods', led to some minority groups to leave the SDF.[87]

Indeed, the Scottish District Council (SDC) of the SDF was fiercely opposed to the Boer War and also opposed to the SDF's membership of the LRC. When the SDF left the LRC at the end of 1901, the SDC was only partly appeased and immediately found itself opposed to those, including many rank-and-file members in Lancashire and some of the national leaders, who felt that departure from the LRC was unwise. The SDF membership began to divide between those who wanted the Federation to be a pure revolutionary organization with revolutionary trade union connections, those who wished it to remain a vanguard party working within the existing trade unions, and those who wished to rejoin the LRC.

Theodore Rothstein opened up this debate after the 1901 conference, proposing a synthesis between political and economic action, and attacked the Scottish views which favoured industrial action. He regarded these 'impossibilists' as political 'virgins who, for the sake of their immaculate chastity, are ever ready to immolate themselves on the altar of sterility'.[88] He advocated the capturing of trade union support though not the return to the LRC. Others offered a variety of shades of opinion all of which were anathema to the Scottish 'impossibilists'. From then onwards, matters moved apace.

The struggle in the SDF between 1900 and 1903 that led to the formation of the SLP reflected the mounting opposition to Hyndman's leadership by young working-class militants disgusted at the SDF's political opportunism and particularly Hyndman's abandonment of opposition to the Boer War as 'a waste of time and money'.[89] The opposition of the Scottish SDF to the Hyndman leadership also reflected the ongoing struggle led by Lenin within the Second International against revisionist and opportunist tendencies. This involved concern at the fact that Millerand, the French socialist, entered the French government at the height of the Dreyfus Affair. This was raised at the 1901 SDF Conference when the Scottish delegates attacked the support given by the 1900 International Congress to the Kautsky resolution which allowed socialists to participate in capitalist governments. This resolution was regarded by Lenin and the Scottish SDF as support for the forces of revisionism and opportunism in the International. The Scottish SDF saw the Hyndmanite support for Kautsky's resolution as clear support for opportunism in the International. This, together with mounting evidence of the SDF's opportunist practice in Britain, led many Scottish SDF members to question the value of the Federation.[90]

The Scottish SDF began to go its own way and the Scottish District Council produced its own paper, the *Socialist*. Three 'impossibilists' got on to the SDF executive at the end of 1902 and close links were set up between the Scottish SDF and some sections of the London SDF branches. In open conflict with the national organization, two groups seceded from the SDF.

In May 1903 the *Socialist* announced the formation of the SLP and branches were set up in Edinburgh, Falkirk, Glasgow and Leith, with others forming elsewhere later. Small as it was, the SLP played an important part in the distribution of Marxist literature written by Marx, Engels and Kautsky that had previously been unavailable in Britain. This organization became committed to industrial unionism and was important in Clydeside during the First World War. It certainly played a part in the massive wave of industrial unrest that occurred from about 1909 to 1914, although most of that unrest had little to do with syndicalism.[91] Although many leading members of the SLP participated in the negotiations that saw the formation of the CPGB in 1920, the vast majority refused to do so. Indeed, Raymond Challinor makes it clear that the SLP objected to the formation of a CPGB with policies that the BSP supported and that Lenin imposed. At the same time, he notes the SLP's charge that the Second International had degenerated into reformism and its belief in forming a revolutionary party as an élite vanguard force to lead the working class to victory.[92]

The London rebels remained within the SDF until 12 June 1904 when they left to form the Socialist Party of Great Britain. It refused to offer palliatives and seems to have adopted the idea that it should act as a publishing company, spreading the gospel of socialism, and should contest parliamentary elections, with the intention of turning over the entire political and social system once it had a majority in Parliament. It survives today and still produces its *Socialist Standard* but, as yet, has not won a single parliamentary seat.[93]

The SDF faced constant internal arguments and divisions, although it appears to have sustained an average of about 9,000 members throughout the period 1890–1914. They were organized into numerous small branches, the number of which occasionally rose to more than 200. T.A. Jackson, in his *Solo Trumpet*, gives a description of SDF branch life, revealing the propagandist nature of the activities of the dozen or so members who attended:

The customary routine was, after the minutes and correspondence, to fix arrangements for the Sunday propaganda meetings, and for any weekday meetings there might be. The life activity of the branch centres around these propaganda meetings. . . . The speeches at these open-air meetings usually took the form of a general statement of socialist aspirations, a general criticism of capitalism and its evils, and a special application to current happenings – particularly the doings of the local Borough or Town Council.[94]

The SDF's socialist membership had increased but compared unfavourably with the 20,000 to 30,000 members that the ILP had between 1908 and 1911. In addition there were 1,200 Fabians, about 150 to 200 members each of the SLP and SPGB, socialists in the Clarion movement and many other unattached socialists. Thus it is not surprising that the SDF (whether as the SDF, the Social Democratic Party or the British Socialist Party) was at the forefront of attempts to unite socialism. This was not to succeed since most socialists would not contemplate the attempt by Hyndman and the SDF to hijack British socialism as a whole into the Marxist camp.

Socialist Unity, *c.* 1893–1914

Socialist Unity became an issue for the British left within a year of the formation of the SDF because of the secession of William Morris and the formation of the Socialist League. The formation of other socialist parties, such as the ILP, led to further disunity within the British socialist movement. Notwithstanding the proliferation of British socialist societies with their distinctive credentials, there were several attempts to form a united socialist party in Britain between 1893 and 1914. They were normally encouraged either by the advocates of the 'religion of socialism', such as Morris, Blatchford and Victor Grayson, or by Hyndman and the SDF. The aim was to strengthen socialist organizations, whether in periods of success or failure, but in every instance they failed due to the intractable problem of bringing together socialists of distinctively different persuasions under the umbrella of one party. These failures have led recent historians to debate two major questions. Firstly, they have asked at what point did Socialist Unity cease to be a viable alternative to the labour alliance between the ILP and the trade unions. Yeo feels that Socialist Unity became impossible after the mid-1890s; Howell, however, suggests that this 'suppressed alternative' became unlikely about five to ten years later, as the leaders of the ILP opted for the trade union rather that socialist alliance; while Crick feels that Socialist Unity was still a viable alternative until at least 1911, if not 1914, when a determined effort was made to form the BSP, the one socialist party and the forerunner of the Communist Party of Great Britain.[95] Thus 1895, 1900 to 1906 and 1911 to 1914 are offered as alternatives for the point at which the prospects of Socialist Unity in Britain reached a watershed. Historians have been equally divided on the second, and related, question of why was Socialist Unity not achieved. In particular, they have focused upon two subsidiary questions. Firstly, why did the Independent Labour Party choose the alliance with trade unions and the parliamentary route to power rather than Socialist Unity? Secondly, how important was the intransigence and narrowness of the SDF in thwarting moves towards Socialist Unity? Some writers have noted the steadfast opposition of the ILP leadership as the main problem while others have focused upon the inflexible and domineering nature of Hyndman and the SDF, offering the 'image of the Social Democratic Federation as a narrow and dogmatic sect unsuited to the rigours of British politics'.[96]

In fact there was little real prospect of Socialist Unity being achieved in Britain after the mid-1890s and the reason for its failure is to be found in the diverse and compromising nature of the ILP and the continued intransigence of the SDF. Even if the domineering influence of Hyndman has been blown up out of all proportion into a marvellous myth, it is clear that even in 1912 his antipathy towards industrial action was a block to Socialist Unity, as was his attitude towards defence and foreign policy.

As Yeo suggests, by the mid-1890s, with the political failure of the ILP in the general election of 1895, Hardie and the other ILP leaders were forced to choose between the business of 'making socialists' and the need to make a political party. Up to the 1890s socialism was about the former and it did not matter to which socialist organization an individual belonged. Yeo argues that after the 1895 general election and the death of Morris in 1896, the ILP and other socialist groups chose to become entrenched in an alliance with trade unions that focused upon parliamentary and local political organization. Electioneering and the need to win elections replaced the ethical aspects of socialism, which had focused upon leading the ethical life of a socialist. The general drift of Yeo's argument seems fair, even if the fine detail has proved contentious. Indeed, he has argued that party connections became much more important to socialists towards the end of the 1890s. Howell accepts much of this and feels that the alliance with trade unions meant that Socialist Unity became a less likely option.[97] This view seems plausible but it is difficult to concur with the argument put forward by Crick, who seeks to extend the Socialist Unity debate to at least 1911 and possibly 1914. His argument is that many socialists were unattached; that the ILP and the SDF worked closely together in Lancashire; that the socialist revival of the 1904 to 1909 period ensured there was an alternative to the alliance with trade unions on the eve of the First World War; and that the SDF was far more flexible and less sectarian than is often supposed. Nevertheless, his supporting evidence could be interpreted in another way. As Jeff Hill has noted, the SDF in Lancashire appeared to be detached from the policies of its parent organization and its success may have been in spite of the actions of its national body.[98] It was also possible that the vibrancy of socialism was just as likely to produce sectarian rigidity as it was to engender a desire for Socialist Unity, since each organization viewed its own individual successes as confirmation of the correctness of its policies. In the final analysis, the intransigence of both the ILP and the SDF, and the success of the ILP and trade union alliance in 1906, made Socialist Unity a highly unlikely proposition and confirmed the experience of the previous twenty years that socialism in Britain was to be characterized more by schism than by unity. Indeed, there was little prospect of Socialist Unity being achieved in the 1890s and none after 1906 once the LRC/Labour Party had established its trade union credentials and parliamentary ambitions.

In August 1911, Victor Grayson wrote that 'The time for the formation of the British Socialist Party has definitely come.'[99] He then called for others to follow his example and to withdraw from the ILP, vowing never to join another socialist organization until the BSP, the 'one socialist party', had been formed. Grayson's appeal worked briefly. There was a period of ecstatic enthusiasm leading to the Socialist Unity conference in Manchester in September 1911, when a clamour of support emerged. Within a week of his appeal Grayson was writing that 'the British Socialist Party is practically an accomplished fact . . . the response has been extraordinary'.[100] After the Unity Conference, Grayson wrote that it 'was the most harmonious and unanimous Conference of the kind that has ever been held'.[101] It seemed that the dream of uniting socialists of all persuasions under the umbrella of one organization was to become reality. The attempt had been made several times previously but this moment seemed propitious for Britain was experiencing a period of serious industrial unrest and both the ILP and the Labour Party were under attack because of their failure to lead in the fight for socialism. Yet support for the BSP seemed to evaporate almost as quickly as it appeared. The vast majority of ILP members were not attracted to it and the BSP was soon little more than the old SDF/SDP. Yet for a brief moment, carried forward by the impetus of Grayson's enthusiasm, the BSP promised to be something more. The BSP was eventually undermined and destroyed by the bitter disagreements that had blighted earlier moves towards Socialist Unity.

The idea of forming a united socialist party was clearly not new in 1911 and, indeed, it was fitting that Grayson should begin his campaign in the *Clarion* for it was Robert Blatchford, its editor, who had set the precedent by his staunch advocacy of the ideal during the 1890s. In 1894, Blatchford had called for the formation of 'One Socialist Party'. He desired that the ILP, SDF and the Clarion Scouts should submerge their differences and unite all genuine socialists into one party. It was an extension to the provinces of ideas that had already occurred in London in 1892 and 1893 when Morris and the Hammersmith Socialist Society promoted the idea of a union between themselves, the SDF and Fabians. The result of the Morris initiative had been the rather vague and imprecise *Manifesto of English Socialists* issued on May Day 1893. The main weakness of the document is that it excluded the national ILP. Blatchford's appeal was an attempt to rectify this omission. However, the campaign proved to be mistimed and Blatchford's faith was unfounded. The idea of creating some type of mass party concerned more with fellowship than political organization simply did not appeal to Hyndman or Hardie.

Nevertheless, socialist defeats in the 1895 general election revived the prospects of Socialist Unity. Hardie was rather reluctant to push the ILP in this direction, preferring to work for an alliance with the trade unions, but agreed to support the idea of an 'informal conference' with other Socialist organizations on 29 July 1897. At first, the SDF was reluctant to respond to these overtures but financial difficulties forced its leaders to think anew. As a result it decided to send five delegates to the 'informal conference' where it was agreed that a joint committee would be set up until decisions were made about the nature and name of the new arrangement. An additional committee was formed to deal with arbitration in election disputes. Subsequently, H.W. Lee, secretary of the SDF, gave his support to attempts to create real unity between socialists.[102] There was then a referendum of the joint membership of the ILP and the SDF which voted 5,158 to 886 in favour of fusion. However, the decision was never implemented. Hardie intervened to inform the ILP that less than a third of its paying membership had voted and a decision on the ballot was delayed until the next annual conference. In the meantime, Hardie campaigned strongly against fusion and suggested that the methods of propaganda of the SDF and its stagnant membership would 'check rather than help forward our movement'.[103] This was a view supported by J. Bruce Glasier, whose paper to the April 1898 ILP conference in Birmingham maintained that Federation and continued separate existence would be advantageous to the ILP for 'the ways of the SDF are not our ways. If I may say so, the ways of the SDF are more doctrinaire, more Calvinistic, more aggressively sectarian than the ILP'.[104]

The ILP leadership supported Hardie's demand for Federation rather than fusion. It called for a vote by ILP members in July 1898, which resulted in 2,397 voting for Federation and 1,695 for fusion. It had thus blocked the prospect of creating a united socialist party and the issue expired when Lee stressed that the SDF was still 'in favour of fusion'.[105] The belated efforts of Blatchford to revive negotiations failed, even though a poll of *Clarion* readers produced a vote of 4,429 for fusion and 3,994 for Federation.[106]

The ILP leadership had thwarted the attempt to form a united socialist party but there is much evidence to suggest that the rank and file of the ILP was very mixed in its attitude towards Socialist Unity. There appears to have been support for the

Socialist Unity idea in many parts of Lancashire. Littleborough ILP called for 'one militant socialist party'. The branches at Bolton West, Everton and Blackburn opposed the ILP leadership and Stockport ILP announced its intention 'to withdraw from the party' as a result of the undemocratic action of the NAC'.[107]

At the other extreme there was far less support for Socialist Unity in the textile regions of the West Riding of Yorkshire. In Bradford, the ILP's rejection of Socialist Unity was based upon the fact that, even in decline, it had about 1,000 members while the SDF was almost powerless, having started in Bradford in August 1895 with six members, averaged fifteen members and expired in 1897. The ILP had nothing to join with. Not surprisingly, in 1896 the local Labour paper argued, with some justification, that 'the time has not come for the thorough fusion of forces which the creation of such a party would demand. . . . The formation of such a party before the time was ripe would bring nothing but mischief.'[108] The July 1898 issue of the *Record*, organ of the Halifax ILP, did refer to the 'One Socialist Party' campaign going on in Bradford but played down its importance, doubting its 'practical superiority' to the existing situation. The report suggested that the term fusion indicated a hardening of social policies which did not fit the more general approach favoured by the members of the Halifax ILP. Also, most ILP members spent a working week protected by trade union surveillance, and weekends attending Labour church activities, glee club meetings and rambles. Satisfied with their achievements, they were not inclined to join forces with a society that had little presence in Halifax and that appeared to play down the importance of trade unionism. On the whole one is left with the impression that Socialist Unity barely merited serious consideration in the ILP strongholds of Bradford and Halifax. Not surprisingly, the Yorkshire Divisional Council of the ILP had rejected the idea by thirty-two votes to sixteen, as early as October 1894. In Bradford, Halifax and more generally throughout the West Riding of Yorkshire, there was little or no inclination to join with an organization that carried almost no political support. Martin Crick has suggested that the movement for Socialist Unity was probably a movement from the bottom up but even this is partial and barely evident in some areas, most notably in the West Riding of Yorkshire.

There was, therefore, little prospect that Socialist Unity would be achieved in the late 1890s. There were four main reasons for this. In the first place, the ILP leaders and many of their supporters had attached their flags to the trade union mast that the SDF had eschewed. Secondly, there were intense rivalries within the broader socialist movement between Hardie and Blatchford on the one hand and between Hardie and Hyndman on the other. Thirdly, if the ILP was driven by political expediency, so was the SDF, whose leadership showed no inclination towards Socialist Unity until it began to lose members in the late 1890s at a time when it was faced with financial embarrassment. Finally, while just under half the rank-and-file members of the ILP favoured fusion the other half, or possibly the majority, favoured federation and it was the second body, firmly based in Yorkshire, which carried most political clout with the ILP leaders.

It is true, as Crick suggests, that there was nothing unusual in socialists having dual membership of the ILP and SDF. Quite clearly it did not matter to many socialists which organization they joined for to them a socialist Britain was imminent. But after the 1895 general election defeat it was more difficult to sustain hope for the immediate success of socialism, and electioneering and leadership considerations got in the way of sustaining any hopes of socialist success. Indeed, the experience of Lancashire should not be emphasized too much for, as Jeff Hill suggested, there are two factors that need to be taken into consideration when looking at the area. One is that the Lancashire SDF branches acted more flexibly than the parent organization, and some branches still continued to remain in the LRC. Secondly, they paid a price for their flexibility for 'though on the one hand local autonomy was a source of strength in that it allowed social-democrats to adapt to their immediate environment, on the other hand, it produced a movement notoriously prone to internal divisions over strategy and one which ultimately was unable to preserve its identity as a united socialist force'.[109] Even if Socialist Unity had been achieved it seems unlikely that it would have survived. Most probably the ILP would have split, with Hardie leading the West Yorkshire contingent and his other supporters into an alternative organization. In effect the SDF would probably have been left with its own supporters and a few other socialists, much as occurred when the BSP was formed in 1911.

There was a second phase in the development of Socialist Unity at the beginning of the twentieth century. The LRC was formed as a result of a conference held in February 1900 and, at first sight, appeared to have met the needs of both alternative strategies for the progress of the labour movement. On the one hand, it was an alliance between the trade unions and the socialist parties, and on the other, it brought the socialist parties, including the SDF and the ILP, within one organization. Although the LRC was not a socialist organization at this time, five of the twelve members of the executive committee were socialists and there was a prospect that this alliance could be the basis of closer cooperation between the SDF and the ILP. Yet within eighteen months of the founding conference the SDF voted to secede. This decision was taken because 'we were being committed to the support of men and measures with which we do not agree'.[110] Indeed, the ILP and the SDF clashed from the outset when the ILP failed to support the SDF resolution committing the LRC to socialist objectives.

The SDF's secession from the LRC was a mistake for it now cut itself off from the most influential independent political organization of the working classes, although its action is explicable in terms of the internal difficulties within the party which led to the secession of two groups who formed the SPGB and the SLP, organizations usually dubbed the 'impossibilists'.

By 1907 the SDF seemed to have revived an interest in Socialist Unity but, according to Howell, such a prospect had effectively been ruled out by the formation of the LRC: 'The logic of national events . . . combined with local developments . . . to erode the United Socialist alternatives, even in an environment where it had developed a significant presence.'[111] Only Crick seems to doubt this judgement, basing his assessment upon the situation that existed in Lancashire, referred to above, and upon the Dewsbury parliamentary by-election of 1902 where Harry Quelch obtained 1,597 votes as the SDF candidate, 517 votes more than E.R. Hartley had secured in the 1895 general election despite the hostility of the ILP. Referring to the Dewsbury contest, A.M. Thompson, of the *Clarion*, wrote that it was:

> . . . a crushing blow to the conflicting 'Leaders' and a triumphant vindication of Socialist Unity . . . The rank and file of Dewsbury have shown the way. Socialists of all denominations have shut their eyes to the scowlings and nudgings of rival party officials and stood shoulder to shoulder for Socialism.[112]

The problem with Crick's approach is that the Lancashire SDF began to decline after the secession of the national SDF from the LRC, and the Quelch affair produced a damaging conflict between the SDF and the ILP rather than the climate that would have produced Socialist Unity. In any case, this second phase of Socialist Unity, if it can be regarded as such, did not get very far.

Crick is quite correct to suggest that there were strong moves towards the further advocacy of Socialist Unity between 1904 and 1911, although this is not to suggest that it was a viable proposition. The SDF certainly changed its attitude towards Socialist Unity and fully embraced the Amsterdam Conference resolution of 1904, which instructed socialist parties in all countries to amalgamate. However, even though it made approaches to renew negotiations with the ILP in 1907, the SDF conference did so in the face of opposition from Hyndman, who opposed the idea of fusion between the two parties.[113]

There was clearly some sectarian opposition to the idea of Socialist Unity within the SDF and this surfaced when the Labour Party applied for affiliation to the Second International in 1908. Hyndman opposed this move which was put forward by J. Bruce Glasier of the ILP and supported by Karl Kautsky. Hyndman felt that the Labour Party should not be allowed to join until it was a socialist party while Kautsky felt that even though the Labour Party did not recognize the class struggle, it operated it. Lenin gave Kautsky support: he still felt the Labour Party had not broken free of the Liberal Party but believed it would do so if it was informed that it had to accept socialist principles or keep away from the International Socialist Movement. In the end, Kautsky's motion of support for the affiliation of the Labour Party was passed.[114] All this, of course, was to the displeasure of Hyndman who bitterly denounced the action taken in *Justice* in 1908, attacking the International Socialist Bureau as 'whittlers away of principle to suit the convenience of trimmers'.[115] It is also clear that Hyndman was willing to raise the issue of the Labour Party's affiliation at the next Congress of the International at Copenhagen in 1910.[116]

Nevertheless, in 1909 and 1910 there were renewed negotiations between the SDP (the old SDF until 1907) and the ILP, although the ILP laid down the precondition that the SDF should re-affiliate with the LRC. Socialist Unity was on the agenda but it would appear that the SDF became internally divided over the issues of industrial conflict and international relations as new figures in the party, such as Zelda Kahan, began to challenge Hyndman and Quelch. Undoubtedly, the rising emphasis which the SDF placed upon Socialist Unity was a distraction from these internal conflicts but it was hardly going to offer a solution to the conflicts of the SDF/SDP nor to the problem of policy as it emerged in the BSP. The SDF/SDP may have become less narrowly economically deterministic in its attitudes but Hyndman's view was still dominant in the vital years when the BSP was being formed.

There were quite clearly other factors which encouraged the idea of reviving Socialist Unity apart from the convenience it offered to the SDF/SDP. The membership of all socialist organizations rose between 1906 and 1909 and the return of twenty-nine LRC MPs to Parliament in 1909 brought an optimism about social change that was not going to be realized, even by a Labour Party working upon a reforming Liberal government. The contrast between Labour Party inaction and rising socialist ambitions certainly increased tensions between some members of the ILP and the Labour Party. Victor Grayson echoed this disillusionment with the Labour leaders following his success in the Colne Valley parliamentary by-election in 1907, where he had been returned without official Labour Party support. His views were outlined in a book entitled *The Problem of Parliament – A Criticism and a Remedy* (1909), dedicated to 'H.M. Hyndman, Robert Blatchford and J. Keir Hardie, who can give this country a Socialist party tomorrow if they care to lead the way'. At much the same time, E.R. Hartley was arguing in a debate at Manchester that the ILP was 'swamped' within the Labour Party.[117] Indeed, between 1909 and 1911, forty-six branches of the ILP collapsed. The moment seemed propitious for a renewal of the Socialist Unity debate.

Criticism of the ILP intensified. Towards the end of 1910 four of the fourteen members of the NAC of the ILP signed the pamphlet *Let Us Reform the Labour Party*, better known as the 'Green Manifesto'. It attacked the ILP and the Labour Party for sacrificing socialist principles in order not to embarrass the Liberal government.

Subsequently, Fred Jowett criticized these men for their lack of loyalty and all lost their seats on the NAC at the ILP annual conference in 1911.

Also, social representation committees were emerging in towns such as Birmingham and Manchester to unite socialists of all persuasions, including many who were not attached to any particular organization. The United Socialist Propaganda League was formed to combine them and to spread the message to the rural areas.[118] There was sufficient evidence to persuade Grayson, now free of parliamentary duties and the political editor of the *Clarion*, that a call for Socialist Unity would be well received. Within three months he was claiming that about 30 per cent of ILP members had joined the BSP.[119] This seems excessive and percentages of 20 per cent for Yorkshire and about 25 per cent for Lancashire seem more accurate.[120] Within a couple of years these levels were to diminish significantly as individuals and branches drifted out of the BSP. Ultimately, the BSP was to become the SDF/SDP under a new name, under the domination of Hyndman and the old SDF/SDP leadership who appear to have used the new movement to meet both the demands of SDF/SDP members and to thwart the threat that Grayson posed to their control of the membership of the SDF/SDP itself.[121]

In the meantime the Socialist Unity Conference was held at Manchester on the weekend of 30 September to 1 October 1911. Delegates claimed to represent 35,000 members coming from 41 ILP branches, 32 Clarion clubs and fellowships, 85 SDF/SDP branches, 50 local socialist societies and 12 branches of the new BSP, plus other organizations. The BSP was later to claim 40,000 members and 370 branches, although its total dues of £650 based upon 1*s* membership subscription suggests that there were only 13,000 paying members.[122] Matters went well but the provisional committee soon ran into trouble when Grayson realized that the SDF/SDP would not cease to exist immediately. Grayson left the BSP and many of his supporters did the same.

Other problems were added when Hyndman addressed the first annual conference of the BSP in April 1912. While noting the success of the new body, he admitted that there had been difficulties and he attacked syndicalist ideas on the need for industrial unionism, stating that 'of the futility of resuscitated syndicalism it is needless to speak. There is nothing real and nothing ideal in the floundering and hysterical propaganda of segregated grab.'[123] Such a statement from the chair made the 'old guard' position clear. It would concede that 'the political and industrial organizations of the working class must be complementary to each other', but its view that the main function of the BSP was 'the organization of an independent political party of the working class' remained unchanged. Leonard Hall, a syndicalist committed to industrial action to change society, moved an amendment at the first annual conference to gain equal recognition for industrial as well as political action but was defeated by 100 votes to 46. The syndicalist debate continued for several months but they broke from the BSP in

October 1912 when the BSP *Manifesto* was issued, emphasizing the primacy of political over industrial action. Many BSP branches were divided on the issue. The Huddersfield BSP, led by Arthur Gardiner, was a strong advocate of industrial action, partly owing to the pioneer propaganda work of syndicalist E.J.B. Allen, who lived locally. It passed a resolution committing itself to socialist representation and 'to assist in the building up of a powerful union movement'.[124] In other areas there was serious division within the local BSP branches. In Birmingham there was split because of the 'Graysonian clot' on the party.[125] This split was just one of several tensions that divided the BSP. Another major division was the conflict between Hyndman and Zelda Kahan over increased government naval expenditure.[126]

The end product of the infighting was the decline of the BSP. It faced financial problems with Twentieth Century Press, which produced *Justice*; the 'enrol a Million Socialists' campaign, begun in April 1912, failed to get anywhere near the 100,000 members it wished to win in less than a year, never mind the 1 million it hoped for in five, and in fact its total membership fell from a claimed 40,000 in 1912 to a mere 15,313 by 1913.[127] In 1914, the BSP began to woo the Labour Party and the ILP, worked to form the United Socialist Council, organized joint socialist demonstrations with the ILP and the Fabians, and voted by 3,263 to 2,410 in favour of affiliating to the Labour Party.[128] It applied to join the Labour Party on 23 June 1914 and affiliated in 1916. In October 1916 a not very effective United Socialist Council was also formed.

Yeo has written that the formative socialist period of the 1880s and the 1890s was 'too exciting to last' and that 'Socialism in that period had not yet become the prisoner of a particular elaborate machine – a machine which would come to associate its own well-being with the prospects of Socialism'.[129] He was right for by the mid- and late 1890s party electioneering was rapidly taking the place of the task of 'making socialists'. By that time, also, the ILP and the SDF had become almost sectarian in their approach which meant that there was little prospect of obtaining Socialist Unity. If it was the ILP leaders who were intransigent opponents of Socialist Unity in the 1890s as they sought the support of trade unions, the SDF/SDP leaders in the 1911 and 1914 period were also intransigent for there was little evidence that Hyndman was going to change his mind on the issue of industrial action and defence. Hyndman's control of the SDF/SDP might not have been total but it was still sufficient to thwart attempts to unite and keep socialists in one mass party.

In the final analysis, Socialist Unity was a non-starter after the formation of the LRC in 1900 if not before, killed by the rigidity of both ILP and SDF leaders. As the Communist Party of Great Britain was to find, mass party socialism within a united socialist party in Britain has proved always to be an appealing illusion.

Conclusion

Marxism had developed in Britain to a significant extent between the 1850s and the First World War. By 1914 there were about 16,000 active Marxists compared with a few hundred in the 1860s. Nevertheless, Marxism had not developed well in comparison to other sections of the labour movement. Marxist organizations had, by and large, emerged outside the mainstream of the political labour movement dominated by the Labour Party, and the socialists dominated by the ILP. Its links with the trade union movement were also tenuous and constantly strained by Hyndman's hostility to industrial action which created serious divisions within the ranks of the BSP. Hyndman's essentially reactive – rather than pro-active – policy meant that Marxism languished as other sections of the labour movement developed. Given the split between the nationalist and internationalist sections of the BSP, the outbreak of the First World War was a problem to be faced, rather than an opportunity to be seized, by the BSP. World war did, however, help to bring about the Russian Bolshevik Revolution of 1917 and thus eventually changed the direction of Marxism in Britain. Yet, despite the Bolshevik Revolution, Marxism in Britain seemed to retreat, rather than advance, over the next twenty years; its development was greatly influenced by the decisions made in Moscow.

II

The Emergence and Development of the Communist Party of Great Britain, 1914–32

The First World War brought to account the policies that had dominated the Second International ever since it was founded in Paris in 1889 as the forum of socialist parties throughout the world. The Second International condemned the use of standing armies and favoured the creation of citizen armies, assuming that these would prevent capitalist wars and only fight the 'just war'. It also passed peace resolutions. Its efforts were coordinated by the International Socialist Bureau, formed at the Paris Congress in 1900, and yet the tensions between national groupings, most obviously between the German socialists and Hyndman's BSP, and the French internationalists and the German nationalists, meant that there was no coordinated socialist response to war. Internationalists wanted peace while nationalists were prepared for war. In the case of Britain, the First World War divided the BSP along nationalist/internationalist lines and it was not until 1916 that the internationalists prevailed.

The First World War also shaped the development of the Communist Party of Great Britain, which emerged out of the Bolshevik Revolution of 1917 and the pressure applied by Lenin. However, this attempt to create a mass Marxist movement in Britain never succeeded. Many possible reasons for this were rooted in the early years of the movement: most obviously the Marxist and quasi-Marxist movements in Britain had failed to sink roots within the working class between the 1880s and the war. Perhaps there was little that could be done to retrieve Hyndman's negligence. But there were other difficulties. Existing Labour institutions, such as the Labour Party and the trade unions, did not wish to work with Marxist organizations. There was also the well-founded suspicion that the CPGB was controlled by the Comintern (the Communist or Third International formed in March 1919) and the changing policies of the Comintern did not help the CPGB. Indeed, Class Against Class

(1928–33) proved to be an immensely divisive event in the history of the Party with battles raging over 'ultra-leftism', 'right tendencies' and 'Hornerism' and the challenge to trade unions and the Labour Party. It made the position of the CPGB even more tenuous as membership began to fall and produced a spurt of campaigns that the dwindling CPGB membership was unable to sustain in a destructive sectarian atmosphere. Nevertheless, one should be careful of dividing CPGB history into 'good' and 'bad' periods[1] and the importance of the Comintern should be acknowledged 'in laying the basis in Britain for the growth of an effective revolutionary party'[2] even if its activities failed to flourish.

The Outbreak of the First World War

The declaration of war on 4 August 1914 brought to a halt any semblance of anti-war unity among British socialists. The Labour Party supported the war effort while the ILP leadership supported a peace campaign. Hyndman, firmly to the right of the socialist spectrum on the question of war and intensely nationalistic, led the 'old guard' of the SDF/BSP to a pro-war position. At first, the BSP manifesto of 13 August 1914 urged moderation: 'We appeal to you to distinguish soberly between the mass of the German people and the Prussian military caste which dominated the German Empire'.[3] However, Hyndman soon adopted a jingoistic tone. The BSP manifesto of September 1914, which suggested that members should get involved in military recruiting campaigns, brought an outcry from the internationalists, including John Maclean, the Glasgwegian revolutionary, and fifteen of the eighteen London branches.[4] In order to gain support for his chauvinistic views, Hyndman organized five BSP regional conferences in February 1915 instead of the usual national gathering, but these simply revealed a divided party. The Lancashire BSP branches and the Leeds conference supported Hyndman, Arthur Gardiner of Huddersfield being provoked into suggesting that red, white and blue ribbons should be distributed to the delegates of the Leeds conference. The Hyndmanites ran *Justice* and also controlled the central (London) branch of the BSP.[5] In contrast, there was strong opposition to Hyndman's views in London and Glasgow, and the new Executive Committee of the BSP came to be dominated five to four by the internationalists.

This divisive situation worsened when, following an essentially pro-war Conference of the Allied Socialists in London, the Allied internationalists met at Zimmerwald in September 1915 in an attempt to forge a united socialist demand for peace. The Zimmerwald Manifesto criticized the way in which 'Socialist societies have disregarded their obligations' and called for them to 'take up the struggle for peace without annexation'.[6] Hyndman rejected the manifesto but other sections of the BSP were supportive. Now pro-war sections of the BSP began to form into new organizations, most particularly into the Socialist National Defence Committee whose purpose, according to *Justice*, was to 'resist anti-British, pro-German pacifist elements in this country' and 'to insist that the war be pursued to a complete triumph'.[7] This committee formed the British Workers' League *en route* to becoming the National Democratic Party. It attracted many patriotic socialists including Robert Blatchford from the *Clarion* and Will Thorne of the BSP. Hyndman gave his support but did not join the organization and soon dissociated himself from it.

There were many other points of conflict between Hyndman and his anti-war socialist opponents. These reached a crescendo when the state began to arrest some of the anti-war elements of the socialist movement and to introduce both military and industrial conscription. Indeed, it appears that Hyndman collaborated with the British government to inform it of the activities of anti-war socialists and was largely responsible for the arrest and deportation of Peter Petroff, a supporter of John Maclean in Scotland, as a result of an article in *Justice*.[8]

The BSP Conference held at Salford on 23 and 24 April 1916 was to be a decisive moment. The executive of the BSP, no longer dominated by Hyndman, asked for a vote to hold the meeting in secret because of fear of arrest under the Defence of the Realm Act and, though opposed by Hyndman who was by now considered to be almost a spy for the state, this proposal was supported by a vote of seventy-six to twenty-eight.[9] Then, following a pre-arranged plan, twenty-two pro-war delegates walked out of the conference. Hyndman led them to the Deansgate Hotel, Manchester, where he announced the formation of the National Socialist Advisory Committee, soon to become the National Socialist Party (NSP).[10] The remaining internationalist section of the BSP recognized that its power base was small and it affiliated to the Labour Party in 1916, pressing for peace within the ranks of the pro-war Labour Party.

Nevertheless, there were many prominent members of the BSP who continued to fight for revolutionary change. John Maclean was one of the most important of these figures. A schoolteacher, he was active in the industrial dispute on Clydeside in 1915 and 1916, edited the Marxist journal *The Vanguard* and, for his efforts, was imprisoned on five occasions between 1916 and 1922, before his early death in 1923. While active in the BSP he built up the tradition of Marxism on Clydeside and emphasized the revolutionary potential of war which could only be resolved by the working class conquering state power. In many respects he was Glasgow's Lenin, although he was to reject some of Lenin's views on the formation of the CPGB.[11]

Despite the efforts of Maclean to drum up support, by 1917 the BSP was down to 6,435 paying members and the NSP had fewer than 2,000.[12] The future of Marxism in Britain would have been bleak had it not been for the Bolshevik Revolution of 1917.

The Bolshevik Revolution, the Workers' and Soldiers' Councils and Industrial Experience

The downfall of the Tsar in February/March 1917 and the creation of a Provisional Government in Petrograd, offering the prospect of a democratic government in Russia, was well received across almost the whole spectrum of political opinion in Britain. In May, Arthur Henderson visited Russia on behalf of the British government, which wanted an offensive on the Eastern Front: he was criticized by the Bolsheviks and came back convinced that the Russians would only stay in the war if a conference of all socialists was held at Stockholm, an event which never came about although the Bolsheviks, voted to attend.[13]

In this atmosphere of euphoric support for the February Revolution, the ILP and the BSP, through their United Socialist Council, organized the Leeds Convention in June 1917. It was a large meeting, which brought together all the sections of the Labour movement and passed four resolutions: hailing the Russian Revolution; advocating moves towards establishing a general peace based upon the rights of nations to decide their own affairs; demanding the creation of a charter of liberties by the British government; and advocating the formation of a council of workers' and soldiers' delegates in every town, urban and rural district.[14] It was rather less revolutionary than it appeared and it has been suggested that the workers' and soldiers' council movement was designed to press for a negotiated settlement to the war rather than to bring about revolutionary change.[15]

The groups who attended the Leeds Convention did so for varying reasons. The ILP saw it as part of its effort to bring about peace, while the BSP considered the Leeds meeting 'a distinctly revolutionary event, the beginning of a trail which would lead to a revolution in Britain . . . by convincing British workers of the possibility for success of a mass uprising, that is, a "social" revolution rather than the "political" revolution which could be engineered by a minority party'.[16] Sylvia Pankhurst saw the convention in a similar light.[17] The SLP, of course, boycotted the conference and the Bolsheviks seem to have regarded as leftist posturing the role played by 'social chauvinists', such as Ramsay MacDonald and Philip Snowden.[18]

The Workers' and Soldiers' council movement generated by the convention soon faded away. In July 1917 the Labour Party had declared that none of its branches could work with the councils, and many of the delegates who attended as trade union and trades council representatives were doubtful of the value of the conference as they feared that it might challenge their dominance in organizing workers. Returning from the event, the President of the Halifax Trades Council, G. Kaye, reported his disquiet, stating that he did not support the workers' and soldiers' council resolution and that the 'place for these people was in the Labour and socialist movement'.[19]

The Leeds Convention was a product of the Russian Revolution of February 1917 which had blurred political differences within the British labour movement. It achieved little because of the conflicting objectives of its participants.

The Bolshevik Revolution of October 1917 initially changed little but, after a bout of enthusiasm in Britain, fundamentally split the vast majority of anti-Bolsheviks in the British labour movement from the much smaller pro-Bolshevik section.[20] Initially, the Bolshevik Revolution – the single most important event in the international socialist movement – was well received in Britain. There was a spontaneous singing of the 'Red Flag' at the Labour Party conference in January 1918 and cheers at the mention of the names of Leon Trotsky and Maxim Litvinov. The BSP gave its whole-hearted support to the Revolution and, at its Leeds conference in 1918, E.C. Fairchild declared that the party would have to 'apply precisely the same methods the Bolsheviks were applying in Russia. There would have to be a definite break with constitutional methods, and a recourse to the revolutionary process.'[21] Meanwhile, the Socialist Labour Party simply claimed to be the 'British Bolsheviks'.

The BSP's links with Russia were strengthened when M. Chicherin and Peter Petroff, former Russian exiles, were deported from the UK in January 1918, only to assume prominent roles in the revolutionary government in Russia. Joe Fineberg, another Russian exile, also returned to Russia and prepared the way for the arrival of Bolshevik propaganda in Britain. Theodore Rothstein, who had spent many years in Britain, became the chief Bolshevik agent in the UK and directed Russian funds to British revolutionary movements – although the sums were relatively small and the process was opposed later by Rajani Palme Dutt who felt that 'You will get the only loyalty worth having if not a penny passes.'[22]

Russian foreign policy became increasingly important to the Allies who feared the Russians would withdraw from the war and adopt the 'revolutionary defencism' policy of Lenin, which meant that Russia would fight only if her borders were threatened. The Treaty of Brest-Litovsk, which the Bolsheviks were forced to conclude with the Germans in March 1918, saved the Soviets and ended Russia's participation in the war. This decision reflected the weak situation of Bolshevik Russia at this time but provoked the hostility of the British government and the Allies.

At this point the Labour Party began to question what the Bolshevik Revolution meant and to examine the attitude it should develop towards Russia. Despite some doubts it urged the recognition of Soviet Russia and was committed to the 'Hands Off Russia' campaign to stop any Allied intervention in the country at the end of the war. The 'Hands Off Russia' campaign had first emerged in 1918. It was led by W.F. Watson of the London Workers' Committee (LWC), which was affiliated to the Shop Stewards' and Workers' Committee, and Sylvia Pankhurst, who was organizing the Workers' Socialist Federation (WSF) in the East End of London. They worked with the People's Russian Information Bureau, which was set up in July 1918. The 'Hands Off Russia' conference was held on 18 January 1919 at Memorial Hall, London. It brought together the BSP, the SLP and the Industrial Workers of the World, along with a smattering of trade union delegates, representatives from ILP branches, the Women's Co-operative Guild, the Herald League, the No-Conscription Fellowship and other similar organizations. In total there were some 350 delegates who resolved to call a general strike against the fact that Russia had been invaded at the end of the war by fourteen Allied armies, and that Britain had also supplied arms to Poland.[23] It also set up a committee of fifteen London members, including Watson, Pankhurst, Albert Inkpin and Harry Pollitt.[24] *The Masses*, Watson's short-lived industrial unionist paper, also campaigned.[25]

The campaign widened in the summer months and a new 'Hands Off Russia' committee was formed, which included prominent trade unionists such as C.T. Cramp of the National Union of Railwaymen and Alf Purcell of the Furnishing Trades and the TUC Parliamentary Committee. Harry Pollitt was appointed full-time national organizer in September 1919; he was based at Openshaw, near Manchester, was paid out of Russian subventions, campaigned strongly, and distributed Lenin's pamphlet *Appeal to the Toiling Masses*. The Polish attack upon Soviet territory at the end of April 1920 raised the campaign to an even higher pitch and on 10 May, three days after the fall of Kiev, the London dockers refused to supply coal to the SS *Jolly George*, which was loaded with munitions for Poland. The British labour movement supported this direct action and over the following months a central Council of Action was formed by the TUC/Labour Party and 350 local councils of action were set up. Demonstrations were held throughout the country, particularly on Sunday 8 August 1920 and, also in August, the Council of Action threatened a general strike if war occurred. On 17 August it issued a leaflet demanding *Peace with Soviet Russia*.[26] In the event, the invasion of Russia came swiftly to an end, the crisis subsided, and Lenin claimed that 'English Mensheviks' had been forced to follow the 'English Bolsheviks' and that Britain was now at the stage that Russia had been in February 1917.[27]

The Formation of the Communist Party of Great Britain, 1919–21

The successful 'Hands Off Russia' campaign pointed to the need for a more unified Marxist organization in Britain. At the end of July 1920 members of the BSP, some members of the Socialist Labour Party (who had formed the Community Unity Group), the WSF, the shop stewards' movement, the Plebs League, and other small socialist groups and societies, met to form the CPGB in London. The Party's combined strength was about 4,000 at that time but had fallen to 2,500 when it was relaunched at Leeds in 1921.[28]

The history of the CPGB's emergence has been examined in enormous detail in other books and only the essential points need to be presented here.[29] From the outset, the newly formed CPGB was dominated by the old BSP whose secretary, Albert Inkpin, became its business organizer and secretary. It had emerged from a bewildering array of discussions before the First World War within the United Socialist Council, at the fifth and sixth conferences of the BSP in 1916 and 1917, and between various socialist parties, including the SLP and the ILP following the Bolshevik Revolution of 1917. These efforts to form a united communist party came to fruition at the first unity meeting held in London between the representatives of the BSP, SLP, ILP, WSF and the South Wales Socialist Society (SWSS) on 13 May 1919.[30] Here the BSP and the SLP representatives agreed to join the Comintern and to work for revolutionary change through the organization of soviets or workers' councils. The other societies also moved in this direction. Yet these meetings could not reach agreement about tactics. The BSP and the SLP favoured parliamentary activity while the WSF and the SWSS did not. The BSP supported Communist affiliation to the Labour Party, to which it was already affiliated, while the other bodies rejected such an association. As a compromise it was suggested that all the organizations should consult their members about their willingness to merge into one body and that the question of affiliation to the Labour Party should be settled by a referendum of the new party three months after its formation. But matters did not run smoothly.[31] The SWSS did not hold a ballot and almost ceased to exist,[32] and while all the other societies agreed on unity, the BSP continued to be the only body favouring affiliation to the Labour Party.

By early 1920 little had changed and meetings of the Unity Committee on 8 and 24 January achieved nothing.[33] Matters were made worse by the fact that the Western European Committee of the Communist International was formed in Amsterdam and, exceeding its authority, opposed British communists' affiliation to the Labour Party. The BSP resisted this move and deadlock was reached; the SLP declared that it stood 'firmly on the bedrock of no compromise'.[34] The 13 March meeting of the four main organizations took matters no further.[35] There was also some opposition from John Maclean who left the BSP in April 1920, outlined his objections to Lenin about the formation of the CPGB and attempted to form the Communist Party of Scotland. However, swift progress was made from that date onwards.

The SLP negotiators called those in the SLP who supported unity to their own unofficial unity conference at Nottingham in April 1920 at which the Communist Unity Group (CUG) was formed.[36] At the same moment the BSP resolved, at its ninth annual conference, not to permit points of tactical detail to stand in the way of forming the 'United Communist Party'. As a result at a unity conference on 24 April 1920, all the socialist societies agreed to unity, the final decision being taken on 9 May. On

29 May it was further agreed that the tactical differences would be resolved at another Unity Convention called for the beginning of August 1920. Any organization willing to accept the three principles of affiliation to the Communist International, dictatorship of the proletariat and the creation of soviets would be invited to send representatives.

During June and July 1920 a joint provisional committee undertook preparations for CPGB formation but faced many problems. The WSF withdrew from the unity committee and the SWSS was replaced on the committee by the South Wales Communist Council. But eventually on 7 July 1920 the official invitation to the Unity Convention was issued along with a *Call to the Communist Party*. On 8 July 1920 Lenin wrote a letter to the joint provisional committee supporting the Unity Convention and indicating his support for parliamentary activity and affiliation to the Labour Party.[37] Despite the opposition of the official SLP and the WSF, which organized an alternative conference and published Sylvia Pankhurst's oppositional 'Open Letter to Comrade Lenin' in the *Workers' Dreadnought* of 17 July 1920, the Communist Unity Convention took place.

It was held at Cannon Street Hotel on the 31 July and at the International Socialist Club at East Road on 1 August. There were 160 delegates, 96 from the BSP and 22 from the CUG. Among the introductions and greetings was a supportive statement from Lenin advocating affiliation to the Labour Party on the 'condition of free and independent Communist activity',[38] although Lenin saw affiliation to the Labour Party as a matter of tactics to win support, rather than as a matter of principle.[39] Lenin thus steered the CPGB in that direction and later encapsulated his ideas in *Left-Wing Communism, an Infantile Disorder*.[40] In this and the *Draft Theses for the Second Congress of the Communist International* he strongly attacked the 'infantile left' as the ultra-leftists who wanted to progress along the straight road to socialism without having to work within the Labour Party, trade unions and other reformist organizations.

During the same period as the London Unity Convention was meeting, the Second Congress of the Comintern was being held (19 July–7 August 1920) at which Willie Gallacher and Sylvia Pankhurst opposed parliamentary activity and affiliation with the Labour Party while the BSP delegation and J.T. Murphy of the SLP supported these policies. After Lenin had spoken, the session of the Second Comintern Congress devoted to the affiliation to the British Labour Party question ended in a vote of 58 to 24 in favour.[41] Lenin had won support for his view and even persuaded Gallacher to change his stance and join the CPGB.[42]

Meanwhile, at the London Unity Convention in July and August 1920 the CPGB committed itself to using soviets or workers' councils to win political power for the working class and further declared itself in favour of the dictatorship of the proletariat for combating counter-revolutionary action in the transition from capitalism to communism. The fundamental strategy was clear but the issue of tactics had still to be decided. There was a heated debate over parliamentary action, which was agreed to by 4,650 votes to 475 (186 cards to 19). The more contentious issue of affiliation to the Labour Party was carried by the narrow margin of 100 votes to 85. The CPGB was now in business and a provisional executive committee was formed, consisting of six members elected by the convention who would be added to the existing members of the joint provisional committee. Albert Inkpin was to act as its secretary.

Within less than six months the Party met again at the Leeds Convention (29–30 January 1921). This event arose from the Comintern's call for further unity with the CPGB immediately after the end of its Second Congress. The fact is that there were other small socialist and Marxist groups operating outside the CPGB. Scottish revolutionary groups and the Scottish shop stewards had formed the Communist Labour Party in September 1920 and had called a conference in October under the leadership of J.R. Campbell, a prominent communist journalist in later years. This party contained many anti-parliamentarians and anti-Labour Party people, but wanted unity and moved towards negotiations with the CPGB. There was also the self-styled Communist Party (British Section Third International) – formed in Manchester on 18–19 September 1920 and including Sylvia Pankhurst among its members[43] – which agreed to unity negotiations at its conference at Cardiff on 4–5 December. These two bodies, along with others, joined with the CPGB to publish a circular letter on 15 November calling for a meeting on 11–12 December 1920 at which it was agreed that they would move to unification at the new Unity Convention at Leeds on 29–30 January 1921.[44] At this convention the wider CPGB was formed and *Communist* was adopted as the official organ of the new party.[45]

Debates

At this juncture it is useful to reflect upon the historiography of debate concerning the CPGB. The major question has been: was the CPGB an artificial creation forced upon Britain by Lenin or did it arise from an indigenous revolutionary movement? Martin Crick has suggested that there is sufficient evidence that an indigenous Marxist movement had developed by 1917, that it had dropped the social democracy of Hyndman, and that it was accepting the Bolshevik approach: 'What is important is that between 1914 and 1919 the Marxists of the BSP came to accept the Bolshevik viewpoint not because it was imposed upon them but because they accepted its validity.'[46] This theory obviously rejects the ideas of Walter Kendall and Raymond Challinor, both of whom believe that the Soviet Union dictated events and imposed itself upon an indigenous revolutionary movement. Kendall believes that a native British Marxist tradition was developing around John Maclean but that Theodore Rothstein, an exiled Lithuanian who was active in the SDF/BSP and later became the chief Bolshevik agent in Britain, was responsible for diverting the BSP from a revolutionary tradition into Comintern sectarianism.[47] Challinor generally concurs with Kendall, but suggests that Rothstein misled Lenin about the situation in Britain and argues that the SLP, not the BSP, was the true originator of British Bolshevism.[48]

This conflict of opinion raises several other related debates. For instance, there is Kendall's implication that the situation in 1918–20 held revolutionary potential, that it was the 'missed revolution, which the British revolutionary groups failed to recognize'. In contrast, Crick suggests that it seems unlikely that a revolution could have occurred given the weakness of the BSP, the division of the opponents of the war and the failure of industrial action on Clydeside and elsewhere. It would seem that the weak indigenous movement missed the revolutionary opportunity and that the success of the Russian Bolsheviks provided the basis for subsequent domination by Moscow.

There is also the Trotskyist argument that there was revolutionary potential at this time, that it was wasted, yet in spite of this the CPGB had built up considerable influence within the British Labour movement between 1922 and 1926. Unfortunately the CPGB, under Stalin's direction, did not capitalize upon these successes in the General Strike of 1926 when it failed to develop a revolutionary situation and merely called for 'All Power to the General Council'.[49]

Returning to the main debates it seems almost axiomatic that the CPGB was formed because of Lenin's pressure rather than as a result of the desire of British Marxists to unite. The intention was to form a mass party: the second main question facing historians is – why did the Communist Party fail to become the party of the working classes? Many explanations have been put forward, ranging from the poor economic conditions of the inter-war years and the bureaucratic degeneration of the Communist Party to the suggestion that Marxism was alien to the British social and political system, manipulated as it was by Moscow. Ross McKibbin has said that there were many conflicting social interests within the working class that cut across the possibility of the CPGB developing into a mass revolutionary working-class movement.[50] There may be some truth in all these explanations but probably of more importance is the fact that the CPGB was formed too late to exert much influence on the trade union movement and to make good the connection which previous Marxist organizations had often neglected, despite the exaggerated successes of the Minority Movement.[51] As John Callaghan suggests, without the trade union movement the CPGB was unable to win the support of the working classes.[52]

Nevertheless, there were some areas of communist support, the 'Little Moscows', which Stuart Macintyre suggests may have been the tip of a proletarian culture based upon Marxism.[53] There is no doubt that communist communities, such as Mardy in South Wales, and Lumphinnans and the Vale of Leven, in Scotland, did emerge. Yet such islands of support were not typical of Britain as a whole and may have been rooted in problems peculiar to those communities. Even so, one cannot assume a continuity of communist influence in these 'Little Moscows' because the movement had to be fought for against a background of police prosecutions and the expulsion of members from the trade unions and the Labour Party, which meant that even in communities such as Mardy communist support fluctuated considerably. The detailed records of the Party are a constant reminder of the difficulty that the CPGB faced in trying to secure and maintain a sizeable active membership, something it was never able to achieve in the 1920s and the early 1930s.

It is important to keep both debates – on the formation of the CPGB and its failure to become the mass party – in mind when examining the history of the CPGB between 1921 and 1932. However, what is obvious from the outset is the feeling of revolutionary imminence that many Marxist felt in the decade following the Bolshevik Revolution of 1917.

Communist Party of Great Britain, 1921–28: Politics, Trade Unionism and Auxiliary Bodies

The CPGB was formed as a result of the activities of the Comintern. Through this organization Lenin, Trotsky and Zinoviev had sought to bring together Marxists of all countries to fight for world revolution. It was considered essential that a communist party should be formed in every country, including Britain. As Kendall and Challinor have stressed, it was Lenin and the Comintern who persuaded British Marxists to form the CPGB.[54] The Soviet Communist Party directed 'Moscow money' to certain sections, most notably to the old BSP leaders, and the Comintern, at its Second Congress in 1920, laid down twenty-one conditions that were designed to ensure that only truly communist organizations became its members. There were always groups within the CPGB that were prepared to criticize the official line of the Comintern but once the Comintern changed its mind the official attitude of the CPGB followed, despite some temporary dissent.

In addition to its own representatives, such as Peter Petrovsky, the Comintern operated influence in Britain through Rajani Palme Dutt and Harry Pollitt: the latter, despite his occasional protests, always acknowledged his 'primary allegiance to Moscow'.[55] Salme Dutt completed the 'Holy or Unholy Trinity' of the Dutts and Pollitt: they acted as a caucus to change the leadership of the CPGB in the 1920s. Indeed, they worked together to create a Leninist Party in 1922 and, in 1923, Dutt proposed Pollitt as the General Secretary of the Party to replace Inkpin and to challenge the old leadership.[56] From the mid-1920s until 1936 the Dutts lived in Amsterdam because of Rajani's ill-health, earning a living by writing and receiving a £10 monthly salary from the Comintern.[57] The relationship between the Dutts and

Pollitt was not free from dispute.[58] There were clashes over Comintern policy, particularly on the implications of the Class Against Class policy – on which Rajani and Harry were initially united in 1928 – and again in connection with the changing CPGB policy towards the Second World War.[59] In 1928, Pollitt complained of an article that Dutt had written in *Labour Monthly*. Dutt replied, 'Your letter leaves me staggered.'[60] Dutt later objected to Pollitt's support for the Party's criticism of himself.[61] However, good relations were soon restored.

The Comintern was a constantly evolving organization which exerted considerable influence upon the CPGB, for example with the change of line from united front to Class Against Class in 1928. It felt that the great danger was monopoly capitalism which it believed created international tensions, wars and instability. It therefore maintained that reformist trade unions and socialist parties were merely appendages of the bourgeois state operating inside the workers' movements. It also suggested that the capitalist state, no matter how democratic it was, was merely a reflection of the control and dictatorship of monopoly business and finance. True democracy could only be established in a soviet republic. Therefore, what mattered was the acquisition of power by the revolutionary party for this was the measure of progress towards socialism. Leninism was thus to turn British Marxism into a doctrine of action. No longer were British Marxists to await the inevitable economic collapse of capitalism, in the style of the SDF; they were now committed to revolutionary action. Dutt, Pollitt and Harry Inkpin, in their famous *Report of Organization* (usually known as the Dutt-Pollitt Report), sought to Bolshevize the CPGB by getting rid of inactive Party branches and creating in their place active groups of members who would be responsible for promoting the campaigns of the Party. In effect the report was an attempt to prevent the CPGB from collapsing by modernizing it with the aim of attracting mass support. The slogan of the paper was 'Down with the old style branch' and the aim was to set up a 'network of influences through the working class and its organization'.

Dutt claimed that with the report 'a transformation took place in the life and work of the Party', although he recognized that there had been some falling back under the 'right-wing leadership' after 1926.[62] This was a clear reference to the reluctance of the Communist leaders to implement the suggested reforms. Yet there was some early criticism that all had not gone well, with J.T. Murphy stating that: 'If I were asked what are the principal defects of the party today, I would answer unhesitatingly, formalism, organizational fetishism and the lack of political training.'[63] Pollitt dismissed Murphy's criticisms and was not inclined to hold back on the 'Bolshevization' of the Party.[64] Murphy simply retorted that all the Party did was mechanically follow through the Comintern resolutions and reflected that in the CPGB 'there were few in it who had more than a nodding acquaintance with the writings of Marx'.[65] Murphy was right but the CPGB remained relatively unified as it followed uncritically the bureaucratization process within the Comintern presided over by the triumvirate of Stalin, Kamenev and Zinoviev. However, there does seem to have been some slippage in membership; it fell to fewer than 3,000 by 1930. Not surprisingly the Political Bureau was worried and its minutes, particularly for 1930, expressed the view that the 1922 reforms had not been carried through in many branches.

The *Workers' Weekly* appeared in February 1923 as part of the drive to transform the Party and replaced the fading *Communist*. Dutt acted as editor and raised circulation from 19,000 to 51,000 in eight weeks.[66] It was seen as 'an organ of working-class life and struggle deep rooted in the factories'. However, reorganization and propaganda alone would never be sufficient to achieve political power. The problem of how to win mass support in Britain remained. Socialist developments were still dominated and controlled by the trade unions and the Labour Party.

Lenin encouraged the CPGB to apply for affiliation to the Labour Party to strengthen its appeal, but there was some reluctance within the CPGB leadership to pursue this policy. Indeed, at a special ECCI (Executive Committee of the Communist International) Commission in July 1923 the Party was sharply criticized for its 'inadequate and aimless' application of the United Front tactics of working with the Labour Party and was encouraged to make more of an effort.[67] However, Labour Party conferences rejected all CPGB affiliation attempts between 1920 and 1924, opposing the last by 4,115,000 votes to 224,000.[68] At that point the Labour Party conference added a rule to its standing orders preventing the issue being voted on for another three years.[69] There was, of course, little chance that the Labour Party would ever allow the CPGB to affiliate and thus permit itself to be used as a platform for communist expansion. And the hostile attitude of the CPGB to the first Labour government of 1924 did not help matters.

The CPGB had initially welcomed the fact that the minority Labour government had taken power. The Party expected that Labour would put forward a socialist programme and improve the position of the working classes. However Labour then appeared to be acting against working-class interests: the outcomes of the rail strike of January 1924, the dockers' strike, the London Traffic strike and the builders' strike all revealed the Labour government to be encouraging the trade unions to settle on poor terms. The continuation of British imperialism in India in unremitting terms against the independence movement and the relatively bullish nature of British foreign affairs gradually turned the CPGB against Labour, even though it had officially recognized the Soviet Union. The Party issued *The Future of the Labour Government – A Call to All Workers*[70] in which it stated that :

The Labour Government is in existence at a time when the workers are in a state of revolt against the intolerable conditions imposed upon them during the last three years. Yet instead of the Labour Government openly taking the side of the workers, and using the whole resources of the government on their behalf, they have already threatened on two occasions . . . to use the forces of the state against the workers . . . the Labour Government has shown itself the servant of the bourgeoisie . . . the Labour Cabinet Ministers have become the missionaries of a new imperialism.

Relations with the Labour Party remained poor but the Sixth Congress of the CPGB in May 1924 decided to continue to apply for affiliation and directed criticism at Ramsay MacDonald rather than the Party itself.[71] However, Labour was still not prepared to consider CPGB affiliation and the events of the Campbell Case confirmed their prejudice against communism. This famous dispute began on 25 July 1924 when the *Workers' Weekly* published an 'Open Letter to the Fighting Forces' (written by Pollitt) and demanded that the armed forces should not turn their guns on their fellow workers, calling instead for them to organize committees in barracks, aerodromes and ships. J.R. Campbell, the acting editor, was arrested on 5 August 1924 in the place of Dutt who was out of the country, and charged under the Incitement to Mutiny Act of 1797. After some pressure from the labour movement, and fearing that the case would collapse, the government dropped charges against Campbell. However, the handling of the case became the basis of a motion of censure against the Labour government on 8 October 1924, and led to its collapse. In such a climate of hostility, much less a general election with the distraction of the Zinoviev Letter (the infamous forgery which called on the Communist Party to prepare for an armed insurrection), it is hardly surprising that relations between the CPGB and the Labour Party were poor.

It is hardly surprising, given the opposition of the Labour Party and thus the majority of working-class voters, that the CPGB was never able to establish a parliamentary group. It returned only J.T. Walton Newbold (Motherwell) and S. Saklatvala (Battersea) at the 1922 general election and S. Saklatvala (Battersea) at the general election in October 1924.[72] Saklatvala was defeated in 1931 but the CPGB won another parliamentary seat in 1935 when Willie Gallacher was returned for West Fife.[73]

The CPGB, the National Minority Movement, the General Strike and the National Left-Wing Movement

Rejected by the Labour Party and failing to secure a parliamentary niche, the CPGB employed 'auxiliary' bodies to strengthen its position. In 1921, the Comintern encouraged the formation of the British Bureau of the Red International of Labour Unions (Profintern). The London committee was formed on 6 March and assumed responsibility for circulating the objectives of the Red International of Labour Unions (RILU) to the 'Trade Unionists of London'. The intention, of course, was to establish trade union solidarity with the CPGB.[74]

This strategy presented the Party with the problem of how to deal with the trade unions. Supporting rank-and-file strike activity that was in conflict with the views of the trade union leaders was seen as damaging to the prospects of developing trade union support for the CPGB. Yet the rank-and-file approach was pursued in the case of the miners' strike and 'Black Friday' in April 1921 and with the engineering lock-out of April–June 1922. Despite its efforts, which included an extensive campaign based upon the slogan 'Stop the Retreat' in the engineering lock-out, there was little the CPGB could do to prevent the victory of the employers. The employers' offensive gathered further momentum in 1923 and led to the dockers' strike in the summer of 1923. Faced with a reduction of 1s per day in pay, from 11s to 10s, and a lengthening of the hours of work from eight to nine per day dockers throughout the country began to strike spontaneously in July 1923. However, by August it was only the London dockers who were still out. Ernest Bevin, the Secretary of the Transport and General Workers' Union, urged them to return to work while the CPGB encouraged the Dockers' Unofficial Strike Committee to extend the dispute to other ports rather than to break away from the union. The Unofficial Committee stated: 'The Dockers' strike is a spontaneous revolt, not against the Union as Mr Bevin claims, but against wages that just mean starvation.'[75] In the end, Bevin prevailed upon the men to return to work on 21 August 1923.

By this time Pollitt was playing an increasingly important role in the CPGB's trade union and strike policy, stressing the need to work inside, not outside, the unions; this was known as the Minority Movement. He wrote:

The minority movement inside the unions is growing. Moving up and down the country, coming into contact with the workers everywhere, one can sense the new feeling of discontent that is rapidly springing up. The minority movement in the various industries must harness this discontent and guide it along the right lines.[76]

In 1923 Pollitt, the Comintern and the CPGB decided to form the National Minority Movement (NMM or MM) to unite trade unions more effectively with the communist cause. The NMM was instituted in January 1924 and declared its aims in August 1924. These included:

a wage increase of £1 a week, with a minimum wage of £4; a 44-hour week, and no overtime. Workshop and Factory Committees with members guaranteed against victimisation; Workers' Control of Industry; a stronger TUC, with control over the

Labour Party; industrial unionism; the affiliation of the National Unemployed Workers' Committee Movement and the trades councils to the TUC.[77]

It also committed itself to more revolutionary aims:

> to organize the working classes of Britain for the overthrow of capitalism, the emancipation of the workers from the oppressors and exploiters, and the establishment of a Socialist Commonwealth; to carry on a wide agitation and propaganda for the principles of revolutionary class struggle . . . and against the present tendency towards social peace and class collaboration and the delusion of the peaceful transitions from capitalism to socialism; to unite the workers in their everyday struggles against the exploiters; to maintain the closest relations with the R.I.L.U.[78]

To these ends, the NMM set out guideline lectures for metal workers, railway workers, miners, transport workers and other occupational groups.[79] At its 1927 conference it declared its intention to fight against the capitalist offensive on wages and hours, declared its commitment to working with the unions and proclaimed its intention to 'agitate for one union for each industry, a centralised General Council and a single Trade Union International'.[80]

In addition to the NMM, the CPGB also helped to organize the unemployed through the National Unemployed Workers' Committee Movement (NUWCM, later NUWM) formed on 15 April 1921. Led by Walter Hannington and other leading members of the CPGB, it supported the unemployed occupation of the Wandsworth Workhouse in July 1921 and the Poplar struggles (September–October 1921) over the level of benefits for the poor. Its first major activity was to organize a national hunger march, when 2,000 people from all over the country descended upon London on 17 November 1922 to present the Prime Minister with a petition.[81] The NUWCM also organized 'Unemployed Sunday' for 7 January 1923 and campaigned intensively for the jobless over the next few months. There were numerous local hunger marches in the late 1920s and five more national ones in 1929, 1930, 1932, 1934 and 1936.

There were also many other communist initiatives to widen support. The CPGB set up a Women's Department in 1922[82] and the first National Conference of Communist Women was held on 18–19 May 1924 at Manchester as part of the Sixth Party Congress; this was at a time when only about 14 per cent of the membership was female. Yet the CPGB's women's organization was always weak and was forced to go through several revivals in the early 1930s. The Young Communist League of Great Britain (YCL) was also formed in October 1921.[83] It soon began to produce its newspaper, the *Young Communist*, and held its first national conference in August 1922.[84] The YCL aimed to win support within the trade unions and in the factories but like other communist organizations it faced the problem of a wildly fluctuating membership and had to be radically altered in the early 1930s.

These 'auxiliary' organizations exerted a limited influence within the wider labour movement. Nevertheless, the NMM claimed extensive trade union support – 1 million of the 5½ million trade union members in 1926 – and Pollitt suggested that it 'could capture the TUC if it continued working along existing lines'.[85] J.R. Campbell also felt that the 1925 TUC had 'trod the path of the class struggle by adopting some of the leading aims of the Minority Movement'.[86] However, Campbell's comments were about a TUC that, in reality, aimed to prevent trades councils and trade unions sending communists as delegates and Roderick Martin has demonstrated that the NMM exaggerated its influence, particularly once the CPGB supported the formation of independent trade unionism in the Class Against Class period.[87]

Part of the NMM's problem was that the General Council of the TUC recognized that the National Federation of Trades Councils, formed in 1922, had been taken over partly by the communists and that trades councils were sending communist representatives to the TUC. In 1926 the General Council decided to take action, following votes at the 1925 and 1926 TUC, and instructed that trades councils could not be members of the NMM. This decision was partly influenced by the CPGB's hostile attitude towards the TUC's conduct of the General Strike of May 1926.

The General Strike was a setback for the CPGB. At the outset of the dispute it had used the slogan 'All Power to the General Council' (of the TUC). However, the force of this commitment was undermined by the fact that a dozen of the CPGB's leading figures, including Pollitt, had been arrested for seditious libel, found guilty and imprisoned for six months to one year before the dispute began. Nevertheless, the remnants of the Communist leadership helped organize support. Robin Page Arnot, released from prison on the eve of the dispute, was active in running the strike in the north-east and communists got involved in the work of councils of action throughout the country. However, the fact is that while there were many communists helping the strike effort throughout the country there is little evidence that they led the councils of action or strike committees. Only in Battersea, London, did the CPGB carry significant influence, with ten communists on the committee of 124, of whom four were on the seven-member executive committee.[88] But communist support was accepted because it was aimed at maintaining the strike effort, not because of its revolutionary potential. Indeed, James Klugmann, a prominent CPGB member and its historian in later years, wrote that:

The Party well knew that on the eve of the strike the workers were eager for action, but not in the sense of a revolutionary mood. They were ready to fight on economic issues, to show their solidarity with the miners to defy the threat of government – but they were *not* ready to challenge the social system. The Party knew, too, that many of those taking part in this great unprecedented strike, particularly those most deeply involved in it, could in a few days develop further politically than in the years of more 'normal' times. Its problem was how to help to organize the struggle, develop the local leaderships of the Councils of Action, lift the level of the strike, put forward step by step, new lines of action and prepare, as far as possible, for continued struggle when, as it had so often warned, the General Council capitulated. Not easy![89]

Klugmann's comments are not entirely unmindful of the debates which had been going on within the Comintern throughout the dispute. The General Strike had, in fact, become another source of conflict in the struggles within the Bolshevik Party and the ECCI (Comintern) between the left opposition, led by Trotsky, and the duumvirate of Stalin and Bukharin. The former suggested that the General Strike should be pushed to revolution while the latter opposed such a policy as they were eager not to upset relations with the TUC leaders on the Anglo-Russian Trade Union Committee. It was Stalin's and Bukharin's position that prevailed.[90]

CPGB support for the General Strike held good until the dispute was called off on 12 May 1926 after only nine days, during which time up to half the Party membership had been arrested. A Party infuriated by the call for an end to the dispute attacked the TUC:

> The General Council's decision to call off the General Strike is the greatest crime that has ever been permitted, not only against the miners, but against the workers of Great Britain and the whole world. The British workers had aroused the astonishment and admiration of the world by the enthusiasm with which they had entered upon the fight for the miners' standard of living. But instead of responding to this magnificent lead by a call . . . the General Council has miserably thrown itself and the miners on the tender mercies of the workers' worst enemies – the Tory Government.[91]

The Party's attack upon the TUC made it difficult to maintain any significant CPGB support within the trade union movement, although it did move to reduce the criticism at the end of May 1926 and allowed George Hicks, of the General Council, to write in the Party's papers that the General Strike had been a 'great victory'.[92] However, the CPGB membership did rise to about 10,000 by the end of 1926, mainly as a result of recruitment in the mining areas of the South Wales and the north-east coalfield, but these figures soon dwindled away.

The CPGB's estimation of its own performance in the dispute was very critical. The Central Committee report to the Eighth Congress (1926) suggested that:

Communications were a problem from the outset, as it became clear that we had not sufficiently mobilised even the very scanty resources at our disposal. . . . The Party entered the General Strike with political and organizational slogans that were inevitably defensive in character . . . once the masses were on the streets the business of the Central Committee was to extend these slogans, at the same time making them more aggressive in character.[93]

Party criticism of the TUC speeded up action against its members. By 1927 the trades councils were beginning to make moves against their Communist delegates and in May 1927 the Communist majority was removed from the executive of the London Trades Council. This action gained wide approval within the trade union movement, including support from Herbert Smith, the miners' leader whose union had its fair share of Communist influence, and the Miners' Minority Movement.[94] The National Union of General and Municipal Workers suspended C.J. Moody, a communist member of its general council, and seventeen other members in February 1927.[95] Walter Citrine, General Secretary of the TUC, also launched a sustained attack upon the Minority Movement in *Labour*.

Given the difficulties of sustaining trade union support it is perhaps not surprising that there were now renewed efforts to influence the Labour Party through 'auxiliary' bodies. In 1925 the National Left-Wing Movement (NLWM) was developed by communists within the Labour Party, following the Labour Party's Liverpool Conference, the purpose of which was to develop a link between the left wing of Labour and the CPGB. The communists were attempting to penetrate the mass Labour movement through the trade unions and the constituency Labour parties.

Following its formation the NLWM gathered some support in the Labour Party in South Wales and London. Shortly after the General Strike, the Greater London Left-Wing Group formed the National Left-Wing Movement which held its first national conference at Poplar Town Hall, London, in September 1926. It then held a number of district conferences – one particularly successful one at Newcastle. By the time of its 1927 annual conference it was claiming 150,000 members, including many non-communists, such as Alex Gossip, Secretary of the Furnishing Trades Association, and Will Lawther of the Durham Miners' Executive. Yet the NLWM did not develop much further. There appear to have been two reasons for this. Firstly, the Labour Party expelled twenty-seven constituency associations connected with the CPGB between 1926 and 1929 and threatened dozens of others with expulsion.[96] The expelled organizations included the trades council and Labour Party organizations for Battersea, Holborn and Bethnal Green in 1926; Rhondda West Divisional Labour Party in 1927; and Southport Trades Council and Labour Party in 1929. The majority were, however, local Labour parties in London where 434 out of 1,105 CPGB members were active in constituency Labour groups.[97] The attack upon them was led by Herbert Morrison, secretary of the London Labour Party. Secondly, the NLWM was affected by events within international Marxism. The Comintern officially withdrew from its united front policy with reformist parties at its Sixth Congress in the summer of 1928, although the alternative Class Against Class line had been developing for several months before. This move had been provoked by a number of developments within the Soviet Union: Stalin had expelled the Left Opposition from the Communist Party of the Soviet Union (CPSU) and then turned upon the Right Opposition led by Bukharin. As Soviet domestic policy moved leftwards with the adoption of the first Five-Year Plan, Stalin and the Comintern leadership 'groped towards a new tactical orientation'.[98] In order to justify the attack upon the Right Opposition within the CPSU, Stalin urged the Comintern to attack social democracy in both its parliamentary and trade union forms.

The CPGB, once it accepted this line, decided to abandon the attempt to work with and within the Labour Party. As a result, Pollitt was convinced of the need to wind up the NLWM, although there was resistance to this policy from Dutt. In a letter to Pollitt on a statement connected with Class Against Class, Dutt explained 'Only you can't say "liquidate the NLW" as a slogan because (1) it is murdering a baby (2) we still want to have a left-wing opposition fraction within the LP even after the final break.'[99] However, Dutt became disillusioned with the NLWM once it began to present itself as an alternative political party. Commenting upon a press report he noted that the '"Left Wing is selecting candidates for Parliament" not just seeking to work within the Labour Party'.[100] He noted that this would mean that there would be three political parties – the Labour Party, the NLWM and the CPGB – competing for parliamentary votes at the next general election. The CPGB recognized the dangers and accepted the need for vigilance in ensuring that the National Left Wing did not 'develop as an independent political leadership inside and between the Communist Party and the official Labour Party'.[101] The CPGB agreed to suspend the NLWM on 18–19 November 1928 and it collapsed in 1929.[102]

Little seemed to be going well for the CPGB. However, as John Callaghan suggests that the real problem ran deeper than the failure of communism to develop trade union and left-wing connections: there were no bitter and massive splits in the Labour movement comparable to those that occurred in Europe during the First World War and led to the emergence of mass communist parties. To Callaghan, British quasi-Marxist organizations were too small and had failed to detach the working class from the existing political system. Lenin's revolutionary approach was thus a non-starter in Britain.[103]

The continued failure of the CPGB to become a mass party provoked detailed examination throughout the 1920s and an internal leadership struggle. The

Comintern appointed British commissions to examine the whole position of the CPGB in 1921 and again in February 1922. This led to the decision to commission and implement the Dutt-Pollitt Organization Report, already referred to. However, some members thought the failure lay in the CPGB's advocacy of social democracy. By the late 1920s the most vociferous critics of social democracy were Tom Wintringham, Esmond Higgins and Dutt – all of whom had been at Balliol College, Oxford – as well as Robin Page Arnot of the Labour Research Department, Salme Dutt, Pollitt, and a number of young middle-class women, including Rose Cohen. The alliance between Pollitt and the Dutts was the core of this group's activities[104] and Salme Dutt may have been the most influential figure here since her husband, Pollitt and Wintringham acknowledged that they could not make decisions without her approval.[105]

Palme Dutt, with the support of Gallacher, who was the Party's vice-chairman in 1921, began the moves which led to an internal power struggle in 1922 and 1923. In a coordinated movement against the old leadership, Gallacher called for an organization commission to be formed in March 1922. Dutt, chairman at the insistence of the Comintern, and Pollitt were the leading members of that body. Following the guidelines laid down by the Comintern's Third Congress, the Dutt-Pollitt Report suggested that branches of active members should be formed and that their views should move upwards through various organizational layers.

In a confused round of meetings within the CPGB, it is clear that the Dutt-Pollitt Report was formally accepted but ignored. When the reformers appealed to the Comintern to replace the old leadership of the CPGB their demands were simply rejected.[106] It appears that the Third Plenum of the Comintern, in June 1923, still felt safer with the existing leadership and believed that any changes should be directed towards setting up a special left-wing industrial organization (the National Minority Movement). Nevertheless, the reformers gained a majority on the Political Bureau, a full-time organization which had just been formed to act as the CPGB's day-to-day executive authority. Pollitt became national organizer of the CPGB and was given responsibility for the industrial work. Nevertheless, Dutt felt that he and the reformers had been 'completely beaten'.[107]

Internal disputes continued within the Party over the next few years even as Pollitt threw himself into industrial work and the Dutts moved to Amsterdam, where they remained until 1936. Dutt remained a member of several CPGB bodies, wrote many reports for the CPGB, continued to edit the *Labour Monthly*, and attempted to keep the CPGB in line with the Comintern's policies. However, it was not until the introduction of the Comintern's Class Against Class policy, which classed all social democratic parties as bourgeois formations, that Dutt, Pollitt and the reformers truly came to the fore.

CPGB: the Evolution of Class Against Class, 1928–30

At its Sixth Congress in July 1928 the Comintern adopted the policy of Class Against Class. This new sectarian tactic claimed that the capitalist world was on the verge of new revolutionary upheavals and that the main obstacles to revolution were the reformist socialist and labour parties, which were labelled 'social fascist' organisations. Historians have recently acknowledged the immense damage done to the CPGB by the new policy.[108] Kevin Morgan regards the Class Against Class period as a watershed in the Party's history: 'My own belief is that it brought the CP to such a pass that, but for the Soviet subventions, it would virtually have collapsed.'[109] However, at the outset the situation appeared far from serious to those demanding change.

Between 1920 and 1927 the CPGB had made slow progress. Its membership was low although it enjoyed some internal unity. It was under attack from the TUC leadership, rejected by the Labour Party and was increasingly concerned about the NLWM. It was at this juncture, at the end of 1927, that the Comintern, encouraged by Bukharin,[110] advocated the policy of Class Against Class and the rejection of the united front with social democratic parties. Eventually, the Sixth Congress of the Comintern, held between July to September 1928, endorsed this 'new line'.

The Ninth Congress of the CPGB was still pursuing the 'old line' at Salford on 8–9 October 1927 but a telegram from Bukharin, President of the Comintern and its Political Secretariat, alerted the leadership of the CPGB to imminent changes. On 1 October the CPGB executive received Bukharin's telegram, which emphasized the need to step up the 'fight against the bourgeois leadership of the Labour Party' and the need to fight as an independent party at the coming elections.[111] It seems that the CPGB leadership suppressed this telegram and Willie Gallacher, speaking to the ECCI Political Secretariat on 18 November 1927, suggested that the Party 'will not take the letter seriously'. Pollitt, also in Moscow in October 1927, was harangued by both Stalin and Bukharin on the need for the 'new line'.[112] Eventually, on 15 December 1927, the Presidium of the EECI held in Moscow declared that the CPGB should not support the return of a Labour government and introduced the slogan demanding a 'revolutionary Labour government'.[113]

This change of policy was not popular with the old leadership of the Party and its British advocates were in the minority. For three days in January 1928, the CC of the CPGB discussed the 'new line'. This led to much soul-searching in which Campbell argued that the new leftist attitude would make the CPGB a socialist sect: 'We might get a larger membership amongst proletarian intellectuals desirous of making the CP a socialist monastery, but we would lose our influence in the working class immediately.'[114]

The Class Against Class line was still a minority view being expressed by Dutt and Pollitt. Indeed, Dutt, writing to Pollitt just before the meeting, referred to it as 'our line' and added that 'We need not be troubled if we are defeated this time. The issue will arise again, and can only end in one way.'[115] Pollitt drew up a statement on his position and signed it on 24 January 1928, advocating the end of the attempt to work with the Labour Party and the end of the NLWM.[116] Dutt also outlined the new position further, damning the Labour Party and the trade unions as the 'pseudo left', and arguing that:

> The question now arises whether the time has not come to advance to a new stage, a stage of direct and open fight against the reformist leadership of the Labour Party, while continuing to the maximum extent the policy of the united front from below with the workers in the Labour Party.[117]

He proposed that Labour Party candidates should be opposed at the coming general election, maintained that the political situation had changed between 1920 and 1928 and that the decline of capitalism and the Labour Party's abandonment of socialism meant that the 'new line' had to be pressed forward.[118]

The dispute within the CPGB became somewhat academic when the Ninth Plenum (of the Comintern) was held in Moscow in February 1928. At this meeting, Campbell and Gallacher fought for the 'old line' but found their views rejected in favour of the 'new line' put forward by Arnot on behalf of the absent Dutt and Pollitt. The CC of the CPGB still expressed doubts at this development but by the summer the Sixth World Congress was accepting Class Against Class as a guideline for all communist parties in European countries.[119]

The Comintern's official adoption of the Class Against Class line forced the CPGB to re-evaluate its future direction. The Central Committee meeting of 18–19 November 1928 resolved that a party congress would be held in January 1929 when the demand for affiliation to the Labour Party would be dropped, trade unions would be urged to disaffiliate from the Labour Party and workers encouraged to keep paying their political levies to trade unions in the hope of eventually gaining some local Communist control.[120] In fact the Comintern was not yet prepared to abandon affiliation to the Labour Party and the matter was dropped from the Congress, although the NLWM was wound up against the advice of the Comintern. However, relations with the Labour Party continued to deteriorate and, following Comintern advice and the Central Committee meetings on 23 March 1929 and April 1929, it was decided that communists would abstain from voting for the Labour Party candidates in the general election of 31 May 1929 and would put forward their own potential MPs.

The CPGB produced its *Class Against Class* election manifesto, which argued that the Labour Party was to be regarded as the third capitalist party in Britain and outlined a sixteen-point programme for a Revolutionary Workers' Government which would declare Britain to be a Workers' Socialist Republic, nationalize banks, repudiate the national debt, and establish a seven-hour working day.[121] In the event, the CPGB put forward 25 candidates at the general election, secured 50,000 votes – an average of about 5.3 per cent of the vote in the contested constituencies – and won no seats. This failure prompted some doubts about the wisdom of adopting the 'new line' and the reconstructed Political Bureau, which was dominated by supporters of the 'old line', hinted that the dissolution of the NLWM was 'open to reconsideration'.[122]

During the general election, Pollitt had himself experienced a humiliating defeat in the Seaham contest against J. Ramsay MacDonald. Pollitt attacked sham elections and preached 'Down with Conservatism, Liberalism and Labourism – the three allies of the united front of mondism and empire!' but admitted that 'it was impossible to raise any enthusiasm for our policy'[123] and recorded that at his adoption meeting for the election held at Dawdon Miners' Hall not one person turned up, indicating the negative effects of the 'new line' as practised in the recent Dawdon miners' dispute, which occurred in the Seaham constituency.[124] The political humiliation was felt throughout the Party which now also faced serious problems with its industrial policy.

Indeed, there were serious implications for trade unionism arising from the 'new line'. Most obviously, there was the view in RILU circles that the CPGB and the Minority Movement should develop 'independent leadership' on the factory floor in order to eventually develop a revolutionary trade union movement, although it was felt that work should also continue within the reformist trade unions to expose the treachery of the leaders and to win over the rank and file to the new revolutionary trade unions. This view was put forward by A. Lozovsky (General Secretary) to the Fourth Congress of the RILU in April 1928. It was resisted by Arthur Horner, leader of the Miners' Minority Movement, and later by Pollitt, both of whom felt that the trade union movement should not be split. Nevertheless, pressure to create independent trade unions continued. The British ECCI (Comintern) delegation in Moscow passed a resolution in favour of formation of a 'red' seamen's union in the place of the 'fascist character' of the present one, which had been the only union to oppose the General Strike in 1926. The resolution called for a Minority Movement conference to make such a call but the Political Bureau (21 August 1928) opposed this and the Central Committee wrote a letter on the matter to the ECCI Political Secretariat declaring that 'we had absolutely no organization of any description at all amongst the seamen' and to 'attempt to form such a union would make the . . . Minority Movement look ridiculous'.[125] The Political Bureau referred the matter to the Central Committee meeting on 24–6 September 1928 where it was noted that there was no prospect of forming a new seamen's union. There were better prospects elsewhere.

Communists had gained control of the Fife Miners' Union in 1928, but a breakaway union of right-wingers was formed and recognized by the Scottish Executive of the Miners' Federation in February 1929. This prompted the Fife Union to become part of the independent United Mineworkers of Scotland (UMS) in April 1929. Also, following an unofficial strike by the tailors and garment workers, the United Clothing Workers' Union was formed in London under Communist leadership.[126] When these developments were combined with pressure from RILU to promote 'independent unionism', it is not surprising that in August 1929 the Sixth Annual Conference of the Minority Movement accepted the principle of 'independent leadership'.

The 'new line' also ensured that there would be a change of leadership within the CPGB. Pollitt was placed upon the Secretariat (of three and later five): it decided that Dutt would join the new PB and that he should stop editing *Labour Monthly* in favour of editing *Communist Review*.[127] At this time the Secretariat ran the Party, a Political Bureau of ten members acted as a small executive committee, and a Central Committee of thirty-one members, drawn together to represent the regional interests of the Party, was the larger executive committee to which, theoretically, the PB referred for final decisions. Adding Pollitt to the full-time Secretariat was a stage in the move to ease Albert Inkpin out of the secretaryship. In fact this was not achieved until later in the year and the new Secretariat was composed of Pollitt, Campbell and Inkpin. Gallacher and Murphy, who were critical of the 'new line', were dropped from the PB after a meeting of the CC on 15–16 June 1929. At this meeting, which followed discussions at the Tenth Plenum in Moscow and took into consideration comments from the districts, it was finally agreed that Inkpin would leave the Party administrative structure and that Pollitt would take over. The Leeds Congress of the CPGB in November 1929 confirmed these moves and maintained that the reason for the decline of communist membership from 7,000 to 3,000 in the previous eighteen months was the failure to apply the 'new line' properly. An article in the *Communist Review* reflected that 'the old Party leadership was decisively defeated', and that congress was correct to carry over those from the old leadership who could contribute to the development of the 'new line'.[128]

The Leeds Congress was a significant turning point in the history of the CPGB for it sought to reverse the decline of Communist membership by embarking upon numerous sectarian campaigns, most of which failed. The Party's actions thus produced further recriminations and dissension, and provided fuel for British Commissions of the Comintern in 1930 and 1931 that sought explanations for the continued decline of British communism without focusing upon the obvious problems created by the 'new line'. In the meantime, however, the process of transference from the old to the new leadership was finally completed.[129]

Dissension and the Failure of the Industrial Campaigns under Class Against Class, 1929–32

The failures of Class Against Class provoked one of the most bitter and controversial periods in the history of the CPGB. In this climate no one was free from criticism as campaign after campaign and strike after strike failed.

Pollitt, now General Secretary, was not above reproach largely because while supporting the mass industrial action of workers within factory groups and cells, he did not wish to conflict with the trade union leadership. The Dawdon colliery strike of March to June 1929 revealed Pollitt's position. The strike resulted from a threatened cut in piece-rate payments and saw the miners reject, in three ballots, the new terms recommended by Miners' Federation of Great Britain. Maurice Ferguson, the Tyneside district organizer of the CPGB, demanded independent leadership but Pollitt argued that the old strike committee should be continued and that a 'vigilance' committee should be formed to influence and monitor the strike's leaders. Pollitt and the Tyneside Communist leadership were thus in conflict, the latter noting bitterly that Pollitt's Seaham election campaign (of May 1929) 'would have done credit to the ILP in its better days'.[130] Yet it must be remembered that the Tyneside district of the CPGB was fully behind the formation of a vigilance committee to 'keep an eye on your interests and see your leaders don't arrange a "Sell Out"'.[131]

Pollitt's support for the old reformist trade unionism was criticized in the PB, although he was brought into line when Lozovsky, on behalf of the Comintern, intervened to stress independent leadership of trade unions at the conference of the Minority Movement in August 1929.[132] Dutt also detected Pollitt's 'right tendencies' and defined them to him in the following manner:

> In essence the Right tendency is over-estimation of the strength of capitalism . . ., underestimation of the radicalisation of the working class, wrong relationships to social democracy, lack of confidence in the leadership of the Party; and on the basis of this, *surrender to depression, pessimism, scepticism, passivity.*[133]

A few months later, Dutt wrote to Pollitt that he got from his letters 'an impression of despondency and disbelief in everything about the Party, personal secrecy of things, overwhelming in detailed troubles, and no clear political line'.[134] Pollitt attempted to follow the 'new line' with the ritualistic utterances against reformist trade unions from the end of 1929, partly demoralized by the constant inner Party strife that was turning his image from a 'Prince Rupert' into a 'social fascist'.[135] However, he continued to deflect the Party from independent unionism whenever it was possible to do so.[136]

From the summer of 1929, the CPGB, encouraged by the Tenth ECCI Plenum of 3–19 July 1929, began to accept D. Manuilsky's belief in the need to examine every gesture, statement and action of its members in the self-critical way the German communists did. The Tenth Plenum also moved to radicalize the Comintern's trade union tactics whereby every strike was to become part of the struggle to bring about revolutionary change. With the defeat of the Bukharinites in the Russian Communist Party, Lozovsky, head of the Red International Labour Unions, demanded the formation of separate 'red unions' and the CPGB was informed that it needed to move more quickly to achieve this. *Communist International* and *Inprecorr* published many articles in the summer of 1929 noting the revolt of the membership against the 'old line'. The Comintern instructed D. Petrovsky (under the name A.J. Bennett) to ensure that three members of the Political Bureau (Inkpin, Rothstein and Wilson) were removed from office.[137]

Pollitt was also under scrutiny and at the Eleventh Congress of the CPGB his opposition to the imminent launch of the *Daily Worker* was rejected and his views were described as having the 'essence of the Right danger'.[138] In contrast to Pollitt's view, William Rust, later editor of the *Daily Worker*, painted an heroic image of the paper's efforts to publish in the face of police harassment in 1931,[139] though he had to admit that it 'was not yet a paper for the masses'.[140] Indeed, there were complaints that the publication was losing £500 per week, that sales had fallen from 44,000 to 39,000,[141] and that it was 'neither aggressive enough nor coherent' .[142] There was also criticism of its arid style and its tendency to act as a CPGB newsheet. After nearly six months of publication, Dutt reflected that 'the paper will never obtain a mass circulation so long as it remains a narrow Party political bulletin. Talk to any group selling the paper; talk to workers who buy the paper . . . and they will admit that the paper is taken out of loyalty'.[143] The *Daily Worker* made many adjustments in staff, staff pay, and production but still did not break even. By June 1930 circulation was down to 25,000. Nevertheless, the Party endorsed its work. At the end of the decade, the publication was still relying upon a fighting fund of £1,500 per month to survive as well as subventions from Moscow.

The industrial policy of the CPGB continued to create problems as it still failed to capture the mass support of the working class. In the face of the severe depression that had been prompted by the Wall Street Crash of November 1929 it seemed, according to the Comintern (which issued a resolution entitled 'The Maturing of the World Economic Crisis: Mass Unemployment and Strike Action' in February 1930) that the world economic crisis for capitalism was at hand.[144] The Party accepted the theory and saw the wage reductions demanded by employers as evidence of it. Given that the Party – rather than the trade unions – was now resisting employers, it felt that it was bound to attract mass support. Independent leadership was thus on the agenda.

Many industrial campaigns were now launched and fought, almost on a weekly basis. However, underlying the industrial policy of the CPGB was the Workers' Charter. It appeared at the end of July 1930 and expired in the early months of 1932. It was the child of the Fifth World Congress of RILU which argued that the:

Minority Movement must formulate a broad united front programme of action – the Workers' Charter – around which to rally and organize the employed and unemployed, organized and unorganized workers. The programme must contain a small number of simple and popular demands embodying the most important needs of the masses affecting wages, working conditions, unemployment, struggles against anti-labour legislation and arbitration and colonial repression.[145]

Initially, it demanded the introduction of the seven-hour day, opposition to the speeding up of work, increased unemployment benefits, a fight against increased insurance contributions, a minimum £3 national weekly wage, the repeal of the Trades Disputes Act of 1927, and opposition to imperialism and tariff attacks upon the workers. Other issues were added to this appeal to the masses from time to time.[146] However, at the end of 1930 it was admitted that:

It is not yet clearly understood that the campaign for the Charter is the means for winning workers inside the Labour party, the ILP, the Co-op, guilds etc. to fight against the Labour party and the TUC policy and against the Labour Government, and of mobilizing the masses for independent struggle.[147]

The Workers' Charter emerged at a time when the Party was trying to apply the 'new line' but making few gains in membership. The Party organized the unsuccessful 6 March demonstrations against the Labour government but declared that it found a 'general under-estimation of the willingness of the mass of the workers to struggle. March 6th showed the Party generally lagging behind the masses.'[148] The hunger march of 1930, directed against the Labour government's unemployment policy, fared no better despite the presence of a women's contingent.[149] At the end of January 1930, the event had been forced upon a reluctant Hannington, who felt that there was insufficient time to organize it. He noted that the previous national hunger march had occurred under Baldwin's Tory government and had been aided by some Labour organizations 'which [sic] would not render assistance in a demonstration against the MacDonald Government'.[150] In the event, it was the least effective of all the inter-war hunger marches with only a few hundred participants descending upon London.

The 1 August demonstrations, when the Workers' Charter was put forward, fared no better. Indeed, afterwards Dutt wrote to Pollitt about the failure of the Party to attract and keep new members, noting how new recruits wanted to be part 'of a living revolutionary movement' but were made to feel 'outsiders' by a 'handful of all-knowing old members' and were effectively ignored.[151]

Failure led to a British Commission being formed by the Comintern. It met on 6 August 1930, reported in September and asked 'Why in a favourable situation our Party was [sic] in such grave danger of being isolated from the working-class movement?' The commission stubbornly suggested that the 'new line' was not wrong 'but that what was wrong was the method by which it was being applied' and it maintained that the Workers' Charter was the way forward, since it would provide the necessary links between the Party and the workers. However, it added that there had been 'a great tendency to look at trade unions as played out. If comrades did work in the trade unions, they are sneered at as trade union legalists. . . . We have to take a decisive turn to bring our comrades back into the trade unions.'[152] This cut across the idea of independent unionism.

Notwithstanding such endorsement the Charter campaign faltered. The *Workers' Charter* pamphlet sold about 120,000 copies and the National Charter Convention of April 1931 attracted more than 800 delegates.[153] But such success was illusory. J.T. Murphy suggested that the convention was more a meeting of the Minority Movement than a Charter Conference, as there was little broadening of influence.[154] Pollitt's claim that Charter had done much 'to break down the dangerous isolation which existed, and the strong tendencies towards sectarianism' was clearly an exaggeration.[155] Indeed, only a few months before Dutt had informed the Party that the Workers' Charter Campaign was not related to the political situation except in a 'mechanical' way.[156] The fact is that Charter was eventually subsumed by other campaigns, such as the 'Five Slogans' or 'Five Points' effort directed against the 10 per cent cut in unemployment benefit imposed by the National Government in the autumn of 1931. The Workers' Charter eventually faded away.[157]

One constant difficulty the Charter's supporters had faced was the confusion of roles. The Minority Movement and the Charter committees were effectively doing the same job in seeking mass support. On the one hand, an open letter from RILU (Profintern), circulated in April 1931, restated that 'The Minority Movement must be the leader of the fight for the Workers' Charter.'[158] Dutt, on the other hand, felt that this was the duty of the Charter movement,[159] although he warned that 'we must not try to use the Charter campaign as our universal maid-of-all-work organisation for every single job that arises, as if it could for all practical purposes replace both the Party and the MM'.[160] Where did primacy lie?

All the policies connected with the Class Against Class line were failing. Scapegoats had to be found. This was most evident in the change of leadership and the expulsions, threatened expulsions and disciplining that occurred in the failed strike initiatives that littered the CPGB's history between 1930 and 1932.

The removal of the old leadership set the new tone of conflict and recrimination. The Comintern sent Walter Ulbricht to Britain in July 1929 to assist in the task of removing the old guard and two-thirds of the Central Committee.[161] In the early months of 1930 the Party was occupied in dealing with the issues surrounding the dismissals of Albert Inkpin, J.R. Wilson, Ernie Cant and Beth Turner.[162] They were removed from office in the Party, often with little prospect of outside employment. Pollitt, virtually alone, fought for the four to be given employment in some other area of Party work, not wishing 'to be associated with the comrades responsible for carrying out such a policy' of victimization.[163] His actions increased the suspicion that he was also a right-winger.[164]

Those removed soon proved hostile to the changes in the CPGB. Inkpin's 'attitude was even more vicious than previously' and he suggested that 'the Secretariat was more like Fred Carno's organization than a political organization'. Wilson reacted by suggesting, with some justification, that 'comrades at present in the leadership of the Party made more mistakes, right mistakes, than himself'.[165] Ernie Cant was less vociferous than the others but complained that he had little prospect of gaining employment in Nottingham where he had been sent by the Party.[166]

The eviction of the old leadership was but the tip of the iceberg of internal disputes. A more obvious cause of conflict was the failure to win mass support via individual leadership. This failure was immediately evident in the case of the Bradford woollen strike of early 1930 which saw the castigation of both the local leaders and national leaders for 'right tendencies'. The strike began in April 1930 when about 250,000 woollen workers faced wage reductions.[167] The Minority Movement held a conference on 23 March from which a committee of action was formed later – it became the central strike committee. This body issued a call for the formation of a mill committee for each mill but, given that its membership was dominated by unemployed woollen workers and sympathizers and contained only one delegate from the mills, it is hardly surprising that its appeal was ignored. Nevertheless, the central strike committee did organize picketing, collected money, conducted marches and invited prominent Communist activists to help. Indeed, Gallacher noted that mill committees were being formed and that 'Fairly good progress was being made in Bradford, whose Council of Action was issuing the manifesto and bulletins; non-Party elements were being drawn into the meetings called.'[168] Yet there were problems. E.H. Brown, organizer of the Bradford district of the CPGB, expressed his alarm at 'the non-representative character of the main strike committee', and Gallacher felt that while 'the strike situation was very strong' the Bradford organization was very poor compared with that of the Shipley strike committee.[169] The strike had encouraged a growth in the membership of the

Bradford branch of the CPGB from 66 to 300, yet, as Idris Cox noted, 'ten Communist cells had been formed in Bradford and seven in Shipley but so far no mill committees were in existence, and no steps were being taken for their formation'.[170] Gallacher accepted this point at the end of May.[171] At this juncture the CPGB anticipated a 'complete betrayal of the strike by the trade union leaders'.[172] It was right: the various textile unions authorized separate negotiations with the individual employers and brought their action to an end.[173] The woollen workers returned and within weeks half of the Bradford CPGB's 240 new recruits had fallen away.

Hamstrung by the 'new line' of independent leadership the CPGB looked to a scapegoat for the failure. Brown was attacked in the first month of the dispute when Pollitt described him 'as an unscrupulous opportunist of the worst type' and Rust referred to him as ' a political and personal opportunist.'[174] Brown admitted that he had never been clear on how to form the mill committees and that despite his efforts, 'at practically every mill in Bradford', little had occurred. He was supported by J.T. Murphy who suggested also that there had been no chance of getting a mass mill committee 'because it was feared that this would lead . . . to ideas of a new union'. The 'new line' had not made matters easy but Brown was criticized from two opposing, incompatible, directions – that he had not made enough effort to win support within the unions and that broad mill committees had not been developed as an alternative to the reformist trade unions.[175]

The bitterness at the failure of the woollen textile dispute was later compounded by the defeat of Willie Gallacher in the parliamentary by-election at Shipley on 6 November 1930 when he gained only 701 votes, or 1.7 per cent of the vote.[176] On election day Murphy suggested, 'Until we tackle the Bradford leadership and Comrade Brown, it will be impossible to change the situation. . . . Unless we get from 3,000 to 4,000 votes in the Shipley Election it will be a blow to the Party.'[177] The following week Rust mounted a personal attack upon Brown, blaming him for the failure of the Bradford strike and dismissing Brown's suggestion that the reason for the failure was the reluctance of the centre of the CPGB and the *Daily Worker* to make it a national campaign.[178]

The main lessons learned from the woollen textile dispute were that Communist activists had to be involved in the workplace and that there had to be some type of relationship with the existing reformist trade unions. Obviously, this was something that the 'new line' was inhibiting. The problem with the 'new line' became even more evident in the case of the South Wales miners' dispute of early 1931, which gave rise to the term 'Hornerism'. This term was later defined by Will Paynter as 'politics takes second place to the trade union job, and when they conflict, as they did on occasion for Horner and myself, loyalty to the trade unions comes first.'[179]

This strike had arisen from the 1930 Coal Mines Act, which reduced the mining hours per shift from eight to seven-and-a-half and prompted the South Wales mine owners to reduce wages from 1 January 1931. The miners struck for two weeks but were urged back to work by the Labour government and trade union officials to await the arbitration award of March 1931, which advocated that the miners' wages be reduced by 6 per cent. This was accepted by a narrow majority of the South Wales Miners' Federation (SWMF) on 20 March. The communist Central Strike Committee asked the miners to continue with their strike action but only six pits remained out and the strikers soon drifted back to work.

In effect, the Party played little part in the dispute. It had already come into conflict with the SWMF at the end of 1930, when it had suggested that the Federation's Rhondda 100 per cent union membership campaign was a ploy to restrict communist influence; there was also ill-feeling connected with the exclusion of the communist-controlled Mardy branch from the union.[180] Despite the restrictions these developments put upon the CPGB, Arthur Horner, the secretary of the miners' section of the Minority Movement, was blamed for the Party's poor performance. He had been a member of the Central Committee in 1929 but had gone off to work with the RILU in Moscow, returning to Britain in December 1930 before assuming his new position. He quickly organized a conference at Cardiff on 10 January where the 55 delegates, allegedly representing 20,000 miners, had set up a strike committee with himself as chairman. Yet the strike committee carried no significant influence and only one communist was present at the meeting one week later when the SWMF decided to return to work. Horner then asked to be relieved of his position as chairman of the Central Strike Committee. His complaint was that 'the role of the SWMF was practically disregarded' and that the Minority Movement was isolated.[181] This was a view supported by others.[182]

The Party attacked Horner, criticizing his assumption that it was impossible to carry on independent struggle.[183] Pollitt remarked that 'the General impression of the South Wales comrades' was that 'nothing would be done to weaken the Federation'.[184] Pollitt's comments emerged from the report that Idris Cox had produced on the situation: on 27 February the PB published a statement attacking the defeatist role of Horner, based upon the Idris Cox report.[185] It stressed that the line of the PB was one of relentless struggle against the Labour government and the trade unions on the basis of the independent leadership of the struggle by the Minority Movement's independently elected strike committees. It added that:

Comrade Horner accepted this line in words. In practice he sabotaged the policy of independent leadership . . . in fact, it can be said that Comrade Horner at no time freed himself from the belief that the bureaucracy could be compelled to fight for the workers, and he betrayed at every step a complete lack of confidence in the fighting power of the masses, and the ability of the MM to lead the struggle independently, and a failure to understand revolutionary perspectives in Britain.[186]

Campbell added that 'he was always harping back to the great possibilities of the trade union movement'.[187]

Such statements fuelled further conflict within the Party over its industrial strategy. Horner blamed the Party leadership for not getting involved in preparing to win mass working-class support and was specifically opposed to the Idris Cox report on the South Wales situation, which he referred to as a 'mass of misrepresentation and lies'.[188] Referring to the PB statement, Horner reflected, 'This is not a political decision – it is your defence for the attack on me, finding me as a scapegoat for the mess in South Wales.'[189] He later asserted that neither 'the Central Committee nor the Local were in possession of the full facts, and to some extent they were moved on inaccurate information'.[190] He reflected that: 'It is clear that the resolutions calling for my expulsion are to some extent instigated by the leadership and I regard them as such.'

In May 1930, Horner was brought before the Central Committee where he rebutted the accusations made against him but was bitterly attacked by Cox and Pollitt who claimed that he was 'opposed to the line of independent struggle and leadership' and the Class Against Class policy.[191] In the end, it was decided that he would have to go to Moscow for re-education. After discussions extending over six weeks he returned to Britain and made a statement in September 1931 agreeing that his political line had been mistaken – 'I am now convinced that my line, the line pursued in the South Wales strike was not compatible with the line of the Communist International' – and expressed his belief that 'the line of the PB' was correct.[192] One month later, he stood for East Rhondda in the general election, winning 10,359 votes (compared to the Labour candidate's 22,000), the highest vote gained by a Communist in that general election; the 26 Communist candidates in fact secured 75,000 votes, 7.5 per cent of the total poll in the constituencies for which they stood.

Like Brown before him, Horner had been brought into line for being too committed to working with the reformist trade unions and for not developing independent leadership of trade unionism. It was therefore ironic that, at the same meeting at which Horner accepted that he had failed to follow the 'new line', Campbell should talk of the flexibility in the 'new line' and a more 'confident approach to trade union branches'.

The fact is that by the end of 1931 the Party's efforts to make the Workers' Charter succeed, to organize the unemployed and women, and to create a mass base of support had failed. The Party was simply not attracting and retaining new members; in addition, it was losing old ones. Towards the end of 1931 it claimed about 4,500 members (up on the 2,555 of 1930 but well down on the membership for 1928); there were in fact more than 4,500 on the register and only 3,200 paid up.[193] During the previous year the Party had attracted 2,500 members but 2,000 had left; well over a third of the members were unemployed and 700 were housewives who were not in a position to influence factory groups or trade unions. The ability of the Party to gain mass support was still extremely restricted. The Comintern therefore set up a British Commission which met in the autumn of 1931 and reported in mid-January 1932. This commission decided that there were too many slogans and not enough action, and that there were insufficient street and factory cells. Yet the greatest significance of this Commission was that Pollitt managed to get the ECCI of the Comintern to change its position, thus enabling the CPGB to abandon the independent leadership line.

Pollitt challenged Lozovsky at the RILU Central Council session: he pointed out that trade unions were not a barrier to the growth of the Minority Movement and other communist organizations but were institutions through which the Party could grow. When the British Commission published its findings as the 'January Resolution' it referred to the need to fight for the 'transformation of the trade union branches from organs of class collaboration into organs of class struggle':

> We must get comrades elected as shop stewards and on every force and aspect of organization that may exist – on a work's committee, pit committee, departmental committee . . .
>
> The question of our work in the reformist Trade Unions particularly is open to misinterpretation . . . The Central Committee of RILU is going to see, at all costs, that internationally a drive is made for carrying out relatively mass work in the reformist trade unions, plus the line we have tried to indicate in regard to work in the factories, as being the two main essentials by which we shall lay a firm basis for independent leadership for independent struggles . . . there has been a conception in our Party that the new line meant the desertion of work in the reformist trade unions. There is a feeling that the unions are played out in the Party. A war must be waged on these two conceptions . . . It would be wrong to try to separate the work of the unions from the work in the factories. They are both part of the same fight and process. There . . . must be no intended re-formulation of the phrase that the trade unions are schools of communism.[194]

This general line was presented in the *Communist Review* and the *Daily Worker* over the next few months in an attempt to inaugurate a new phase in the Party's relations with the trade unions.[195] The messages were clear: distinctions had to be drawn between the Party line and the reformist line; mass influence had to be 'rooted above all in the factories and trade unions'; and 'the greatest defect of the Party's work during the past few years is that it had not carried on any systematic revolutionary mass work in the reformist trade unions'. In addition, it was stated that 'Every party member and all workers who sympathise with the party must be members of the reformist trade unions in order to carry on the struggle against the trade unions and for the transformation of the trade union branches from organs of class collaboration to organs of class struggle' and 'the most important concrete task of the British party in the immediate future is correct work in the preparing and carrying through of the strike struggles of the workers'.[196] It is perhaps no surprise that Communist activists were perplexed at the changes and reflected, as one South Wales comrade did, that the 'new line' 'is a return to the old line' and that 'the resolution [January Resolution] justified the opposition of Horner'.[197]

However, an about turn could not be done to order. Party members had often neglected trade union work and Pollitt reflected that only two of the 700 delegates at the 1932 TUC were communists.[198] This lack of trade union presence was further illustrated by the failure to achieve much in the Lancashire cotton strike. The cotton textile industry was badly affected by the economic depression during 1930–1 and the employers decided to rationalize the industry by reducing wages, increasing working hours, raising the number of looms worked by each weaver, and introducing other cost-cutting activities. Little progress was made in reducing costs and therefore national action gave way to local action – the Cotton Spinners' and Manufacturers' Association allowed all local associations to impose these conditions mill by mill. From May 1932 the employers attempted to introduce wage reductions of 10 to 15 per cent and to force the adoption of the more-looms system. Strike conflict broke out in Great Harewood, Burnley and Blackburn.[199] There was a rolling system of strikes throughout the region, although in Burnley there was effectively a local 'general strike' during the summer of 1932.

The CPGB showed great interest in this dispute but exerted little influence. Although Arnot pointed out the successes achieved at some Burnley mills in fighting off increases in hours in February 1932,[200] Pollitt, referring later to the recent strikes in the Manchester region, reflected that 'we do not yet know how to lead a strike: we had a strike committee set up in Hawley Syke and one in Sampson and Baldwins, but did we really lead the strike? No, we did not. It was the trade union officials who led the strike.' He suggested that Party had neglected trade union work because it felt that all the lower trade union officials were class traitors.[201]

The failure of Communists to win significant support for strike action also reflected the hesitancy in the Party about the new approach to trade unions in what Dutt referred to as the 'recent tendency to reverse our whole trade-union line'.[202] There ensued a major debate in the *Daily Worker* between September and November 1932, in which Pollitt and Dutt sparred over the trade union policy, Pollitt claiming that he was intent upon destroying the influence of trade union leaders rather than the trade unions.

This was, of course, all shadow-boxing in anticipation of the Twelfth Congress of the Party held between 12 and 15 November 1932, which put forward the development of rank-and-file movements as the future basis of the development of independent leadership through the factories and within the trade union movement. The subsequent report of the meeting noted that 'The January resolution was a real Leninist document, pointing out clearly that the role of the Party was to be the vanguard and organiser of the working class and showing concretely how this was to be done.'[203] This was quickly accepted as the mainspring of the Party's future industrial policy. Thus, this Congress gave rise to the demand for rank-and-file organizations within the reformist trade unions.[204]

This rank-and-file movement was already operating before December 1932, revealing itself in the formation of the Members' Right Movement in the engineering industry. This was created in the summer of 1931 after the Amalgamated Engineering Union had made the decision to sign an agreement with employers to reduce wages without consulting the union membership. The Minority Movement led protests from some members and many of them, including Edmund Frow of Manchester, were expelled. Rather than form another union they set up the Members' Right Movement to fight for their reinstatement and published their own paper, *The Monkey Wrench*. The movement was successful and those expelled were reinstated in July 1932.

There were other similar developments. The railwaymen's Vigilance Movement met in 1932 and produced a monthly entitled the *Railway Vigilant* with a circulation of 12,000. The London busmen, part of the Transport and General Workers' Union, also formed a rank-and-file movement when the London General Omnibus Company decided to introduce wage cuts in 1932. The CPGB had exerted little influence upon the busmen until that time but revived the *Busmen's Punch* on 12 July 1932. When it emerged, a fortnight later, that the union was going to accept wage reductions, thirty-three garages met to form a body which later became known as the Rank-and-File Committee, led by the communist Bert Papworth. Soon afterwards a four-to-one ballot led to the rejection of the wage reduction; the Central Bus Committee of the TGWU called an official strike and the company withdrew its wage reductions. The Rank-and-File Committee claimed victory and some leading communist members worked their way on to the Central Bus Committee.[205]

Despite the confusion and equivocation in the CPGB's trade union and industrial policy it is clear that the Party had committed itself to working with the trade unions well before Hitler's rise to power in Germany brought a sea-change in attitudes to social democracy and the demand for the 'United Front against Fascism'. This does not mean that the Party relented over its attitude towards the Labour Party which it still considered to be a 'social fascist' party until 20 October 1934.

The ILP, the Labour Party and the NUWM

There were many other domestic issues that dominated the CPGB during the Class Against Class period. There were campaigns connected with the Invergordan Naval Mutiny of September 1931, which had arisen over a pay cut. There were campaigns connected with the arrest of Communists who were fighting for Indian independence, demanding that soldiers and sailors join them in their fight against capitalism, and also for the release of those arrested and imprisoned on charges of seditious conspiracy.[206]

More importantly, the collapse of the second Labour government (1929–31) provided the CPGB with an opportunity to gain support. However, Party candidates contesting the general election of October 1931 performed poorly, being swept away in the reaction against the Labour government at that time. The Party was equally unsuccessful in dealing with the ILP, which seceded from the Labour Party on 31 July/1 August 1932. Although more efforts were made to secure ILP support in 1933 and 1934, it is clear that the ILP leadership was being attacked, and exposed, before secession in an attempt to attract some of the support from a party which in its decline still had a substantially larger membership than the CPGB.

The CPGB was also at odds with Walter Hannington and the NUWM. The NUWM had not wished to organize the 1930 hunger march and was constantly criticized by the communists for its reluctance to extend its influence among the unemployed.[207] The arrest of Hannington and other leaders of the NUWM during the 1932 hunger march against the means test provoked another period of blood-letting between the two organizations and a Party campaign throughout 1933 and 1934 to move control of the NUWM away from Hannington.

The Soviet Union, War and Imperialism 1929–32

In the welter of other developments that occurred during these years there were two major foreign affairs issues that occupied the CPGB. The first was the threat of war – capitalism appeared to be moving into economic crisis and Japan invaded Manchuria in 1931. It was felt that such actions could lead to an attack upon the USSR. The second foreign issue was concern about Britain's imperial presence in India and the fight for Indian independence with which even the second Labour government did not appear to be concerned.

The Soviet Union had been concerned about the possible threat from foreign powers ever since it had been invaded by armies from fourteen countries at the end of the First World War. This concern intensified when the Mukden Incident occurred in September 1931 and triggered Japan's invasion of Manchuria. This signalled a renewal of CPGB campaigns against war. Some of these drives were run in conjunction with the League

Against Imperialism, which had been set up in 1927 and included some ILP and Labour MPs but had been proscribed by the Labour Party in 1930. It was in connection with this campaign that the expulsion of J.T. Murphy from the Party occurred in May 1932. In April he had written an editorial in which he had suggested that British trade credits for the Soviet Union might allow the British working class to become involved in the industrialization of the Soviet Union; he suggested that this was 'waging the class war as decisively as the waging of a strike' and would yet allow war to be avoided.[208] In other words, he argued that international trading relations would reduce the danger of war. He was attacked for holding such views in a meeting of the PB and expelled a week later.[209] Unlike the Horner case, the departure was swift with Murphy indicating that he could no longer accept Party discipline, adding that he felt that 'the trouble with the party is that it was now in the hands of pigmies'. The CPGB struck back by stressing that it was more interested in preventing the outbreak of war against the Soviet Union by strikes and related action, since imperialist nations could not be relied upon. Murphy was thus found guilty of right tendencies.[210]

The concern about imperialism was also very much focused upon the question of Indian independence.[211] With both Dutt and Saklatvala concerned in Indian independence it was not surprising that the CPGB should become involved in many incidents, particularly in trying to establish trade union rights in Calcutta and Bombay. The most famous event was the Meerut conspiracy. This arose from the fact that, in March 1929, thirty-one people, including two CPGB members and twenty-nine members of the trade unions based in Bombay and Calcutta, were arrested. (Lester Hutchinson, a journalist, was also arrested later.) They were charged with 'conspiracy' in attempting to deprive 'the King-Emperor of Sovereignty over India' and tried without jury at the remote military station of Meerut. In January 1933, after nearly four years, they were found guilty and given severe sentences. An international outcry led to the quick release of some and to the eventual release of them all within a few months.

Conclusion

British Marxism was transformed between 1914 and 1932. It became more united, was more associated with international rather than national interests, and was greatly influenced by the success of communism in the Soviet Union and the formation of the Comintern. Nevertheless, it remained a small and marginal force in British life. It sought to win mass, working-class support but failed to do so. Part of the reason for its failure to progress was the sectarian resolutions pouring from the Comintern, which cut across the desire of some British Communists to continue to work within the trade unions and the Labour Party. The Class Against Class, or 'new line', policy damaged the development of the Party in the late 1920s and early 1930s and produced deep divisions. Indeed, when the

Tenth Congress of the Party decided to abandon the National Left-Wing Movement, by 55 votes to 52, ignoring the fact that the Comintern did not sanction such action, it is clear that the Party was pretty equally divided on the application of the 'new line'. Many members, and some leaders, of the Party did not see any wisdom in cutting the links with social democracy. Inevitably, the Party's influence within the Labour Party diminished quickly once the NLWM was abandoned.

It is also clear that if the Party was to create mass revolutionary support it would have to win over trade unionists. It made some small headway towards this in the 1920s through the National Minority Movement, but after the General Strike of 1926 and the problems that Class Against Class created for Party policy towards trade unionism it is hardly surprising that it was unable to gather support. The constant failure of the 'new line' led to divisions, confusion and exasperation within the Party. This is captured by D.A. Wilson, of Bradford, in a letter to Dutt, in which he noted that opportunism 'was an abuse of principle, but I am not yet quite clear as to exactly what is Rightist Leftist Left Sectarianism Opportunist Conciliator Liquidator?'[212] One might be forgiven for thinking that even the leadership did not know what it meant as it bandied around these terms of abuse willy-nilly. Such confusion and conflict did not augur well for British communism, although there is no denying the lengths to which CPGB members went in attempting to follow in Lenin's footsteps. It was only the rise of Hitler and the emergence of the United Front Against Fascism that saved a desperate and ailing party from descending into the political abyss.

III

The United and Popular Fronts against Fascism and the Outbreak of the Second World War, 1933–41

In March 1933 the Comintern announced the inauguration of the United Front against fascism and the CPGB adapted, albeit slowly, to the changes this made in the Comintern anti-fascist strategy. In January and February the Party remained content to carry out the 'Prague resolution' of 1931, through which the Comintern ordered all communist parties to mass revolutionary activity. Rank-and-file trade unionism was to the fore, encouraged by the January Resolution of 1932 and the events surrounding the London busmen's strike.[1] The Central Committee of the CPGB was committed to supporting mass revolutionary trade unionism and to implementing the decision of the Twelfth ECCI Plenum which 'placed before the Parties as a principal task in this period the development of the revolutionary trade union movement into an organization capable of . . . leading the struggle of the workers against capitalism'.[2] This whole approach was dramatically transformed once Hitler became German Chancellor on 30 January 1933, although it is clear that both the Comintern and the CPGB were slow to implement the new ideas.

Hitler's rise to power was to lead to the complete abandonment of revolutionary policies. It not only dealt a death blow to the German labour movement but also forced the Comintern to discuss the possibility of uniting with the Second International. The burning of the Reichstag on 27 February 1933, and the false arrest of communists for the deed, forced the Comintern to produce its manifesto of 5 March 1933 outlining the United Front against Fascism policy and encouraging all communist parties to unite with social democratic parties to fight fascism, while criticizing the German Social Democratic Party for its part in permitting Hitler's victory.[3] The Seventh, and last, Congress of the Comintern, held in July and August 1935, took the policy further by pushing forward the proposal of a Popular Front against fascism; for some months the idea had been brewing of bringing together all those people and parties opposed to fascism irrespective of whether they were socialist. The mood of the CPGB changed as it responded to the demands of the Comintern. These new policies occurred at a period when Communist membership was beginning to increase steadily. However, this was due more to the membership campaigns of the Party, work within the trade union movement, and to events such as the Spanish Civil War, than to the United Front and Popular Front movements, which gained little support within Britain.

With the outbreak of the Second World War the CPGB was shaken by another grave internal crisis. Pollitt and the CPGB initially supported the British government against fascism but had to reverse the policy and oppose the war and the administration's stance as a result of the Soviet-German Non-Aggression Pact of August 1939.[4] The CPGB thus suffered a serious setback in its credibility in the period between October 1939 and June 1941. By the end of the period, however, the Party was beginning to acknowledge the dangers posed by Hitler, particularly after the fall of France in the summer of 1940, and found itself truly in a Popular Front against fascism by the summer months of 1941.

These dramatic switches in CPGB policy have given rise to considerable speculation about the precise extent and influence of the Comintern and Soviet foreign policy upon the actions of the CPGB. It was once fashionable to suggest that the Comintern was dominant[5] but in recent years some historians, most notably Morgan, have been prepared to argue that there was more flexibility within CPGB policy than is normally admitted and that there were many contradictions and inconsistencies in the action which it, and its members, took, particularly over the Party policy debate at the beginning of the Second World War.[6] Indeed, Andrew Rothstein has argued that the Comintern simply reinforced the widespread communist revulsion against the CPGB's support of the war. More recently, however, Monty Johnstone has suggested that Stalin, Russian foreign policy, and thus the Comintern, were decisive in changing the CPGB policy to the Second World War in 1939. The Georgi Dimitrov diaries – those of the most trusted supporter of Stalin – reveal that on 7 September 1939 Stalin gave the instruction to change the line and Johnstone stated that 'I would claim that there is no longer any room for doubt as to the pre-eminence of the role of the Comintern in securing the change'.[7]

There are also other debates among historians concerning this period in the CPGB's history. Most obviously there is the question of the extent of opposition to the British Union of Fascists. Was the CPGB leadership as committed to opposing this organization as were the district members in London and the provincial centres? It is also generally accepted that the United and Popular Fronts failed, but why? Was this because of the failure of leadership by the CPGB or because – unlike in France and Spain – the circumstances were not in their favour, with the Labour Party remaining hostile, the ILP and Socialist League creating difficulties, and the Moscow Show Trials provoking criticism? Also, why did Communist membership rise from 3,000 to about 20,000 between 1933 and 1941 despite the failure of the United and Popular Fronts? Was it a product of the support for the fight against fascism and the actions in Spain or was it the result of the increasing work within the trade unions, as has been stressed recently?[8]

The dominating argument of this chapter is that the CPGB responded, however haphazardly, to the demands of Soviet foreign policy and Comintern directives. In doing so it faced many problems and contradictions inherent in its policy and activity, not the least of which were the abandonment of revolutionary aims and the decision to work with capitalist democracies in order to stifle the threat of fascism. The revolution was now on hold until the defeat of fascism and this fact nurtured the international split in Marxism between Stalinism and Trotskyism. Even given the sterling work that was done in trade unionism, Communist membership and influence was still severely restricted and the Party remained firmly rejected by the leaders and mainstream of the trade union movement and the Labour Party.

The CPGB was forced to face up to the dangers of fascism with the rise of Hitler. To most Communists, and particularly to R.P. Dutt, fascism was merely a manifestation of the failure of capitalism which indicated that capitalist society was ripe for revolution, 'rotten-ripe' as Dutt would have it.[9] Indeed, the British re-armament programme of 1936 was also seen as part of the process of the fascization of Britain. It was this line of argument which dictated that the CPGB would oppose fascism in Britain. Nevertheless, the Party also recognized fascism was a major international danger that had to be tackled with the support of social democrats and, eventually, all those peoples who opposed it, whatever their political viewpoint. The aim was to oppose both fascism and war but, ultimately, to fight a people's war if necessary. The CPGB was not driven by thoughts of pacifism and appeasement, as Noreen Branson would have us believe, but by a desire to prevent war against the Soviet Union. As Morgan has suggested, the CPGB's policy at this time was often confused, inconsistent and contradictory, driven as it was by the changing moods of Moscow.

United Front against Fascism, 1933–5

On 5 March 1933 the Comintern issued a manifesto which formally began its United Front against fascism.[10] This removed some of the sectarianism of the Class Against Class policy and called for communist and socialist parties to combine in support of the anti-fascist cause. In a speech to the Central Committee of the CPGB, in March 1933, Pollitt outlined the new policy, although he made it clear that there had been little consultation:

> What is the situation now. The proletariat suffered a terrific defeat as a result of the triumph of Fascism in Germany. If we can't see that we can't see anything. The second most important point is that the C.I. declares that it is permissible for the Communist Parties to approach central organizations of the reformist Parties. This isn't merely a figure of speech. This is not something to be put in there lightly. It is one of the most important things that is in the Manifesto and there isn't one comrade who read it but didn't immediately understand that this was something big.[11]

He then argued for a concrete programme of action and a positive commitment to the United Front – unity, not discord.

There were many critics who felt that the new instruction to work with social democratic parties could be used as a weapon against them and the *Daily Worker* printed the statement that 'Should the Social Democrats not accept the Communist offer, the whole working class, even its most backward strata, will know that it is social democracy which interferes with the rejection of fascism and the defence of the working class'.[12] Pollitt rejected this sectarian view and emphasized that a new positive tone had been adopted in the United Front manifesto. However, it is clear that he was faced with a continuing fight within the Party leadership. The Political Bureau was confused about the ECCI Manifesto during April and May, and Pollitt admitted that the Secretariat was divided and unable to come up with a commonly agreed position on the United Front.[13] Clearly, there were those who were surprised by the change and hesitant about whether to embrace it, since 'the Party, in all its practical work, rejected any possibility of unity with social democratic organizations and the leaders of these organizations'.[14] Indeed, the switch of policy can only be explained within the context of Soviet international strategy.

From the end of the First World War Soviet foreign policy had been based upon the rejection of the Treaty of Versailles and the demand for world revolution. With the rise of Hitler and the challenge of fascism that policy changed towards one of peace maintained by a system of alliances with capitalist countries. Indeed, throughout 1933 the Soviet Union was maintaining friendly relations with Germany and, at the same time, making overtures towards Britain and France as a form of insurance policy in case things did not work out with Hitler. In addition, the Soviet Union joined the League of Nations in September 1934, after Germany and Japan had left it. Nine months previously, on 25 December 1933, Stalin had declared, in an interview for the *New York*

Times, that the Comintern was adopting a more positive attitude to the League of Nations. He later admitted that 'the League may act in some degree like a brake, retarding and preventing the outbreak of hostilities'.[15] Thus from 1934 until September 1939, the Soviet Union relied upon the double protection of the collective security of the League of Nations and a system of treaties with capitalist powers, abandoning Lenin's goal of world revolution in the process. The Comintern resolution of 1 April 1933 set the tone for the years 1933 to 1939 not only by condemning social democracy for leading to fascism but also by trying to block fascism through the United Front.[16]

There was little guidance from the Comintern during 1933 about how to apply the United Front to Britain and the CPGB was left very much to its own devices. The majority of Party comrades were still steeped in the sectarian Class Against Class policy and Pollitt had to battle to get the Party in line with the new directives.[17] Even as late as May 1933 he had to admit that the Secretariat was still divided on the issue.[18] Frustrated at the lack of guidance and limited success by September 1933, Pollitt declared that the United Front was 'as dead as a doornail'.[19]

The CPGB response to the new United Front policy consisted of three policies: working with the ILP, working with the Labour Party, and opposing Mosley and the British Union of Fascists (BUF). The Communist leadership was committed to the first two strategies, which provoked little positive response and gained little success. It is clear that the third strategy was quite successful although it was the rank-and-file, not the national leadership, who made the local and regional campaigns against fascism successful. In fact, the national leadership almost ignored the growth of the BUF, feeling that the real threat of fascism in Britain came from the National Government. Indeed, Ted Bramley, reporting to the Central Committee on the European Anti-Fascist Congress in Paris in June 1933, dismissed the fight against the BUF as irrelevant to the main anti-fascist struggle in Britain and noted that the Party leadership had 'waged a fight against the line of breaking up fascist meetings'.[20]

The CPGB had made some effort to gain support from the ILP – its first United Front policy – well before the latter seceded from the Labour Party in July/August 1932 and moved quickly into action to gain a merger once the split was complete. The Paddington branch of the ILP was willing to join the CPGB in February 1933, as were other sections and regions of the ILP, but the Communist leadership admitted that despite 'the tremendous ferment going on in the ILP . . . our Party is not able to utilise that situation nor to use our ILP workers'.[21] The fact is that Jimmy Maxton, and the leaders of the ILP, wanted joint action not merger. Despite tortuous negotiations and constant discussion within the Party structure on how to win the ILP support to the CPGB and widen the United Front, very little happened. The Easter conference of the ILP in 1933 confirmed its intention to avoid any particular commitment to the United Front.[22] Indeed, the frustrating nature of working with the ILP was revealed in the autumn of 1933 when Pollitt stated that the 'ILP is crumbling but not coming back to us', noting that there was more support within it for the United Front but that in the north-east, South Wales and London there was still considerable opposition.[23] Negotiations between the CPGB and the ILP that took place on 21 September 1933 further indicated that the ILP leaders were not prepared to submerge their interests with the Communist Party, and Jenny Lee warned the Communist leaders not to ask 'too much of the NAC' (the National Administrative Council of the ILP).[24] This disabused the CPGB of expecting too much from the negotiations, which the CPGB hoped would also lead to the ILP affiliating to the Comintern. The fact is that a much reduced ILP membership, following the secession from the Labour Party in 1932, was divided by two-thirds to one-third against the United Front.[25]

The ILP dragged its heels in these discussions with the CPGB, even as its members were leaving the party, and this eventually led the more Marxist element of the party, the revolutionary policy committee (formed to force the ILP to leave the Labour Party), to quit and join the CPGB in the autumn of 1935. It had between 50 and 100 members.[26] There had at least been some reaction from the ILP leadership. There was no such response from the Labour Party leadership – its second United Front policy – even if some of the rank and file favoured the United Front. The Labour Party expressed no support for the idea at either its 1933 or 1934 annual conference and even local labour parties, such as the Bradford one which was in an area where the United Front campaign carried some weight, rejected the scheme.[27] This was not entirely true of the trade union movement which seems to have given more substantial local support to the United Front campaign, encouraging John Mahon to suggest that union work must be 'the main line of the Party'.[28]

There was far more countrywide support for the CPGB's third United Front policy – the anti-Mosley or anti-fascist movement – but the lead does not seem to have come from the Communist leadership, which saw the National Government as the main fascist threat in Britain and failed to realize that popular support might come from the struggle against the BUF.[29] While the Party leadership always recognized the dangers posed by Hitler, it failed to do so with British fascism. Indeed, its first discussion of the subject occurred in connection with the debate about the European Anti-Fascist Congress of 4–6 June 1933 at the June meetings of the both the Central Committee and the Political Bureau. Yet the *Daily Worker* regularly recorded the numerous rank-and-file meetings and activities against the BUF and clearly turned a blind eye to the involvement of Party members in anti-Mosley activities that were being played down by the Central Committee and the Political Bureau.

Indeed, there was considerable opposition to the BUF at this time in most areas of the country. Even in Bradford and Leeds, by no means the most powerful of the CPGB districts, there was significant anti-fascist activity. No fewer than 1,200 workers and

Communists turned up to oppose a fascist meeting in Leeds on 8 October 1933[30] and Maurice Ferguson wrote of the enormous successes of the Bradford district in opposing fascism and creating something of a local United Front movement.[31] There was similar opposition to fascism in Liverpool and Manchester.[32] In Manchester there had been some violence at the first major BUF meeting in the city, held at the Free Trade Hall on 12 March 1933, and this flared again at the end of November 1934, when six anti-fascists were ejected rather forcefully.[33]

The CPGB leadership responded to local support for the anti-fascists' campaign in 1934. The trial of those arrested for the Reichstag fire led to numerous meetings in London in September 1933 'against judicial terrorism' and to Labour rallies at Hyde Park on 24 September and at Battersea Town Hall on 25 September 1933, in which there was a significant communist presence.[34] There was also general discussion of the United Front and fascism when Pollitt spoke at the Thirteenth ECCI Plenum in December 1933.[35] Nevertheless, the BUF was hardly the main concern of the CPGB leadership which was more interested in the 'pro-fascist' attitudes and policies of the National Government. Indeed, at the ECCI meeting Pollitt denounced the social fascism of the social democrats and in his report to the Central Committee in January 1934 argued that the success of the struggle against fascism would only come as communist influence 'overcame and wiped out the influence of social democracy over the organized workers'.[36] The continuation of Class Against Class ideas was evident.

Joe Jacobs, a Communist and a Jew, maintains that much of what was done to oppose the BUF in London was done independently of the Party leadership. The Mosley rallies at the Albert Hall on 21 April 1934 and Olympia on 7 June 1934 were opposed by local individuals who had great difficulty forcing the London District of the CPGB to take action, and it was not until 18 May that the London District agreed to organize a counter-demonstration against the BUF at Olympia.[37] However, it has to be admitted that the CC had shown an interest in making the 9 September counter-demonstration a success as early at April 1934.[38]

After the march of 3,000 anti-fascists on Olympia, and the violence that occurred, the Communist leadership seems to have taken more interest in the anti-BUF campaigns. J.R. Campbell, D.F. Springhall and Walter Hannington spoke at an anti-fascist demonstration at Hyde Park on 16 June 1934, organized by the London District of the CPGB, at which between 2,000 and 5,000 were in attendance.[39] On this occasion, Campbell stated that 'The Olympia counter-demonstration was an inspiring example of the workers' united front in action'. Thereafter, the Communist leadership placed great emphasis upon fighting fascism. In August, the Party declared that it would support a mass anti-fascist demonstration at Hyde Park on 9 September, that it would then convene an anti-fascist conference in November and then fight fascism on a broad front in Britain.[40] Indeed, the 9 September meeting was an immense success.

It attracted about 150,000 people and saw the broadening out of the United Front campaign with ILP leader John McGovern attacking the National Government and the establishment and declaring that 'Fascism is therefore the tool of the ruling class who are driven with their back to the wall'.[41] This occurred at the highpoint 'in the development of the United Front'.[42] However, the lack of support from the Labour Party prevented this success leading to the broadening out of the United Front campaign although many rank-and-file Labour Party members did get involved in anti-BUF activities.[43]

There were, of course, other developments that attracted attention. An anti-war movement was active from 1933 onwards (with much local Communist support), the trade unions seemed inclined to support the United Front in some areas, and there were renewed efforts to work with the Labour Party. The last of these developments seems to have been encouraged by Pollitt's speech to the ECCI Presidium in October 1934 in which he noted the desire for United Front work, and its lack of real impact in Britain, and called 'for a clear line on the United Front tactics in elections'.[44] In the end, however, there was to be confusion for the CPGB: having put forward its own candidates for municipal elections to oppose the 'capitalist candidates' of the Labour, Liberal and Tory parties,[45] it made a complete about-turn on 20 October, withdrawing many Communist candidates in order not to split the working-class vote.[46] The Secretariat created confusion with its instructions for the new electoral tactics and this led to the withdrawal of CPGB candidates in Leeds but not in Bradford.[47] In December 1934, Pollitt reiterated his point: 'After eighteen months campaigning for the United Front making approach after approach we are compelled to say in this grave situation that we have not yet been able to break through the ban imposed by the Labour leaders.'[48]

With the failure of the United Front it is hardly surprising that the moves within the Comintern to widen the United Front into a Popular Front began to gather support in 1934, within an increasingly concerned and frustrated CPGB that fervently believed in the need to protect the Soviet Union against fascism. This was a mood which began to catch on in the CPGB even before the formal acceptance of the Popular Front policy at the Seventh World Congress of the Communist International in July 1935.

The Popular Front against Fascism and Socialist Unity, 1935–9

At the Central Executive of the Communist Party of the Soviet Union on 29 December 1933, Viacheslav Molotov, a high-ranking official and sometime premier and foreign secretary under Stalin, revealed Stalin's new line which stressed the need to work closely with some capitalist states to maintain peace. This policy developed further in 1934 as Stalin moved towards establishing diplomatic alliances in an attempt to maintain some collective security against fascism. With the withdrawal of both Japan and Germany from the League of Nations, France pressed for the Soviet Union to be admitted to the League, an action which occurred in September 1934. On 2 May 1935 the Franco-Soviet Pact was signed and the new Soviet alliance system gained its first success. Lenin's goal of world revolution was thus abandoned and replaced by an attempt to coexist peacefully with the major capitalist powers. Indeed, peaceful coexistence with capitalism became the cornerstone of Soviet diplomacy until the collapse of the Soviet Union.

Soviet anxiety about the threat of fascism was quickly transmitted to the ECCI where, from February 1934 until the end of that year, there was a conflict between the Bela Kun group – who still maintained the old sectarian line that social democratic parties, such as the Labour Party, were social fascists – and Georgi Dimitrov and his supporters, who began to advocate a Popular Front between communists, socialist and capitalist groups opposed to fascism, in place of the United Front between socialist and communist parties. At Stalin's insistence, Dimitrov joined the Executive Committee of the Comintern and became the head of its Central European Bureau. Very quickly the mood of the Comintern, and its affiliated organization, began to change. On 26 June 1934 the French Communist Party reversed its line on the 'United Front from Below' and accepted Dimitrov's Popular Front policy. At the beginning of July 1934 the central committees of the French, British, German and Polish communist parties issued a joint statement that did not mention social fascism or social democratic treachery but appealed for the unity of all the working people 'whatever party or trade union you belong to' and suggested that the workers' parties of each country demonstrate together on the twentieth anniversary of the First World War.[49] The Popular Front was transmitted into the official Comintern position on 21 December 1934 by the Presidium of the ECCI. It was to be formalized at the Seventh World Congress of the Comintern in July/August 1935. It also gained tangible existence with the formation of Popular Front governments in France on 3 May 1936 and in Spain in February 1936.

Internationally, of course, the context in which the Popular Front operated was less favourable after the outbreak of the Spanish Civil War in July 1936. There seems to have been some fear that the intervention of the Soviet Union in the war would harm relations between the USSR and Britain and France, although the collapse of the Spanish Popular Front government would pose a threat to France which would then be surrounded by fascist states. The Soviet Union was thus happy to accept the non-intervention policy adopted by the French on 5 August. It was only after Franco captured San Sebastian on 13 September that the Soviet Union changed its policy: it sent its first shipment of arms to Spain on 18 September 1936. As the struggle continued, however, the Soviet Union placed greater emphasis upon establishing an anti-German alliance with Britain. When this did not materialize the Soviet Union began to look towards winning an agreement with Germany and this culminated in the German–Russian pact of 1939, which brought the Popular Front to an end.

The history of the Popular Front was obviously shaped by the needs of the Soviet Union, which manipulated the Comintern to its own ends. There is little evidence that British conditions were ever a significant influence. At the Comintern's Seventh Congress in 1935, Dimitrov had advocated a policy aimed at bringing together all those who were threatened by fascism.[50] It was clearly a dramatic change of direction but was immediately supported by Pollitt who stressed that the British National Government wanted war and that the Labour Party was obstructing attempts to secure a united front. Obviously, the new line provoked controversy between those, such as Trotsky, who saw it as evidence of the Comintern's subordination to Soviet foreign policy and the abandonment of the goal of world revolution and others, such as Dimitrov, who felt the need to make whatever compromises were necessary in order to fight the threat of fascism. The debate continues today for while there are many writers, such as Branson, Hobsbawm and Morgan, who see the Popular Front as a positive move to defeat fascism, although Morgan does highlight the contradictions in the new policy, others perceive it as a development that hamstrung, rather than aided, the anti-fascist struggle.[51]

The CPGB attempted to operate the Popular Front from the start.[52] The new policy was explained at the Party's National Congress on 5–6 October 1935,[53] and it has been suggested that the CPGB now 'adopted a more realistic strategy based upon taking the masses as they were and not, as previously, as the revolutionary irreconcilables [felt] they ought to have been'.[54] Yet there were many difficulties and ambiguities. The new direction was not based upon British conditions, where the prospects of establishing a Popular Front were poor. The policy also looked odd coming from a revolutionary Party, although the Party was later upbraided for not understanding the full Marxist implications of the Seventh Congress.[55]

Indeed, the Popular Front had little prospect of success in Britain where it was opposed by the Labour Party, the leaders of the trade union movement and, in practice, the ILP. There was also little evidence that the Liberal Party and the anti-appeasement section of the Conservative Party, led by Winston Churchill, were going to accept it even if they agreed about the need to oppose fascism. Also, the attempts to create socialist unity with the Socialist League and the ILP, and the problems associated with Trotskyism and the Moscow Show Trials, seemed to undermine the CPGB's Popular Front campaign.

Nevertheless, the Party developed a two-pronged strategy to win support for the scheme: to gain support, firstly, by affiliating with the Labour Party and working for peace and, secondly, by opposing the 'fascist' National Government.[56] The process for the first of these options began as a result of the move towards the United Front line, after which working with the Labour Party became possible. There were attempts in October and November 1934 to get a municipal electoral alliance where workers' selection conferences would choose candidates, but neither the ILP nor the Labour Party was particularly interested. There were further attempts to work with the Labour Party, most particularly during the 14 November 1935 general election, although the issue of supporting the formation of a third Labour government had been hotly resisted by Willie Gallacher in early 1935.[57] Nevertheless, Communist candidates did contest parliamentary seats and Pollitt requested £2,000 from Moscow to help him contest East Rhondda where, he later stated, 'I am putting every ounce of effort into the fight and going to win'.[58] He was defeated and Willie Gallacher was returned as the only Communist in Parliament, representing West Fife.

As an aside, the CPGB was receiving about £2,000 to £3,000 per month from Moscow at this time, the money being filtered through Stockholm. About two-thirds of the money was spent supporting the *Daily Worker*, some contributed towards the expenses of the Lenin students sent to Moscow and most of the rest went to the Party organization.[59] The suspicion that the CPGB was receiving financial support from Moscow was one reason why the Labour Party and its supporters were reluctant to work with the Communists, since they were clearly dependent upon Moscow for stability. Moscow also helped to finance the CPGB's 1935 general election activities and policies.

The attempt to work a United Front with Labour during the general election failed miserably and an opportunity to promote the Popular Front had been lost.[60] Nevertheless, the CPGB applied for affiliation to the Labour Party for the fifth time on 25 November 1935, the Political Bureau having taken the decision to apply on 21 November. It wished to join the Labour Party but also to remain a member of the Comintern, and committed itself to helping Labour fight against the National Government, fascism and imperialist war.[61] The proposal was rejected by the National Executive Committee of the Labour Party on 27 January 1936 with the suggestion that there were irreconcilable differences between the two organizations, as there had been in 1922. Undaunted, the CPGB launched a further campaign to gain affiliation. The *Daily Worker* recorded its progress throughout the early months of 1936 and listed about 280 resolutions from trades unions, trades councils, co-op guilds and local Labour Party organizations in favour of Communist affiliation.[62] This figure rose to 906 resolutions in June and over 1,400 in September, from 831 trade union branches, 407 local Labour Party groups and other organizations.[63] There was, however, a patchiness about much of this support with most coming from the four Communist strongholds of Scotland, London, South Wales and Lancashire.[64]

The Labour Party conducted a counter-campaign in May 1936. The National Council of Labour (the joint body of the TUC, the NEC of the Labour Party and the Parliamentary Labour Party) did likewise and there was much opposition from Ernest Bevin, who declared that he 'doesn't give a damn if he gets two million resolutions' from within the Transport & General Workers for he and his union would still vote against Communist affiliation.[65]

Bitter conflict occurred, based upon claim and counter-claim about the influence of Moscow. The Labour Party's pamphlet *British Labour and Communism*, published by the National Council of Labour in July 1936, attacked the Communist Party's disruptive influence within the Labour Party and suggested that this was a distraction from the real struggle for socialism.[66] Finally, the Labour Party's annual conference in October voted 592,000 for and 1,728,000 against Communist affiliation.[67] This defeat was partly affected by the Moscow Show Trials, which possibly reduced the votes by between 250,000 and 400,000.[68] The Labour Party later issued a manifesto explaining its opposition to affiliation and the CPGB did not apply for affiliation again until 1943.[69]

The leaders of the TUC and some of the major trade unions were also strongly opposed to the Popular Front and had conducted their campaign against communist influence through the Black Circulars of 1934: these documents were designed to prevent communists infiltrating the trade unions and the trades councils. There was much local trade union and trades council resistance to the Circulars, although the official line of the TUC was generally accepted, and opposition ebbed over on to the issue of the Popular Front. The Popular Front also gained no ground with the ILP, which steadfastly rejected it as class collaboration between workers' organization and capitalists designed to subvert the independence of the British labour movement.[70]

The ILP continued to disintegrate. Fully aware of the situation, the CPGB worked in vain to win the party and its supporters to the communist cause.[71] The constant complaint was that the ILP only wished to unite on specific policies connected with the Popular Front campaigns, and not the full range of activities.[72] This was to prove increasingly difficult by the end of 1936 with the split between the ILP and the CPGB over the Spanish Civil War: the ILP argued for a workers' united front against fascism and the CPGB wanted class collaboration in the form of Popular Frontism. However, at this time a Socialist Unity campaign began to emerge.

This was partly a reaction to the failure of the CPGB to secure the support of the Labour Party and the trade unions for its Popular Front campaign. It was an attempt to bring the ILP, the Socialist League and the CPGB together to obtain the 'Unity of the British working-class movement industrially and politically, on a basis of day-to-day struggle'. Examining the views of the Socialist League and the ILP, the Political Bureau (in fact Dutt) noted, equivocally, that:

There is an entirely different conception, a conception of a Left bloc being formed of these three organizations with, in fact, a separatist tendency, even if nominally professing the aim of unification but as discussions have clearly shown a separatist tendency, to look towards a future workers' party and extreme disagreements between the elements of that small bloc on all the vital issues of policy . . . we welcomed the possibility of going forward with the Socialist League, particularly with Cripps, for a Unity Campaign because it would be an enormous step forward. That is our reason for having wanted to go forward with these negotiations.[73]

In other words, there was the danger of separatism but also the possibility that the Socialist Unity movement might strengthen the campaign for Communist affiliation to Labour, and revive the United and Popular Front campaigns. Indeed, the CPGB's Sheffield conference on 11 October 1936 continued to press for affiliation to the Labour Party as its central objective and would not sanction the formation of a new socialist party that would endanger the CPGB's affiliation prospects. Yet, in the discussion that followed various ideas were put forward and it was eventually felt that both industrial and political means would be used to win support for fourteen points – including opposition to fascism, the abolition of the means test, the nationalization of the arms industry and the advancement of minimum wages in various industries – in the Socialist Unity negotiations that finally occurred.

The negotiations were fated from the start since Dutt, Pollitt and the CPGB leadership were opposed to the formation of a new Socialist Unity party that did not seek to embrace the wider socialist movement while sections of the Socialist League leadership sought to create a new socialist party with the CPGB and the ILP. When the Socialist League approached Pollitt and Dutt in mid-October 1936 and began negotiations relations were guarded.[74] Dutt was cautious from the beginning about the 'narrow separatist basis of only two or three organizations coming together'[75] but a meeting was arranged on 20 November 1936, in which Sir Stafford Cripps (Deputy Leader of the Labour Party), William Mellor and Aneurin Bevan met Pollitt and Dutt to form the Unity Campaign, although the CPGB only agreed to open unity negotiations as long as there was no breakaway from the Labour Party, no attack upon the foreign policy of the Soviet Union and agreement upon British foreign policy.[76] This gagging clause regarding the Soviet Union was fixed by Pollitt.[77] It is clear that the different parties had different agendas and that these created problems. Mellor, in line with the ILP position, did not agree with the Popular Front, while the CPGB delegation could not agree with Brockway and the ILP 'unless it changed its line', and there were differences of purpose and intent. The CPGB was not committed to creating a new socialist party. It also objected to the ILP criticism of the Moscow Show Trials. Nevertheless, the three organizations agreed to meet again but acknowledged that once it was known that the Socialist League was involved in the Socialist Unity campaign it 'will be in a very difficult position with Transport House, for Dalton and Bevin, now representing the dominant leadership will certainly make every effort to get the SL to give up the Campaign or be expelled from the Labour Party'.[78]

The CPGB hoped that the Unity Campaign would permit it to work more closely with the Labour Party and the trade unions, and to widen its base for both the United and Popular Fronts. Cripps, from a Labour Party perspective, looked to it as a means of bringing left-wing blood into the Labour Party and giving the Labour Party 'new life and vitality' as Socialist Unity had done for the Spanish workers.[79] To these ends, the campaign began on 24 January 1937 at the Free Trade Hall, Manchester: Cripps, Mellor, Jimmy Maxton (Leader of the ILP) and Pollitt spoke and 3,763 'pledge cards' were signed by those supporting the campaign. Pollitt argued that the campaign would not weaken the Labour Party but strengthen it, the trade unions and the co-operative movement.[80] Indeed, the Communist leaders laid great store on its succeeding. Idris Cox suggested that it was an attempt to make the Labour Party 'the real united organization of the whole working-class movement in Britain', but this failed to influence Labour.[81] The latter soon forced the Socialist League to disband when its National Executive Committee announced on 24 March 1937 that Socialist League members would not be eligible for Labour Party membership after 1 June. Cripps therefore decided to wind up the Socialist League. However, that was not the end of the Unity Campaign movement.

There were attempts to raise renewed support for the Unity Campaign at the Labour Party conference in October 1937, although Willie Rust acknowledged that 'in the main the Popular Front does not cut any ice at all in the Labour Party'. The Labour Party had in fact launched an attack upon the campaign through the *Daily Herald* and had criticized the CPGB's defence of the second Moscow Show Trial and the execution of the Red Army general staff in June 1937.[82] Even then, the movement did not die away entirely. Indeed, Cripps remained a potential leader for Socialist Unity and made his last stand for it on 9 January 1939 when he demanded a meeting of the NEC of the Labour Party to discuss proposals, effectively a revival of the Popular Front that became known as the 'Cripps Memorandum'. The idea was to unite the Liberals, Communists, ILP, the Labour Party and the youth movement to generate a vote-winning opposition to the National Government. However, the NEC of the Labour Party rejected this proposal on 13 January: Cripps moved his campaign to the country and launched a National Petition for the 'Cripps Memorandum' at the end of January. Eventually, Cripps, Nye Bevan and others involved in the campaign were expelled from the Labour Party on 30 March 1939.[83]

The CPGB leaders were well aware that the campaign would be a failure for in a letter from Pollitt to Campbell it was stated that 'The Cripps campaign would go much better if real live men had the organizing of it. But it is in the hands of dead men from the point of view of drive, etc. Cripps makes good speeches and some would be better if they were not made . . . The Petition is not going well. We were opposed to this.'[84]

Rather than Socialist Unity there was socialist disunity. The ILP supported many of Trotsky's criticisms of Stalin and the Comintern, as did sections of the Socialist League. Trotsky's attack upon the class collaboration policy of the Seventh Congress produced tremendous frustration and resentment within the CPGB, which waged an enormous propaganda campaign to discredit him.[85] But this CPGB campaign was not helped by the first Moscow Show Trial at which Zinoviev, Kamenev and fourteen other old Bolsheviks confessed to an 'implausible range of crimes',[86] nor by the attack levelled against them by Walter Citrine at the TUC following his six-week trip to the Soviet Union.[87] Indeed, the media attacks upon the Moscow Show Trials were so intense that the Comintern reproached the CPGB for not influencing public opinion more effectively in Britain.

Part of the problem may have been that the CPGB and its supporters appeared to be connected with pacifism in the mid- and late 1930s. Branson presents them in that mode, and the associations with the ILP and the numerous anti-war societies that emerged certainly tended to emphasize the point. In fact there was little such association. The issue was the defence of the Soviet Union and not simply the advocacy of pacifism. Indeed, Pollitt commenting to the CC on 4 January 1936, stated that 'More and more the fascist forces will look upon the conquest of the Soviet Union as the way out of the crisis. So the defence of the Soviet Union becomes increasingly necessary.' To this end, Pollitt sought to organize a peace ballot. The Party was careful to distance itself from the pacifist stand put forward by George Lansbury, the old Labour Party leader, which seemed to be capturing some support by 1936. The fact that the National Peace Council grew from 25 local bodies in 1935 (13 in London) to 175 in 1936 (55 in London), and that the Peace Pledge Union had about 150,000 supporters and 600 branches, was of some concern to the Party. From 1936 onwards, the Party decided to not treat Lansbury 'as a buffoon' but to tackle the issue of peace more seriously, within the context of the tactical need to protect the Soviet Union.[88]

The CPGB constantly encouraged and monitored the various peace movements throughout the country. It reported on the activities of the Peace Council Movement and League of Nation's Union, which gathered together 1 million signatures for the 1935 peace ballot.[89] It appears to have encouraged the 'Hands Off Abyssinia' campaign directed against Mussolini's invasion of that country in October 1935. This led to the formation of Local Peace Councils and calls for League of Nations sanctions against Italy.[90] The Party, Dutt, Pollitt, and many other leading officials, participated in these movements and also hoped to bring about an Anglo-Soviet pact to strengthen the existing Franco-Soviet pact. As we shall see, this did not occur and the Soviet Union eventually agreed a non-aggression pact with the Germany on the eve of war.

This preoccupation with international peace, the defence of the Soviet Union and the campaign for affiliation to Labour perhaps explains why the CPGB leadership did not become deeply involved in the anti-Mosley movement in 1935. As in 1934, it appears that the real interest in this came from the rank and file in various districts. Indeed, this was also true when there was an upsurge of the anti-Mosley campaign after Italy invaded Abyssinia in the autumn of 1935.

Mosley and the British Union of Fascists (soon to be the British Fascists) began a new recruitment campaign in early 1936. The BUF's first major meeting was held at the Albert Hall on 22 March and the *Daily Worker* helped organize a counter-demonstration, although the CPGB leadership does not seem to have called for such action.[91] Only about 8,000 anti-fascists turned up at the counter-demonstration. Thereafter the Young Communist League helped organize numerous counter-demonstrations in the summer of 1936. There were sections of the YCL who called for a workers' defence force but these calls were rejected by the CPGB leadership.[92] In one instance, 20,000 anti-fascists shouted down a Mosley meeting in Finsbury Park on 21 June 1936.[93] However, Dave Springhall, in his report to the London Communist Party in late June 1936, made no reference to the anti-fascist activities, mentioning instead the need to build up trade union strength.[94]

There is further evidence of this gap between the actions of the executive and local members regarding fascism at the beginning of June 1936. At this point, the Party was encouraging the membership to support a YCL rally on 7 June rather than a counter-demonstration against a BUF rally in the East End of London. Joe Jacobs, the Jewish Secretary of the Stepney branch of the CPGB, was appalled at such callousness and helped organize a counter-demonstration after the YCL rally had finished against the BUF rally in the East End of London.[95] The fact is that the national leadership did not see the anti-Mosley/BUF movement as particularly important when ranged against the need to establish international peace to protect the Soviet Union and the need to mount a mass movement against the 'pro-fascist' National Government.

This difference between the centre and the rank and file was exposed further in 1936 when the BUF declared its intention to march through the East End of London on 4 October. It seems that this march clashed with the YCL's national 'Aid Spain' rally and that this was the more important event, since the Aid Spain Campaign had attracted over 800 middle-class members into the Party. Indeed, Dave Springhall, Bob McLennon and John Mahon told Jacobs that the YCL march was more important than a counter-demonstration against Mosley and the BUF.[96] However, the threat of rebellion from a large section of the membership forced the Party leadership to change its position and call on workers to oppose the BUF march, the decision being publicized on 2 October in the *Daily Worker* following a change of line by the PB on 30 September.

The BUF march of 4 October was prevented from progressing through the East End by a massive anti-fascist counter-demonstration of 250,000 people in what became known as the Battle of Cable Street. As a result the National Government introduced the Public Order Act which allowed the police to ban marches and mass gatherings. Between December 1936 and November 1937 there were in London 12,021 public meetings, 3,094 held by the Fascists and 4,364 by the anti-fascists.[97] Very few of the anti-fascist meetings are mentioned in the minutes of either the Central Committee or the Political Bureau. There was more interest in other events such as the Spanish Civil War.

The Popular Front did not become more popular in Britain and by 1939 it was acknowledged that its prospects were poor. The Labour Party had rejected it, once again, at its Southport conference and 'was consciously pursuing a policy of eliminating all the left-wing elements in the Labour party. That is why Southport was so terrible. The Communist Party was not there. The Cripps people are not there.' The Southport conference was seen to be as reactionary as any Tory conference ever held and 'in regard to the People's Front the general impression is that Southport had killed it, and that it was a dead issue'.[98] The Central Committee wished to reject that notion and find new ways in which to challenge this impression. In fact it was unable to do so and had to admit that its anti-fascist propaganda was poor and that it could not organize mass protests such as it had done in the past. The Popular Front movement faded away primarily because the Labour Party remained totally opposed to working with the Communist Party.

How does this square with other explanations of the Popular Front's failure? Most certainly it does not appear that the 'familiar and culturally familiar' response of the Popular Front in British politics, which David Blaazer has written about recently, exerted much influence in the 1930s.[99] There was certainly only limited evidence of the CPGB establishing some meaningful alliance in this respect with sections of the Liberal and Labour parties, much less with the Winston Churchill Conservative malcontents. More likely is Ben Pimlott's explanation that the Popular Front failed partly because of pressure from left-wingers whose calls for a Popular Front with non-socialists inhibited the Labour Party leadership from forming an electoral alliance with anti-appeasement Liberals and Conservatives.[100] Yet even this explanation is not entirely satisfactory because the fact is the Popular Front was a Communist initiative and that there was no way in which the Labour Party leadership was going to respond to its policies, whether or not there was pressure from the Left. Their fears about any association with the Popular Front were encouraged by the Spanish Civil War, the Moscow Show Trials and the possible link with political enemies such as the Liberals which horrified the rank and file just as much as the leadership.

The Spanish Civil War, the Moscow Show Trials and Trotskyism

The Spanish Civil War broke out on 19 July 1936 when Franco, and other Fascist commanders, invaded Spain with Moroccan troops and began risings in various parts of the country. The Soviet Union and the Comintern were slow to react, not wishing to upset the pact with France by an immediate entry into the war on the side of the Republican government. Within a month, however, the French and the British were putting forward a non-intervention agreement, which was supported by all the major powers. The Soviet Union did not wish to upset this arrangement by sending arms to Spain but after Franco's successes it began its first shipments on 18 September 1936, although it did not formally declare its independence from the non-intervention policy until 23 October 1936 when both Germany and Italy refused to suspend military aid to the Fascists. Moscow decided to form an International Brigade, to be based at Albacete, and on 12 October asked its sections affiliated to the Comintern to send their own volunteers to fight in Spain against the Fascists.

The CPGB declared its position on Spain from the start, demanding aid for the country and denouncing the National Government for its non-intervention policy. It produced a pamphlet on the situation and soon after the outbreak of war the *Daily Worker*, admittedly not always in tune with the thinking of the CPGB leadership, declared: 'We must force the national government to give assistance to the People's Government of Spain'.[101] Indeed, on 12 August the *Daily Worker* urged every Communist worker to report for the emergency distribution of a manifesto on Spain and it denounced non-intervention with the headline 'Neutrality is Treason' on 15 August. On 19 August the Secretariat of the Comintern was also stressing to Pollitt the need to 'mobilize all the forces' to 'obtain from [the] English Government decisions intervening in favour of [the] Spanish Government and against support [of] Spanish insurgents by Italy and Germany, cessation of politics of Pontius Pilate which [will] lead to defeat of Spanish democracy.'[102] It was seeking to expose the inclination of the Labour Party organizations, which favoured non-intervention; the National Council of Labour declared so on 28 August and the annual TUC followed suit on 10 September. These decisions were reversed on 28 October when both the NEC of the Labour Party and the TUC General Council demanded that the Spanish Republican Government should be allowed to buy arms. The CPGB, however, remained critical.

The support for Spain spread quickly through the British labour movement, with the proliferation of organizations such as Aid-for-Spain, the Spanish Youth Foodship campaign, and the National Joint Council for Anti-Fascist Relief. The CPGB was involved in many of these activities although its primary interest appears to have been to encourage more direct action.

The CPGB and Pollitt declared their interest in sending a British battalion to Spain in September 1936. This seems to have been sparked off by Communist members who were out in Spain at the beginning of the war, most obviously Tom Wintringham, who was a reporter for the *Daily Worker* and active in Barcelona. Wintringham suggested the need for more volunteers from the CPGB.[103] Even before the Comintern gave an official lead for the formation of the International Brigade, on 12 October the CPGB, presumably primed by the Comintern, made the decision to form a British battalion. At a meeting two days previously, where the Labour Party was attacked because of its continued neutrality at a time when Madrid was under attack from the fascists, Pollitt suggested that a British unit had to be formed 'so that we should at least redeem ourselves in the eyes of the international proletariat'.[104] The *Daily Worker* continued to press for a British battalion throughout November 1936; Pollitt made his call for volunteers on 5 December and almost immediately 300 British volunteers went to Spain, soon followed by another 150. By January 1937 the British company, later battalion, of the International Brigade had been formed. Pollitt, Dutt and others had been active in interviewing and selecting these volunteers, although on 10 January 1937 the Foreign Office declared that the enlistment of volunteers was illegal under the Foreign Enlistment Act of 1870. However, Communist clandestine operations continued and eventually about 2,200 volunteers were sent from Britain to fight in Spain to help out 'in the heroic struggle of the Spanish people'.[105] It is estimated that between one-third and a half were Communists and that 526 volunteers were killed.[106] To encourage their activities many of the leading members of the CPGB travelled to Spain. Pollitt was, perhaps, the most frequent visitor and his five visits are recorded in considerable detail in his surviving papers. To him, the defence of the Spanish Republic was one of the supreme issues of the age and, referring to Spain, he stated that 'I personally have never known public feeling so roused as it was in Britain at the time'.[107] Nevertheless, by early 1938, when over 200 comrades had died in the war, Pollitt was receiving letters from the wives of many members who were 'getting very vehement about their husbands having gone to Spain'.[108]

The CPGB obviously gained kudos and respect from its intervention in the conflict. Indeed its membership, falling at the beginning of 1936, picked up quickly from about 6,000 in 1936 to 15,648 by the Fifteenth Party Congress in 1938 and 17,256 by January 1939.[109] The Spanish Civil War and its trade union work were obviously factors that encouraged this upward trend. Nevertheless, there were deep tensions emanating from the Spanish conflict which created problems for the Party, especially when they ran alongside the Moscow Show Trials.

The most obvious difficulty was that the forty or fifty members of the ILP who went to Spain associated with POUM (the Workers' Party of Marxist Unity), which was active in Catalonia. This organization believed that revolutionary change should be fought for in Spain at the same time as the socialists, Marxists and anarchists were fighting the fascists. The Soviet Union, the Comintern, the Spanish Communist Party (PCE) and the United Socialist Party of Catalonia (PSUC) did not agree with this view, wishing to defeat fascism first before bringing about revolutionary change. Naturally, they associated the POUM activities with Trotskyism, with its emphasis upon immediate revolutionary change. The irreconcilable differences between POUM, on the one hand, and the PCE and PSUC, on the other, led to fighting, conflict and the imprisonment of many POUM supporters in Barcelona and Catalonia in May 1937. George Orwell wrote about these events in his passionate book *Homage to Catalonia*, condemning the Comintern for derailing the Spanish Revolution and for the arrest, imprisonment and death of the POUM leader Andreas Nin. POUM had condemned the Moscow Show Trials, leading Stalin to instigate a campaign to destroy it. As MacDermott and Agnew have observed: 'The real tragedy of Spain is that Stalin's declaration of war against Trotskyism shattered any chance of obtaining the elusive goal of broad anti-fascist unity.'[110] For the CPGB this meant that throughout the early months of the war, and particularly 1937, it was sensitive to Trotskyism, the position of the ILP and the Moscow Show Trials.

Stretched over the years 1936 to 1938, the Moscow Trials effectively removed all the potential rivals to Stalin who were described as Trotskyists. The whole process was begun as a result of the assassination of Kirov, the Secretary of the Leningrad Communist Party, in early December 1934. The murder allowed Stalin, General Secretary of the Communist Party of the Soviet Union, to purge those who challenged him. This was carried out in a series of public trials and arrests. The first, in August 1936, saw the trial and execution of sixteen veteran party members, including Zinoviev and Kamenev, for being Trotskyite terrorists plotting to assassinate party leaders. In January 1937 a second trial saw seventeen others on trial for being fascism's fifth column. They all confessed and fifteen of them were executed. Another set of arrests, not trials, occurred in June 1937 when the Red Army General Staff was imprisoned and executed. The third Moscow Trial occurred in March 1938 when Bukharin, former leader of the Comintern, and twenty others were charged with murder and having contact with fascist powers. Eighteen of them were condemned to death. These trials were accompanied by the arrest of millions of party members, many of whom were executed.[111]

Most CPGB members believed that these trials and executions were justified in the case of the accused old Bolsheviks, few of whom had ever supported Trotsky (Zinoviev and Kamenev had supported him briefly in 1926–7 but moved again to support Stalin in 1928 following the expulsion of the Left opposition from the CPSU). However, it is clear that there was acute embarrassment at the fact that close friends and fellow CPGB members were caught up in the cases and there were difficulties in getting the British working class to accept the trials. Pollitt wrote to Arnot on

11 February 1937 referring to the *Manchester Guardian*'s comments and his conversations with a *Manchester Guardian* editor, noting that 'Everything was too complete. It all gave rise to incredulity. The confessions too were more than they could stomach, and in general there was a monotonous regularity about every trial, and underneath they felt that something must be wrong. He was quite frank about it and no amount of argument could shift him.'[112]

Shortly afterwards there was some alarm at the arrest, trial and execution of Petrovsky, who had attended CPGB meetings under the pseudonym Bennett and had been the Comintern agent in Britain for most of the 1920s. Pollitt wrote of Petrovsky that he was 'a comrade and close personal friend' and stated that 'I cannot remember a single instance of Petrovsky saying or carrying out a disloyal action'.[113] Petrovsky's wife, Rose Cohen, was also arrested, and disappeared after protesting for his release. Pollitt went to Moscow on her behalf, but got nowhere at which point there appears to have been a Comintern attempt to remove him as General Secretary of the CPGB.[114]

The Moscow Show Trials, in particular, created difficulties for all European communist parties, and weakened the case for the Popular Front since the trials and the terror associated with them gave the opponents of the Popular Front 'a plausible argument against those pressing for unity with Comintern sections'.[115] The Comintern was concerned to obtain international support for the Moscow Show Trials and was alarmed when, in Britain, there seemed to be little effort to promote them. The Secretariat of the Comintern informed the CC of the CPGB (by secret telegraphic message) that in the trial of 'Trotskyist terrorists', such as Zinoviev, 'There is no response at all from your country . . . Once more, repeat, that necessary action CC party, party organization, mass meetings particularly of social democratic workers with expressions of solidarity with toilers in USSR, leadership of CPSU and leader of international proletariat council. STALIN.'[116] As a result, from the end of August onwards the CPGB began a campaign against Trotskyism. But in September 1936 Arnot reported to the ECCI on the slowness of the CPGB to respond to the 'Trotsky-Zinovievite Terrorist Trial'.[117]

The *Daily Worker* then launched an attack upon Trotsky, Zinoviev and Kamenev, which culminated in the infamous headline 'Shoot The Reptiles', and orchestrated a major campaign. It also attacked the *Daily Herald* for suggesting that the defendants in the Show Trials should have a proper legal defence and accused the *Herald* of using these events to undermine the CPGB's affiliation campaign to the Labour Party.[118] Pollitt later wrote to J.S. Middleton, Labour's Secretary, asking him to curb the *Daily Herald*'s supposed 'biased' coverage of the trial.[119] Along with this there were denials that Trotsky, Zinoviev and the other defendants had ever played a meaningful role in the world communist movement.[120] Nevertheless, there was much criticism of the

Show Trials from within the CPGB and the British media and even Pollitt expressed the view that the first Show Trial had been politically damaging for the CPGB.[121]

At the CPGB's national conference on 11 October 1936, J. Shields gave a secret report 'to prepare the Party for further events which are going to take place in the Soviet Union'.[122] This was clearly a reference to the impending Show Trial of seventeen old Bolsheviks scheduled for January 1937 and contradicts the view of apologists for the CPGB leadership, such as Branson, who claim that Pollitt and the other leaders had no idea about what was going on in the Soviet Union.[123] Indeed, a letter from the Hungarian communist Evgeny Varga suggests that foreign communists who attended the Comintern headquarters and Hotel Lux, where they often resided, were in 'constant fear' of being arrested.[124] Thus it is hard to believe that Arnot and Pollitt, who were regular visitors to Moscow, knew nothing of the mass repression sweeping through the Comintern and Soviet society. It was, therefore, with some cynicism that Shields attacked the labour movement critics of the first Show Trial as 'agents of the enemy inside the ranks of the working-class movement', who needed to be cleared out.[125]

The CPGB stepped up the pro-Soviet publicity campaign in January 1937 at the start of the second Moscow Show Trial. It was an action that almost led to the derailment of the Unity Campaign even before it was formally launched. On the eve of the launch Pollitt criticized the ILP for allegedly breaching the unity agreement by criticizing the Soviet Union. It was Cripps who saved the day by criticizing Fenner Brockway and the ILP for their actions and making arrangements to examine the whole question of Trotskyism to the ILP and the Socialist League.[126]

In this climate, and following instructions from Moscow, the CPGB gave a higher priority to the defence of the second set of Moscow Show Trials than to workers' unity. On 21 January 1937 N. Raylock, probably a pseudonym, delivered a secret report on 'Trotskyism in Britain' to the leadership, in which he referred to the formation of a British Committee in Defence of Leon Trotsky, and suggested that the Party should take action to have Trotskyists expelled from the ILP and the Socialist League although it had no direct influence over these organizations.[127] Raylock's recommendations were taken up and the Party got the *Daily Worker* to mount a campaign against Trotskyism and to produce a special four-page supplement on the subject, while all the Party districts were instructed to hold public meetings in support of the trial once the seventeen old Bolsheviks had been executed. In February 1937, Willie Rust made a vehement attack upon Trotskyism, describing it as an ally of fascism.[128] Later in the year, Dave Springhall made a passionate attack upon British Trotskyists in his report to the Central Committee, estimating that there were about 300 to 350 supporters of Trotsky in Britain, that the Trotskyist Balham group had formed in 1932 as the British section of the International Left Opposition, published *The Red Flag* and had drawn publishers Secker & Warburg into its net.[129] J.R. Campbell continued in the same vein the following year, attacking Trotsky as a fascist agent.[130]

The issue of Trotskyism and the Spanish Civil War did create the tension of the famous case in which Tom Wintringham was ejected from the Party for associating with Trotskyists and for not being prepared to accept Party discipline.[131] This was particularly embarrassing for the Party since Wintringham was a reporter for the *Daily Worker* and had been instrumental in the formation of the British battalion of the International Brigade, an instructor in the Brigade and later a battalion commander.

Thus, throughout 1937 the CPGB injected a fratricidal strife into the ranks of the Unity Campaign with its persistent attacks on the ILP and those who criticized the Show Trials and the repressive activities of the Soviet security organs in Spain. This was accompanied by scores of articles in the Party press defending the Show Trials and attacking critics.[132] Coverage included the headline 'Terrorists on Trial' in the *Daily Worker*, which appeared on the first day of the second Show Trial.[133] Also at the Political Bureau on 11 February 1937, Idris Cox boasted of how in South Wales the Party was waging a campaign of intimidation against a National Council of Labour Colleges lecturer with Trotskyist sympathies, designed to drive 'this fellow out'.

Given all these circumstances, it is perhaps not surprising that the Unity Campaign ground to a halt in 1937 and there was increasing conflict between the CPGB, the ILP and the SL, with the ILP being described as 'a disruptive force within the working-class movement'.[134]

The uneasy situation seems also to have encouraged occasional outbreaks of concern about the structure and purpose of parts of the Party machine. Throughout the 1930s the Political Bureau changed its composition and membership and the Central Committee changed even more so. With the Central Committee the idea was that this Executive Committee of the Party should represent the different sections of the party throughout the country and keep them in contact with the leadership. It is clear, however, that this arrangement was often little more than a process of the leadership giving orders. In a remarkable meeting in July 1938 Finlay Hart led an attack upon the Central Committee, describing it as 'an exhortation committee' where the Inner Executive made decisions without recourse to the rest of the members. Arthur Horner also joined in the criticism, noting that many of the then three-monthly meetings were a waste of time because of the feeling of inferiority inspired by members of the Executive: 'I am not afraid to speak anywhere – but I am full of nervousness speaking here.'[135] However, there is little to suggest that there were anything more than cosmetic changes, like having a different member chairing meetings, and this did not do very much to address the charge that the Party was completely undemocratic.

Yet despite all these problems and difficulties the Party membership increased. The 3,500 members of 1933 rose to about 6,000 by 1936 and to 17,000 by 1939. Indeed, there was a surge in membership in 1938 and 1939 and Marion Jessop reported that 'in the West Riding, the membership of the Party had grown enormously in the last 12 months'. Much of this was clearly due to the expansion of trade union work by the Party, particularly at the local level.

The CPGB and the Trade Unions 1933–9

The United Front and Popular Front policies released the CPGB from the Class Against Class line which had suggested that trade unions were played out as agencies for revolutionary demands and that the working classes had to be won by offering them the Workers' Charter. By January 1932 Pollitt had won some concessions from the Comintern to escape this straightjacket and to allow the CPGB the right to work with the trade unions, and not against them, within the context of the exceptional circumstances prevailing within Britain. There is no doubt that this change of policy improved the position of the CPGB within the trade unions and encouraged a general improvement in the fortunes of the Party.

From 1933 onwards the CPGB began to see its membership increase. The stand against fascism at home and abroad helped matters but evidence suggests that the rise in numbers was also partly the result of increasing Communist influence within the trade union movement. Kevin Morgan alerted historians to this possibility in 1989, writing that:

> There was more continuity to Communist influence in the trade union movement than usually recognised, and if there was a decline of influence between 1928 and 1932, it was probably due to the chronic level of unemployment among Party members as much as it was due to sectarianism.[136]

Since then Richard Stevens and Nina Fishman have sought to examine the rise of Communist influence within the trade unions in the 1930s.

Stevens, examining the traditionally moderate area of the East Midlands, suggests that a small number of Communists were to be found in the trades councils at Derby, Nottingham, Leicester and the surrounding areas. They were small rank-and-file groups that appear to have exerted some influence upon their respective trades councils. Their Communist membership was usually well known and the trades councils, who normally paid lip-service to the 'Black Circular' (there were in fact two, one for the trades councils, number 16, and one for the trade unions, number 17) of 1934 demanding the exclusion of Communists, tended to accept their presence.[137] In the case of the Nottingham Trades Council there were between six and nine Communist delegates on a body of just over 100, with between one and three acting in an official position throughout the period 1933 to 1938. Their position improved slightly in the early 1940s.[138] The Nottingham Trades Council chose to ignore 'Black Circular' 16, one of about eighty to do so, when it was issued by the TUC but was then forced to accept it in April 1935 by 29 votes to 8.[139] Despite that decision the Nottingham Trades Council did nothing to force Communist delegates to resign. Indeed, in the East Midlands the Communists were always a small but active minority. Stevens suggests that these rank-and-file members generally went their own way, were not always responsive to the leadership of the CPGB and survived within trades council activities by virtue of the fact that trades councils were increasingly being urged by the lesser TUC figures, such as Vic Feather, Vincent Tewson and others, to confine themselves to industrial rather than political activity.[140]

It should be noted that a similar picture emerges in West Yorkshire. In Leeds, Huddersfield and Bradford the small numbers of Communists on the trades councils exercised an influence out of all proportion to their numbers. However, it would appear that the Black Circular, in contrast to its effect in the East Midlands, was successful in Leeds in halting CPGB influence on the Trades Council. Whereas in Bradford the CPGB, thanks to the strong support of Fred Ratcliffe who was Trades Council President 1934–5, felt the effect of the Black Circular much less.

While Stevens is primarily concerned with rank-and-file developments and admits to the variable and limited impact of communists within the trades councils in the East Midlands, Nina Fishman is much more focused upon the attempts by the national leadership, and particularly Pollitt and Johnny Campbell, to improve the relationships between the CPGB and the British trade union movement. Despite some obvious difficulties associated with the CPGB's attempt to curb the activities of some of its rank-and-file members, it would appear that the new, more positive, approach by the CPGB to trade unionism was immensely successful in Fishman's view, while it was rather less in Stevens's opinion. Fishman says, 'It is difficult to avoid the conclusion that by 1945 Pollitt and Campbell had achieved their ambition, conceived in 1929–30, to make the Communist Party an important force inside the official trade union movement.'[141] Refining, and confining, the argument further, according to Fishman it is clear that the spadework for this was done in the 1930s, even if the Second World War pushed success along more rapidly. Yet Fishman acknowledges that Harry Pollitt and Johnny Campbell, the main architects of the CPGB's trade union policy, were always on the horns of a dilemma between wishing to support rank-and-file movements and desiring to work with the existing unions in order to extend Communist influence. In the final analysis, however, they 'had no hesitation in placing union loyalty before rank-and-filism'.[142] They often worked to get the rank-and-file movements to discontinue their campaigns. Loyalty to the trade union leadership did not, however, bring a substantial increase in CPGB membership at first. Indeed, realizing that tens of thousands of militants had not joined the Communist Party, Pollitt announced in his New Year statement of 1937 that he wished these activists 'would only realise that joining the Communist Party does not mean weakening the Labour Party, the trade unions or the co-operative organization in which they are already working, but will actually strengthen it'.[143] Pollitt felt that this sense of cooperation was important as the Communist Party attempted to build up its alliances and united fronts against both the bosses and fascism.

Fishman's major argument is elaborated in three subordinate themes. Firstly, she suggests that the pragmatic approach of Pollitt and Campbell worked. They built up the strength of the Communist activists in the industrial workplace and on trades councils. Secondly, she believes that the industrial pragmatism of the Communist leaders was justified by the ultimate prospect of revolution, even though it was not a popular response with 'rank and filism' and 'highly embarrassing and potentially embarrassing for King Street's credibility'.[144] Indeed, the dilemma was evident in the case of the London busmen's strike and the Aircraft Shop Stewards' National Councils' planned strike, both of which occurred in May 1937. The Harworth colliery strike of May and June 1937, which sought to challenge the Spencer unionism in the Nottingham coalfield, did, however, go some way to redeeming the Communist Party if only through the willingness of Communist activists to risk victimization and imprisonment. Thirdly, Fishman argues that the CPGB activists in the trade unions ignored the stated aim of the King Street headquarters that the Communist Party should be a party of the masses and accepted, instead, that they were the vanguard of change. Indeed, this seems to be a view that most Communist activists had come to accept by the late 1920s and the 1930s.

It should also be noted that Party records for 1936 to 1939 are much less concerned with trade unionism and the mass support of the working classes than they were before. In 1933 and 1934 there was a clear emphasis placed upon rank-and-file movements, the *Communist Review* stressing 'the need for the development of all-in rank-and-file strike committees initiated by the militant branches'.[145] After the Comintern's Seventh World Congress in 1935, at which the Popular Front was launched, the CPGB seems to have distanced itself from the militant elements in the rank-and-file strategy. Certainly there was a tendency to emphasize the need to maximize the use of the trade union machinery.[146] The downplaying of rank-and-filism seems to have occurred because, as Campbell indicated to the Party Congress in May 1937, 'A growing number of comrades are being elected to trade union executives and to paid official positions.'[147] Also, as the international situation worsened between 1937 and 1939, the CPGB leadership placed more emphasis upon the struggle for peace: in the summer of 1939 the Central Committee noted that there had been a serious neglect of trade union work in many districts and that 'it is not possible to record any big mass movements on the industrial field'.[148]

Drawn into attempting to establish the United Front and the Popular Front, and to deal with British fascism and the Spanish Civil War, it appears that Pollitt and the leadership were in fact content to issue advice about the need to work with trade unions and then to let the districts and locals assume that responsibility. Just before the emergence of the Comintern's manifesto on the United Front in March 1933 there had, nevertheless, been a statement that the Communist leadership aimed to create a revolutionary trade union organization.[149] The CPGB was steeped in the London General Omnibus Company rank-and-file movement, the Railway Vigilance movement and various other rank-and-file activity and there was a commitment to building up an independent leadership for the working classes.[150] There is also no doubt that the Central Committee and the Political Bureau continued to show a great interest in the Communist Party's contacts with the trade union movement, recording endlessly the number of members who also belonged to trade unions.

There was also significant reporting upon the trade union opposition papers. In May 1933 it was reported that the *Busman's Punch* had a circulation of 10,000, that the *Railway Vigilant* had 5,000 and the support of 100 NUR branches, that the *Cabman's Paper* produced 1,000 copies, the *Unity (Bulletin)* 12,000 and that many other opposition papers had a circulation of hundreds and occasionally a few thousand.[151]

Throughout the period, however, the CPGB was involved in most of the major industrial disputes. Members were prominent in the London busmen's strike of 1 May 1937, which was caused by the busmen's demand for a seven-and-a-half hour day and which was lost after a month partly due to the activities of Ernest Bevin. There were strikes in engineering, partly led by Communists, at Lucas's in Birmingham in 1937 and the famous strike at Harworth in the Nottingham coalfield in which the coal miners wished to leave the Spencer Union and rejoin the Nottingham Mining Association, which was part of the Miners' Federation of Great Britain.

Nevertheless, despite all their efforts and their increased influence, communists remained a small group within the trade unions. They, perhaps, carried influence beyond their numbers, but even that influence was extremely limited in relation to the entire British trade union movement. John Callaghan is right in saying that the CPGB was unable to capture significant trade union support or to offer a realistic alternative to the moderate socialist policies developed by the Labour Party. Even if it had penetrated trade unionism further, it may still have been faced with the problem of breaking down the ties that bound the British working classes to the very institutions which communism was attacking. Yet it is clear that, small as its influence was, the CPGB had made great strides forward in its commitment to trade unionism in the 1930s. In 1932 the Party congress had relatively few trade unionists in its ranks. By early 1934, after the change in direction towards trade unions, progress was still slow. In Birmingham only 8.4 per cent of members were in trade unions[152] and Arthur Horner reflected that:

> I do not think that we have made any appreciable progress in our trade union work. The rank and file is further back than it has been for a long time, but there are great possibilities and we must use them more effectively than we are doing at the present time.[153]

The switch of tactics away from Class Against Class, the January Resolutions and the United Front policy had exerted little initial impact. Nevertheless, matters began to improve dramatically thereafter. By the end of 1934 Pollitt emphasized the strong resistance that trades councils had shown to the introduction of the 'Black Circular'.[154] At the Thirteenth Party Congress in February 1935 of 294 delegates, 234 were trade unionists, 34 being district or national officials of the union and 82 being branch officials.[155] By 1937 the CPGB had even more trade union influence. It had 50 delegates among the 350 of the London Trades Council, the Vice-Chairman of Glasgow Trades Council and 60 of the 400 delegates, the Chairman and 30 of the 200 delegates to Edinburgh Trades Council, Arthur Horner as the President of the South Wales Miners' Federation, and numerous Party groups in the London tram depots and the Glasgow bus connections.[156]

Nevertheless, time and again, the main areas of support still tended to be the long-standing communist centres of London, Scotland, Lancashire and South Wales, with the main activities going on in mining and the bus services, although there was some influence in engineering and the new aircraft industries. In Scotland 581 of the region's 1,550 Communists (657 were employed and 865 unemployed) were members of trade unions in May 1936.[157] In Lancashire in 1937, 587 of the 1,158 members were in trade unions and 182 were also in the Labour Party.[158] By the end of 1938, Lancashire had 1,494 members, of whom 854 were in trade unions, 374 in the Labour Party, 147 in factory groups, 285 were women, 304 in cooperatives, 138 in trades councils and 200 unemployed.[159] Even in the West Riding, one of the CPGB's weaker areas, there were 148 trade union members among the 396 Communists and four factory groups, including one at the huge Montague Burton's factory in Leeds, which had 24 members.[160]

There is thus considerable evidence that the Communist Party had made a bold attempt to increase its trade union presence, and a projection of the above figures against its membership of 17,560 on 31 May 1939[161] would suggest that just under half of its members – 8,000 to 8,500 – might have been members of trade unions. Yet impressive as this figure was for a small party it was but a minor proportion of a trade union movement that had well in excess of 5 million members. The CPGB had expanded its influence within trade unions but its impact upon industrial relations was still small and compromised by the attempts of Pollitt and Campbell to work with the trade union leaders.

The Moves to War

In the years and months immediately preceding the outbreak of the Second World War it is clear that the CPGB was attempting to avert conflict, criticizing the National Government for being a friend of the fascist cause and hoping that a Popular Front movement would be formed strong enough to force the government to sign a pact with the Soviet Union.[162] Such policies, of course, raised the prospect of conflict and confusion within the Party. On the one hand, Willie Gallacher was congratulated by the CPGB for his opposition to Neville Chamberlain's meeting with Hitler in Munich over the situation of Czechoslovakia.[163] On the other, the *Daily Worker* was soon afterwards commenting favourably upon the prospects for peace brought about by the Munich meeting. In addition, the international crisis was hotly disputed by the Central Committee in May 1939 when the issue seemed to be the extent to which attacks should be levelled against the Chamberlain National Government because of Chamberlain's apparent refusal to be involved in pacts that would protect the interest of Czechoslovakia. At this point the Central Committee appears to have been in dispute over how much the Chamberlain government should be criticized. Some members, such as Dutt, wished to maintain peace while others, such as Pollitt, wished both to maintain peace and to condemn the National Government.[164] There was also the issue of conscription, which divided the Party until the intervention of Moscow led to the complete change of the line from opposition to support. Pollitt had originally argued that conscription was designed not for national defence but was directed against the people of Britain to allow Chamberlain to 'complete his alliance with fascism'.[165] However, Campbell returned from Moscow with the new line, announced it in the *Daily Worker* on 15 May 1939 and was instrumental in having it accepted by the Central Committee on 21 May 1939, by 13 votes to 5. The new line, as dictated by Moscow, was then published in the *Daily Worker* of 24 May 1939.

When the threat of war became stronger, and the Soviet Union signed the non-aggression pact with Germany in August, it was clear that the CPGB accepted that the opportunity for an Anglo-Soviet pact had been missed and that the Soviets had opted for the best available alternative. This was seen by the CPGB as a master stroke, although it was merely Stalin protecting his position.[166] However, in less than a month the CPGB was to face one of the biggest crises of its existence with the outbreak of the Second World War.

The Outbreak of the Second World War and the Change of Direction, September–October 1939

The outbreak of the Second World War on 3 September 1939 posed major problems for the CPGB. Although it had previously criticized the Chamberlain government as the friend of fascism and not to be trusted to wage an effective military struggle against Germany, Pollitt and his colleagues produced a manifesto on 2 September stating that 'We are in support of All necessary measures to secure the victory of democracy over Fascism' and issued the pamphlet *How to Win the War* on 7 September.[167] By 2 October 1939 the Central Committee had changed its line completely, criticizing both the war and the National Government. This change was so painful that it was nearly forty years before the old Party faithfuls conducted an airing of the events.[168] Even then there was disagreement about what had happened and whether the various policies were justified.

Pollitt's immediate reaction to the events of September 1939 had been to declare in support of the war against Nazi Germany. This seemed to be the natural progression of a policy of opposing fascism in Spain and advocating the Popular Front, even though a policy of international peace had been the declared policy of the Comintern and the CPGB for some time. In fact the Secretariat of the Comintern had urged communist parties 'to continue even more energetically the struggle against aggressors, especially German fascism' as late as 22 August 1939.[169] The manifesto produced by Pollitt and the CPGB declared the Party's support for Britain in the war. Yet it was to be a war on 'Two Fronts', against both fascism and the National Government. This line changed quickly, especially once the Moscow broadcast of 14 September described the war as an 'inter-imperialist conflict'.[170]

At this point Dutt began to press for the Moscow line and claimed some support at the Central Committee, although this seems to have disappeared at the Central Committee meeting on 24 and 25 September 1939. At this meeting, Dutt offered the alternative view, stating that:

> This war means enormous issues for us. It is firstly the extreme stage of imperialism. . . . Further the imperialists are divided, they have not succeeded in their plan against the Soviet Union. . . . The Soviet Union is enormously strengthened. . . . It is not a war for peace against aggression. We have to recognise quite clearly that the British ruling class which determined this war is conducting it for its purpose. . . . It is the fight for the British Empire against a threatening Empire. . . . Our line, the international line, is absolutely definite. If we accept the analysis of the imperialist war, we have to face the conclusions.[171]

Thus his approach was to attack both Chamberlain and the other imperialist powers. In consequence he argued that the main fight of the working class was against their own imperialist government: 'We do not ignore fascism. But we do direct the fight against the Government as the central fight, that only a people's government can defend the people against fascism.' It was also suggested that 'the retention of Poland's independence is a reactionary slogan', referring to Britain's declaration of war on Germany.

Having reminded his audience that, contrary to rumour, the CPGB was still continuing to support the war against fascism, Pollitt defended his policy.[172] He emphasized the need to protect the British people against fascism just as the Soviet government was defending the Soviet people and favoured the slogans 'Britain for the British' and the 'Fight on two fronts'. He seemed to be keeping the Party to his line rather than that propounded by Dutt.

At the end of the meeting on 24 September, however, David Springhall arrived from Moscow with a clear statement of the Comintern line. The next day he expounded it before the Central Committee. He discussed the conversations that he had held with Georgi Dimitrov and André Marty and referred to the ECCI telegram of 10 September, although it has been suggested that this was actually sent on 9 September,[173] and 'had reached all parties but not us'. Evidently, the Secretariat of the Comintern had met on the 9–10 September and agreed to a short thesis which stated that it was necessary to characterize the war 'not just as a war, but as an out-and-out imperialist war, a war which the working class in no country can give support to' and that communist parties at variance with this should adjust their policies immediately. It was also argued that while Poland was not an imperialist state it could become part of a bigger fascist one. Dimitrov, in his second talk with Springhall, emphasized that there should be no unity with the 'Chamberlain Socialists'. Eventually, after much discussion the fourteen points of Springhall's speech – including the suggestion that this was not a just war, the need to fight against war credits and the fight for peace and an end to the war – were reiterated. Pollitt suggested that the Political Bureau should meet at once: it was agreed that the Central Committee should be adjourned until 3 October – it in fact met on 2 October – and it was felt that the matter should not be discussed in the district committees until the Central Committee had made its final decision.

Nevertheless, the CPGB adjusted its political stance. On 27 September the *Daily Worker* denounced the British government's first war budget and on 30 September the Political Bureau declared the war to be against the interests of the people of Europe. In late September and early October, Salme Dutt, the wife of Rajani Dutt, sent a number of letters to Pollitt suggesting that he was a pacifist, that he should go to his 'Poplar Pals' (referring to George Lansbury and the labour movement in Poplar, which was associated with pacifism) and that his line was wrong.[174] Finally, the CC meeting of 2 and 3 October 1939 changed the Party's cause to the Moscow line with three dissenters – Pollitt, Campbell and Gallacher – although Pollitt asked that Gallacher's name be withdrawn from opposition once the vote had been taken since he had voted more out of loyalty to Pollitt. At this meeting, Dutt presented a powerful speech in favour of the international line and greatly strengthened his position by reading out the ECCI 'short thesis' on the war. He suggested that the whole Party was on trial, to which Gallacher responded, 'I have never at the Central Committee listened to a more unscrupulous and opportunist speech as the one which has just been delivered'. Gallacher added that:

> We started with the idea of support for the war, but fight for a new government to carry it on. We are now asked to go over, oppose the war and use the situation to smash capitalism. . . . We started by saying that we had an interest in the defeat of the Nazis, we must now recognize that our prime interest is the defeat of France and Great Britain because that will furnish the suitable conditions for a revolution in the country. . . . We started out by proclaiming the defence of the British people from fascism, we are now told that the defence of the British people from fascism is imperialism, that there can be no defence from imperialism until there is a revolutionary government in this country. . . . We have to eat all we have said. . . . I am against presenting the Soviet Union as a universal Santa Claus.[175]

Pollitt, more diplomatically, suggested that 'I am a loyal supporter of the CI . . . I am opposed to this thesis, I believe that in the long run it will do the Party very grave harm'.[176] He also suggested that the Soviet Union was not yet out of danger with Germany, objected to the overthrowing of the United Front and Popular Front approaches and reflected that, in discussions with Dimitrov, he had been told that the CPGB did not know how to look after the national honour of Britain.

Pollitt then resigned as General Secretary of the CPGB, although he offered his continuing services to the Party.[177] Immediately afterwards he received several letters of thanks for his work, including one from Comrade Rose, stating that it 'was a big mistake for us all to lose you'.[178] It was not until 18 November 1939 that he could force himself to 'unreservedly accept the policy of the Communist Party',[179] blaming his hatred of German fascism and 'the influence of the fascist war of invasion on Republican Spain' for his aberration. Until the summer of 1941 he was involved in working for the Party in Lancashire.

The Party was now in favour of 'revolutionary defeatism', the belief that the home country should be defeated in the hope of achieving revolutionary change. The new manifesto was published on 7 October 1939 and declared that the CPGB was opposed to both the war and the National Government.[180] It stated that:

The truth about this war must be told. The war is not a war for democracy against Fascism. It is not a war for the liberties of small nations. It is not a war for the defence of peace against aggression. This war is a fight between imperialist powers over profits, colonies and world domination.[181]

The Executive Committee of the Comintern reiterated the point on the twenty-second anniversary of the Russian Revolution on 6 November 1939, emphasizing that 'The ruling circles of England, France and Germany are waging war *for world supremacy*.'[182]

This change of policy led to much confusion throughout the Party in the country. Bill Moore of Sheffield was pleased that the CPGB had returned to its peace policy. Years later, he recalled that the change of line was not due to the intervention of the Communist International: 'When Joe turns we all turn; and I just don't believe it. It would not have had as I remember, total acceptance unless it corresponded with the experience that, I think, all the Party had over previous ten years.'[183] Ernie Trory (Sussex District Organizer) also made similar points, maintaining that it was only on 12 July 1941, when the alliance between Britain and the Soviet Union was signed, that he accepted the need to work with the government against fascism.[184] They felt that the defence of the Soviet Union was all-important. Others disagreed, feeling that the mood of the Party members was with Pollitt on the need to fight the war on 'two fronts'. Jack Cohen maintained, 'I don't recollect any of the enthusiasm for the new line when it was adopted, and I certainly don't agree that it represented the logical culmination of ten years of political activity by the Party.'[185] Others also believed that the Party should support Britain in the war. Many, such as Eddie Frow, felt that had Pollitt, Campbell and Gallacher challenged the International line then many of the Party would have followed but that since they did not Frow, and others, felt that there must be something they did not know and that they should support the international line.[186]

In the West Riding of Yorkshire confusion prevailed. Geoff Hodgson of the Leeds CPGB recalls the majority of the branch loyally supported the Pollitt line of a war on 'Two Fronts' during September 1939; he also remembers the new Comintern line that the war was an imperialist conflict come as something of a shock.[187] In contrast, Ernie Benson, a senior figure in the Leeds CPGB who had been District Organizer in 1935/6 and 1938, recalls in his autobiography:

As I saw it, and also the majority of Party members, it was a war brought about by the clash of rival capitalist powers, and a hatred of the Soviet Union . . . An unjust war was being waged and we could not support such a war.[188]

Indeed, most British Communists accepted the new Party line, even if their support was often given in a grudging manner.[189] Morgan put it bluntly: 'The fact is that Stalin had signed a pact with Germany and the CPGB had to adjust its line accordingly.'[190]

The First Unity Convention held at the Cannon Street Hotel, London, 31 July and 1 August 1920. Delegates from the British Socialist Party, the Workers' Socialist Federation, Communist Unity groups, the Socialist Labour Party and Guild Communist groups met to found the Communist Party of Great Britain. (National Museum of Labour History)

Delegates attending the Leeds Convention of the Party in January 1921, a Unity Convention in which an attempt was made to widen support for the Communist Party of Great Britain. (National Museum of Labour History)

The first Central Committee of the CPGB and staff outside the 16 King Street, London, headquarters of the Party. Front row, left to right: Minnie Birch, Tom Bell, Albert Inkpin (General Secretary), Arthur McManus, Willie Gallacher, F. Peate and Doris Wilson. (National Museum of Labour History)

THE GREAT COMMUNIST TRIAL, 1925.

(Back Row) J. T. Murphy, W. Gallacher, W. Hannington ; *(Middle Row)* H. Pollitt, E. Cant, T. H. Wintringham, A. Inkpin ; *(Front Row)* J. R. Campbell, A. McManus, W. Rust, R. P. Arnot, T. Bell.

Published by THE INTERNATIONAL CLASS WAR PRISONERS' AID.   Lond, Cal. Press. Ltd.

The Communist leaders arrested and imprisoned in 1925 for 'unlawfully conspiring together to utter and publish seditious libel to induce diverse persons to commit breaches of the Incitement to Mutiny Act of 1797'. Some were imprisoned for six months, others for one year. (National Museum of Labour History)

Harry Pollitt, General Secretary of the Party, 1929–56 (except for a period between 1939 and 1941) sitting at the side of Georgi Dimitrov (right) at the Seventh Congress of the Comintern held in July and August 1935 at which the Popular Front against Fascism was proposed. (National Museum of Labour History)

Rajani Palme Dutt, *c.* 1925. Dutt was one of the intellectuals of the Party, on the Central Committee and Political Bureau of the Party from time to time and General Secretary, in place of Harry Pollitt, between 1939 and 1941. (National Museum of Labour History)

Communists protest about the Spanish Civil War and unemployment, c. 1937. (National Museum of Labour History)

Harry Pollitt addressing the British Battalion of the International Brigade in Spain, 1937. (National Museum of Labour History)

The flag of the British Battalion of the International Brigade in the Spanish Civil War, *c*. 1937. (National Museum of Labour History)

A mass demonstration for the opening of a Second Front in the Second World War, c. 1942. (National Museum of Labour History)

The *Daily Worker* was suppressed on 21 January 1941 by the Home Secretary, Herbert Morrison, under Regulation 2D. This ban was not lifted until 26 August 1942. This picture shows a meeting in support of lifting the ban held some time in 1941 or 1942. The events of these days were written up by Willie Rust in *The Daily Worker Reborn* (London, CPGB, 1943). (National Museum of Labour History)

Willie Gallacher helping to launch The British Road to Socialism programme at a meeting in 1951. (National Museum of Labour History)

Mao Zedong and Harry Pollitt meet in 1955. (National Museum of Labour History)

John Gollan, General Secretary of the Communist Party of Great Britain, 1956–76. (National Museum of Labour History)

Abe Moffatt, Sid Easton, John Gollan and John Mahon marching against the Vietnam War, late 1960s. (National Museum of Labour History)

John Gollan at a meeting with Leonid Brezhnev (right), First Secretary and later General Secretary of the Communist Party of the Soviet Union, 1964–82. This photograph was probably taken on a visit by Gollan to Moscow in the late 1960s or early 1970s. (National Museum of Labour History)

The *Morning Star*, reporting critically upon the Soviet invasion of Czechoslovakia, 23 August 1968. (Photograph from the National Museum of Labour History, reproduced courtesy of the *Morning Star*)

Gordon McLennan, General Secretary of the Communist Party of Great Britain, 1976–89, with Mick McGahey, the Scottish miners' leader, probably in the mid-1980s. (National Museum of Labour History)

The *Morning Star*'s float in a demonstration against Margaret Thatcher's Conservative government in 1982. (National Museum of Labour History)

Dr Tony Chater became editor of the *Morning Star* in 1974 and led the 'Chaterite' opposition to the Eurocommunism adopted by the Party in the 1980s. (National Museum of Labour History)

Nina Temple, General Secretary of the CPGB from 1989 to 1991, demonstrating outside a Job Centre in the mid-1980s. (National Museum of Labour History)

The War and Convention, November 1939–June 1940

Over the next twenty months the Communist Party preached revolutionary defeatism. However, the focus of much of its activity was not the defeat of Britain but the need to establish immediate peace with Hitler and to improve the lot of the working classes. Indeed, the Party's application forms at this time contained the statement that:

> The rulers of Britain are using this war to declare heavy blows against their own peoples – employers have launched a sweeping attack on the workers' standards and conditions. The workers must organize to resist the combined attacks of the employers and the Government. If you agree with this you will join the Communist Party today.[191]

The CPGB attempted to make every issue one of working conditions and living standards. Through *The New Propeller* they took up the campaign of the Aircraft Shop Stewards' National Council (formed in 1933) for better conditions of employers. Similar action occurred in other trades. According to the government, 'In industry the Communist Party is making determined efforts to improve its position. Already its representation among shop stewards is out of all proportion to its membership and every grievance is exploited by them.'[192]

There were some problems with this policy. The most obvious was that some trade union leaders went their own way. Arthur Horner returned to his old approach of putting the case of the miners and workmen before that of the Communist Party. This was demonstrated in the South Wales Miners' Federation's wage negotiations in October 1939 in which he argued in favour of the unions accepting two-thirds of the offer that the employers were making in response to the miners' demands. He also supported a situation where the SWMF voted three to one in favour of the war effort 'so long as it is fought against Fascist aggression and for the achievement of a permanent peace', an action in opposition to the official Communist line.[193] The Home Office noted that 'His position as President of the South Wales Miners' Federation brings a good deal of kudos to the Party but he has recently shown considerable unwillingness to accept their instructions.'[194]

Other concerns emerged. There was particular opposition to the possibility that Britain might support Finland in its war against the Soviet Union. In the end this did not occur but Dutt, at the height of the emergency, declared that 'the Finnish conflict means that within less than three months of the beginning of the imperial war, direct war on the Soviet Union had begun'. This did not please John Strachey, one of the intellectuals of the Party, who had only been persuaded to accept the new line in November 1939.[195] Indeed, the Soviet invasion of Finland was the final straw for him and, feeling that the *Daily Worker*'s treatment of the matter was revolting, Strachey indicated his departure from the Party to Dutt in May 1940: 'You must not suppose that I think that the Communist International has sold out to the Nazis. It is merely that it is pursuing its goal for a socialist world by a method (that of objective political cooperation with Nazism involving increasing the risk of subjugation of Western Europe and this country to Fascist rule) which I cannot follow.'[196] There were also other domestic electoral concerns. Pollitt was defeated at the West Ham Silvertown parliamentary by-election in February 1940 and Isabel Brown was defeated at Bow and Bromley in June 1940.

The signs for the CPGB were somewhat contradictory. On the one hand, there seems to have been no great surge of interest in the CPGB and at its May Day activities in 1940, the Comintern policies were largely ignored.[197] Nevertheless, there had been some steady increase in Communist support. In January 1940 the CPGB had about 20,000 members – an increase of 2,000 over the previous fifteen months – and the Young Communist League had about 6,000. The bulk of the increase had, apparently, occurred since the outbreak of the war.[198] The CPGB was also making attempts to win the support of anti-fascist refugees.[199]

The growth of the Communist Party, and its opposition to the war, certainly attracted the attention of the British government which kept detailed notes on all its public meetings. In London these were gathered together by the Special Branch and a distilled report sent to the Home Secretary. Apart from the enormous detail, often verbatim, of the public meetings, an assessment of the Communist Party's position as a threat was often provided. Clearly, the government had agents operating at the highest level in the CPGB, for a Special Branch Report on 15 February 1940 stated that 'The following is a copy of the notes used by Dave Springhall when addressing said meetings which are being held in various parts of the country and are attended by leading members only.'[200] There were also enquiries into whether the *Daily Worker* was receiving foreign subsidies; it was suggested that MI5 should check the accounts at the Westminster Bank.[201]

The CPGB, the War and the People's Convention, June 1940–June 1941

The attitude of the CPGB towards the war changed once again with the fall of France in June 1940 and Hitler's offer of a peace settlement on 19 July 1940. By that time the Party was no longer rejecting the war against the Nazis.[202] Indeed, there had been discussions between the government and the Party with Gallacher sending a letter to R.A. Butler, the Under-Secretary for Foreign Affairs, regarding the need to work closely together, suggesting the possibility that Pollitt, Gallacher, Dutt and Kerrigan should be sent to the Soviet Union to effect a change of policy.[203] A telegram from Cripps to Butler, on 16 July 1940, stated, 'I do not believe that any of those named can influence Soviet foreign policy any more than any other unofficial figures . . . I do not consider any harm would be done by Pollitt coming, for whose honesty and intelligence I have great respect. I should respect any of the other two [sic] coming'. Interestingly there was a letter from Maclean, Senior Principal at the Foreign Office, who saw 'every member of the Communist Party' as 'an agent of a foreign power'. There was also a meeting on 23 July 1940 between Butler and Gallacher at which Butler felt that the CPGB should be anti-Hitler.[204]

Whilst the CPGB was prepared to talk to Churchill's wartime government it is clear that moves in this direction were halting. Gallacher, Rust and Dutt were still distrustful of Churchill's wartime administration.[205] Matters did not improve when the *Daily Worker* was suppressed in January 1941, against the advice given to the Home Office. Indeed, although Sir Alexander Maxwell felt that the Communist Party was becoming 'more actively hostile' and 'defeatist' Viscount Swindon argued that he felt the suppression of the *Daily Worker* 'would be a mistake' even though the leading article of 9 September 1940 had praised three 'worthy strikes' which had taken place.[206]

In this less critical, and more cooperative, atmosphere the CPGB now became convinced of the need to develop an alternative strategy, that of forming a People's Convention to form the basis of a 'People's Government'. This proposal was put forward by D.N. Pritt, Labour and Communist sympathizers and others; the first meeting was organized for January 1941 and held in London.

Pritt had first raised the idea of a People's Convention in June 1940 when he wrote, 'I appeal for the widest support of the People's Convention. Only the people can save themselves.'[207] Dutt also put forward the idea of a broad alliance of Labour interests to be brought together in a socialist-labour alliance. By August 1940 he was thinking of a People's Convention that would be a wider coming together of mass working-class interests. These moves coincided with the fact that in July 1940 the Hammersmith Labour Party and Trades Council set up a people's vigilance committee to mount a campaign on the then demands of the Communist Party. Out of these efforts the People's Convention was held on 12 January 1941. A People's Convention manifesto had been circulated before the meeting suggesting six main points: the defence of the people's living standards, the defence of the people's democratic rights, adequate air-raid precautions, friendship with the Soviet Union, the formation of a people's government and a people's peace to end the war.

The People's Convention filled three halls, attracted 2,234 delegates and purported to represent the interests of 1,200,000 people. It extended the six points to eight and was attended by Krishna Menon, a prominent Indian communist leader, and R.P. Dutt, as well as Pritt and other leading figures. Not surprisingly, it was dubbed the 'People's Reichstag' by the *Daily Herald*.[208] Within a few months the movement had distributed 632,000 pamphlets and 1,336,000 leaflets and manifestos. These included W.J. Square's *The People's Convention Movement*, Edgar G. Young's *The People's Peace*, W. Swanson's *Industrial Problems*, Dudley Collard's *Civil Liberties* and D.N. Pritt's *Friendship with the USSR*. It also produced various leaflets to explain to different groups of workers why they must support the People's Convention. It committed itself to a recall conference in August 1941 but this never took place, owing to the changed political circumstances. The movement for the People's Convention was brought to an abrupt end by Operation Barbarossa, the German attack on the Soviet Union on 22 June 1941.

Conclusion

Kevin Morgan has argued that in the 1930s there were always tensions between the revolutionary objectives the CPGB set itself and the non-revolutionary environment in which it operated:

The picture which emerges is a confused one, of a revolutionary party acclimatising itself to a situation offering few opportunities for revolutionary activity without abandoning its fundamental conceptions and expectations. This contradiction would be resolved, if only partially, in the period after June 1941 when the CP came not only to support the war but to revise many of the assumptions which had formed the theoretical basis of Communist policies for two decades.[209]

This is, perhaps, rather exaggerated since the Comintern abandoned all the revolutionary tenets of Marxism–Leninism at the Seventh World Congress of the Comintern in 1935 and effectively accepted the process of Stalinization begun in the late 1920s. From 1935 onwards the USSR attempted a policy of peaceful coexistence with the capitalist world and the last time that the CPGB ever formally accepted the goal of Soviet power as an objective was at its Thirteenth Congress in February 1935.[210] Yet even the abandonment of revolutionary principles did not bring mass support.

Neither the United Front nor the Popular Front succeeded in greatly extending the support of the Party. The fact is that the CPGB was slower to throw off the Class Against Class sectarianism than has often been suggested and did not accept the United Front fully until October 1934. Also, the CPGB's change of attitude towards the Second World War did not endear it to the vast majority of the British people, and the People's Convention was soon exposed for the sham that it was. In any case, it was blatantly obvious that the Party's policy was dominated by the needs of Moscow transmitted through the Comintern. It had less flexibility in dealing with the

Comintern than is often suggested and it was only the change in the Moscow/Comintern line – resulting from Operation Barbarossa, and the subsequent Anglo-Soviet pact – that transformed its fortunes, seeing its membership rise to well over 50,000 and its policies revised. Overnight, it changed its position and became the most patriotic of parties in the pursuit of increased production to win the war and open a second front to relieve German pressure upon the Soviet Union.

The CPGB simply followed the line of Soviet foreign policy, which dictated Comintern policy. Indeed, Ben Pimlott suggests that 'Communist policy followed faithfully every twist and turn of the Communist International'.[211] The evidence presented here suggests this, although it is clear that there was much more confusion and contradiction than Pimlott would accept and less freedom than some Stalinist writers would have us believe. Indeed, there was keen debate within the leadership of the Party, the Central Committee, the Political Bureau and the Secretariat and, while the Party always eventually fell into line with the Comintern or international position, there were many different groups within the CPGB and it was far from the monolithic organization it is often made out to be.

Why then did the CPGB fail to become a mass party during this period? It is clear that it had made little impact in the 1920s and early 1930s because of the sectarianism of the Class Against Class policy, but the abandonment of Marxism–Leninism does not seem to have allowed it to make any significant advance. Why should the British workers support a Party which was courting middle-class opinion from 1935 onwards and which, by 1937, was to the right of the Labour Party on many policies? The CPGB's uncritical defence of the USSR, particularly in connection with the Moscow Show Trials, confirmed for many workers the truth of the Labour Party's accusations that the CPGB was a creature of Moscow subservient to a foreign state which had little in common with the democratic socialism of the British Labour movement.

IV

War and Peace, 1941–51

The years 1941 to 1951 transformed the position of the CPGB. In particular, they saw profound changes in the CPGB line. On the instructions of both the Comintern and the Soviet Union it declared itself in favour of the British war effort, following the German attack upon the Soviet Union in June 1941. Pollitt was now free to pursue the pro-war stance he had advocated in October 1939 and demand that we 'smash Hitler now'.[1] It was a campaign that won substantial support from workers across the country and saw CPGB membership hovering around 56,000 in December 1942 as a result of a wave of Russophile sentiment which swept through British society, following the Red Army's heroic defence of Stalingrad.[2] Yet the political honeymoon of the Party did not long survive the war. The Cold War of the late 1940s isolated it from the mainstream of the British political system although, ironically, it did choose a non-revolutionary, modified parliamentary route in its *The British Road to Socialism* (1951), which jettisoned the last vestiges of the CPGB's revolutionary heritage by abandoning its commitment to Soviet power and, thus, its acceptance of full-blown Marxist-Leninist ideas. These developments in policy contrasted with the Trotskyite opponents of the CPGB, such as the Workers' International League and the Revolutionary Communist Party, who still believed in revolutionary change and, unlike the CPGB, were prepared to support strike activity during the Second World War. *The British Road to Socialism* was redrafted several times until it was replaced in 1989 by *Manifesto of the New Times*, which dropped any semblance of Marxist-Leninist ideas.

The new approach to the war and capitalism was confirmed by the dissolution of the Comintern in 1943. The CPGB was not invited to join Cominform, the new organization set up by nine communist parties in September 1947. It was rejected on the grounds that it was politically insignificant. Not surprisingly, the decade 1941 to 1951 was to be one in which the Party accepted its political marginality within British society. It turned its attention to emphasizing the need to improve international relations between the capitalist world and the Soviet Union through organizing a movement for international peace.

Operation Barbarossa, the Change of Line and Cooperation

Britain and the Soviet Union announced an alliance on 13 July 1941, following Operation Barbarossa, and the CPGB then announced its patriotic campaign demanding outright war against Germany. The Communist Party condemned the German people as being entirely composed of Nazis: 'Millions of youths behave worse than beasts and the entire nation must take responsibility for crimes committed in its name.'[3] It implored Churchill and Roosevelt to open the Second Front in Europe to relieve the pressure of the German assault upon the Soviet Union. It campaigned for the *Daily Worker* to be allowed to publish, for the banning of socialist anti-war papers,[4] and for the Tory Minister, Sir P.J. Grigg, against Fenner Brockway of the ILP during the Cardiff East by-election of May 1942. This last action led Pollitt to inform the CPGB's one-day national conference in May 1942 that this was 'not an easy task to carry out'.[5]

At first some Communists were suspicious that the German invasion of the Soviet Union was linked with the parachuting of Rudolph Hess, Hitler's deputy, into Scotland. However, such doubts were soon allayed and the Party was quickly in full pro-war mode. According to the CPGB, the vital question now to be asked was – who was for and who against Hitler? The Communists' purpose became the defeat of Hitler and fascism; everything else became subordinate, including the class and colonial struggles. Indeed, Pollitt sent a letter to Jawaharlal Nehru, the Indian Nationalist leader, in 1942 suggesting that, although he continued to dislike British imperialism, in order to defend the Soviet Union 'I am prepared to co-operate with all those who are prepared to fight against fascism'.[6]

In order to pursue these renewed demands for wartime unity, Pollitt gave up his shipyard job on 8 August 1941 and, once again, became full-time secretary of the CPGB. He campaigned up and down the country and produced numerous pamphlets including *Into Battle!*, *Speed the Second Front!*, *Deeds Not Words!*, and *Smash Hitler Now*. He addressed many meetings and dominated several Second Front demonstrations in Trafalgar Square. Indeed, as a Mass Observation observer noted, it was Pollitt who obtained 80 per cent of the applause at the July 1942 demonstration in Trafalgar Square.[7] His message was that the nation needed to sacrifice itself in what was a 'people's war', and it appealed to many Labour activists. Michael Foot, Aneurin Bevan, and a number of Labour MPs joined these meetings demanding that the British government should open the Second Front. Indeed, Bevan, having just taken over as acting editor of *Tribune*, threw his full weight behind the new-found commitment of the Soviets and the CPGB to the war effort.

Denis Noel Pritt, KC and Labour MP for Hammersmith North, was particularly active in encouraging the new attitude of cooperation between the Labour Party, the

CPGB and Soviet Russia. His diary notes reflect his constant concern to nurture the belief that the future of socialism in Britain was through some form of alliance and friendship with the CPGB and the Soviet Union. He lectured on behalf of the CPGB, explaining the Soviet system, and temporarily promoted Stafford Cripps as a possible new Labour leader or Prime Minister. He attended a recruitment meeting for the CPGB at the Palace Theatre, Reading, in March 1942, along with William Rust, one of the 'Young Turks' of the CPGB. At the meeting, which led to a collection of £114 and sixty new members, he commented, 'I spoke to the bourgeoisie on the lines that they ought to understand the Communist Party and what it stands for, and judge it impartially. They now know they had [sic] been fooled over the Soviet Union.'[8] He was also in constant touch with 'Johnny' (Ivan Maisky, a member of the Russian Embassy Staff) who reflected that the Soviets preferred Churchill as British Prime Minister since 'neither Eden nor Cripps is sufficiently big . . . and everybody else just unthinkable'.[9] This followed upon the military failures and concerns of Britain earlier in the year when it appeared, for a time, that Alfred Duff Cooper and Cripps were possible alternatives to Churchill. At that time Cripps was seen as the man who helped bring Russia into the war and Pritt had hopes of joining the wartime government:

An important consideration in connection with joining the Labour Party is the question whether I would be more or less likely to be invited into a government if I were an independent rather than a member of the Labour Party. This again could only be judged later on.[10]

This new spirit of closeness between the British and Russian peoples was further galvanized by the decision of the British government to encourage the film industry to produce suitable propaganda films. The most obvious propaganda work was the 1943 film *The Demi-Paradise*, released to get the British to like the Russians,[11] in which Laurence Olivier played Ivan Kouznetsoff, a Russian engineer who visits the English town of 'Barchester' to negotiate the building of an ice-breaker. To Ivan the English seem distant and old-fashioned, more interested in cricket than the international situation. A failed love affair with the granddaughter of the shipyard owner leads him to return home disillusioned. However, he returns to Britain during the Blitz, finds the English carrying on as usual and, following Operation Barbarossa, admires the shipyard workers toiling around the clock to finish the ice-breaker on schedule, despite the shipyard having been bombed. The ship is launched as *Drushka* (*Friendship*) and Ivan realizes that he has come to regard the English as 'a grand, a great people'. Although the film is more a celebration of England and Englishness than it is of Russia, it, nevertheless, helped to associate the two countries in wartime effort in the minds of the British public.[12]

The Second Front

From 1941 until 1944, the driving force behind wartime Communist policies was the desire to see a Second Front opened in Europe to draw German military pressure away from the Soviet Union. Every other policy – political, industrial and colonial – was secondary to this objective. Preparing for the Sixteenth Party Congress in 1942, which was eventually delayed until a congress 'for Unity and Victory' was held in May 1943,[13] Pollitt stated that 'We now have to agitate, fight, and organize, to compel the Government to open the Second Front. Meetings, deputations, resolutions, demonstrations, every conceivable form of political pressure must be brought to bear.'[14] Indeed, the Sixteenth Congress was to be judged by its 'positive contribution towards a speedier winning of the war and peace', and Pollitt further demanded that Communists and others should volunteer to help in harvesting in Britain and that the Labour Party should encourage unity by allowing the CPGB to affiliate.[15]

The Allied signing of a Second Front agreement on 26 May 1942 gave hope that an invasion of Western Europe was imminent, but this was not to be and the CPGB campaign continued. In the summer months of 1942 it was noted that the Central Committee had declared that the 'central issue for the workers is not wages nor the fight for wage increases. The central fight is for the Second Front now, sustained by arms production and improved transportation of materials to their destination.'[16] There was also continued insistence that Churchill should open the Second Front immediately,[17] and a four-page discussion document in January 1943 reiterated that the real concern of the British people was the need to bring about the 'speediest victory over Hitler' by opening the Second Front. Away from the war there was still a preoccupation with the affiliation of the CPGB to the Labour Party.[18]

The invasion of Italy in 1943 did not satisfy the CPGB because 'Hitler can fight a long delaying action in Italy without having to draw decisive forces from the Eastern Front – at the same time he can compel Britain and America to use key forces and inflict such heavy losses'.[19] It was only with the D-Day landings in June 1944, and the obvious build up to this, that the CPGB turned its attention to other events.

·From 1941 the CPGB stressed the closeness of the British and Russian peoples. Much was made of the impact of the Anglo-Soviet Treaty in uniting the British and Russians, and the CPGB constantly reassured Moscow of the positive intentions of the British people. In a letter sent to Moscow on 4 January 1943, regarding the impending Sixteenth Congress of the CPGB it was stated that: 'This Congress will afford the means of discussing the present stage and development of the war in order to bring about a great further mobilisation of the Party and the forces of the British people in support of an all-out effort to win victory over Fascism in 1943.'[20]

The Party was quick to identify those it saw as the enemies of the Second Front. It identified two main groups. Firstly, there were the old 'Munichites', pro-Hitler and Mosley elements who, apparently, wished for a German-British onslaught against communism.[21] Secondly, there was the small group of Trotskyists, calling themselves the Revolutionary Communist Party (RCP), who were seen to be spreading 'disruption and fascist strikes' on the eve of the Second Front.[22] It might be noted that the RCP was a product of the fusion in 1943 of the Workers' International League and the Revolutionary Socialist League, organizations the CPGB had previously criticized in a circular issued on 10 November 1941.[23] They did in fact become involved in some engineering disputes during the war.[24] It was the possible disruption of wartime production by the RCP and other bodies that worried the Party and shaped its attitude towards its industrial and trade union policy.

Industrial and Trade Union Policy in Wartime

From the summer of 1941 to the end of the Second World War, the CPGB was concerned that industrial production should not be interrupted by strikes that might hinder the speedy defeat of Hitler. Abandoning its previous support for all strikes it substituted support for 100 per cent trade unionism, the creation of improved negotiating arrangements and the belief that strikes were avoidable within the context of winning the war and opening the Second Front. These were policies which played into the hands of employers who wished to control wages and conditions of employment.[25]

In 1942 the Party presented its 'Trade Union Policy in the War against Fascism',[26] recognizing that the 'trade unions are one of the powerful driving forces in war'. However, it also emphasized that war production was vital and it called upon the working classes and the trade unions 'to make sacrifice and to enforce sacrifice on others, to support every measure to win the war'.[27] But that sacrifice had to be a fair one and it was clear that the wartime controls introduced in May 1940, including the Essential Work Order, favoured the employers and restricted the right of workers to move from job to job. In addition the right of firms to charge the full cost of production plus 10 per cent, meant that employers were gaining a high level of profits, regardless of whether or not they had been efficient. The failures of this arrangement were thus outlined in an 'Urgent Memorandum on Production', issued by the CPGB in March 1942.

The Communist answer was the creation of joint production committees (JPCs) at which workers would decide output with employers. The autumn of 1941 saw many meetings with employers to discuss such possibilities. Some on the left criticized such committees, seeing them as class collaboration, but others noted that wartime production had to be improved and that the JPCs could highlight and remedy inefficient production techniques. The CPGB saw them both as a way to defeat Hitler and as a means for trade unions 'to gain for them a more enduring place in post-war society'.[28] There was a significant breakthrough when the Ministry of Supply agreed with the unions to set up JPCs in the Royal Ordnance factories in February 1942. Engineering employers agreed to follow suit on 18 March 1942, with JPCs having equal numbers of employer and worker representatives. Nevertheless, not all workers in engineering wished to establish JPCs with employers and there was resistance to the idea, for instance at the Leeds Royal Ordnance Factory.[29]

The Party also stressed the vital importance of the coal industry to war production. By 1941 there was a shortage of miners despite measures to return ex-miners to industry. The CPGB therefore emphasized the need for Pit Production Committees, set up in 1940, to move from dealing with absenteeism towards dealing with the efficiency of production. Indeed, Arthur Horner re-emphasized this need in 1943 in a Communist pamphlet that anticipated the nationalization of the mines.[30] Relations between the coal owners and the coal miners had not been good since the First World War. Therefore, the Party did call for 'the intensification of the drive for increased production through more responsible attitudes towards Pit production committees' in 1943 and by 1944 was demanding that anomalies should be rectified so that 'every miner feels that he has a real incentive to increase output'.[31] Pollitt and the Party were not particularly convinced that the government was handling the miners' pay awards very effectively and called for the nationalization of the mines.

The Party does seem to have built up its influence in some industrial strongholds. Napier's aero-engine plant at Acton Vale, West London, became a centre for Party activists.[32] Les Ambrose built up CPGB strength within the shop stewards' committee at Austen Aero, and numerous other Communist shop stewards extended their influence in other plants and factories, although there were instances, such as the Barrow dispute in September 1943, where the engineers won despite the CPGB's attempt to end the strike.[33] Indeed, in the Barrow strike a majority of the Barrow CPGB members resigned from the Party and worked with Tom Trewartha, the leader of the dispute, to ensure that they won wage increases after eighteen days of action. Many strikers felt that politics should not intervene in trade union affairs and the CPGB was effectively, if jokingly, referred to as 'His Majesty's Communist Party'.

Clearly, not all was successful, and the efforts to form JPCs in the Glasgow engineering plants largely failed, particularly at Beardmore's where a works ballot rejected the formation of a JPC partly on the basis that it might constrict industrial action.[34] Also, in an engineering strike on Tyneside in October 1942 Communist shop stewards opposed the stoppage and lost their position within the district; the Party never regained its status on the Tyne and Communist organizers were rejected.[35] Indeed, Fred Shaw, Branch Secretary of the Huddersfield Amalgamated Engineering Union, wrote to George Hargrave, Secretary of the Huddersfield Trades Council, on

26 October 1942 presenting a resolution that his branch had passed on 23 October, condemning 'most sharply the attitude of the official trade union leaders who had signed the agreement without consultation with the men concerned, it further condemns the blacklegging and strike breaking policy of the Communist Party. The branch further supports the attitude of the men concerned in their demand for an inquiry to be made into the circumstances leading to the agreement.'[36]

War weariness also seems to have occurred in the last two years of conflict and the CPGB lost some of its membership when it became clear that they were doing little beyond stimulating war production at a time when strike activity was increasing.[37] There was also some disillusionment when engineering output began to wind down in 1944 and 1945, leading to mass redundancies in the industry; in response the CPGB suggested that the engineers use the appeals procedure laid down by the Essential Works Order rather than organize unofficial strike activity.[38]

The Communist Party and the Affiliation to the Labour Party

Part of the CPGB's strategy for creating a unified working class and wartime unity of purpose was to reapply for affiliation to the Labour Party. Communist attempts to affiliate had been turned down during the 1920s and in 1936. Now the CPGB was emphasizing unity as a means to win the war against Hitler; the Central Committee of the Party (which became the Executive Committee in 1943) decided to reapply. Pollitt sent a letter to J.S. Middleton, Secretary of the Labour Party, on 18 December 1942 asking that the CPGB's application for affiliation be put to the Labour Party's annual conference in June 1943, and hoping that there could be interim meetings between officials of the CPGB and Labour. The Labour Party's NEC meeting of 27 January 1943 opposed the application.[39] Middleton's reply to the CPGB suggested that the Party was not free from the influence of the Comintern and, therefore, could not be supported in its application. In response, Pollitt suggested that the CPGB's affiliation with the Labour Party would raise no difficulties with the Comintern and that the Party was self-financing. There ensued a protracted debate between the CPGB and Labour.[40] Notwithstanding the rebuff, the CPGB mounted a further campaign to gain support to which Labour responded with articles in the *Daily Herald* and a pamphlet entitled *The Communist Party and the War – a record of hypocrisy and treachery to the workers of Europe.*

The dissolution of the Comintern in May 1943 did little to deflect Labour Party criticism of the CPGB. Although the CPGB was able to claim that nearly 3,400 local Labour groups had passed resolutions in support of the application by June 1943,[41] the Labour Party conference swept the request aside, with 712,000 votes for CPGB affiliation and 1,951,000 against.[42] Nevertheless, the CPGB maintained the hope of affiliation, although its other political recommendations, most notably the introduction of a new system of proportional representation in parliamentary voting and local conferences of progressive organizations to select candidates in the forthcoming general election, were turned down by the 1944 Labour Party conference.

Labour leaders were inclined to draw a distinction between British Communists and the far more powerful Communist Party of the Soviet Union. By the same token the Labour left, including Fenner Brockway and Emrys Hughes (editor of the *Glasgow Forward*), were far more critical of the capitalistic United States, an 'expanding Imperial power', than of Soviet Russia. They even acknowledged that the USSR may need political reassurance. As Aneurin Bevan wrote: 'It is quite natural and inevitable that Russia should influence preponderantly the life of nations immediately on her borders and that she should seek to prevent them from combinations that may be aimed at her. That is the price we have to pay for the bitter recent past.'[43] However, the Labour Left carried relatively little power within the Labour Party. The majority were inclined to support the Soviet Union in the war effort but not prepared to entertain close relations with the Communist Party in Britain.

The Labour Party and the General Election of 1945

With the D-Day landings and the Allied victories in Europe the CPGB looked towards a postwar general election. On 2 September 1944 it called for the continuation of the coalition government after the war and on 2 October supported an electoral pact between all the progressive forces, suggesting that a national conference be held to establish such an arrangement for the postwar years. These ideas were rejected by the NEC of the Labour Party, which, on 7 October 1944, decided to fight the next general election as an independent party 'based upon socialist principles'. This forced the CPGB to campaign – ur.successfully – to get the decision changed at the Labour Party conference in December 1944 but it continued its campaign up to the Labour Party conference in May 1945.

The CPGB made its position quite clear by calling for 'Labour and progressive unity' and that the wartime government should 'be replaced by a Labour and progressive majority, on the basis of which we believe a new National Government should be formed'.[44] Evidently, it felt that an outright Labour victory was unlikely and that a continued coalition or national government could continue, led by a Labour majority. The Yalta and Crimea conferences played a part in this decision, for if the Soviet Union could live in peace with capitalist powers it seemed logical to press for the continuation of a coalition 'popular front' government. However, the fear of continuing Tory dominance was real. The Political Committee (which had replaced the old Political Bureau in 1943) reflected this concern in announcing that:

To end Tory domination in Parliament will not be an easy task. This is why the present policy of Labour leaders refusing to meet the Communist Party leaders to discuss electoral unity, or to try to prevent it being discussed at the Whitsuntide Conference of the Labour Party is not only criminal, but is giving the Tories a better chance than they already have. We shall continue our campaign for electoral unity between the Labour Party, the Communist Party and all really progressive parties.[45]

Pollitt went further two months later, stressing that 'this [the CPGB's] experience in working with such allies during the war – even when an out-of-date Parliament has given the Tory party the dominant position in the National Government and a majority in Parliament – has proved to be in the interests of the working class'.[46]

To confirm its approach the Party asked its members to vote on the issue of postwar electoral unity at regional meetings on 17 March 1945 and the results were presented to the EC. The outcome was that of 8,684 members who voted, 7,850 favoured national unity, 278 were against and 556 abstained – each district and the Party voted overwhelmingly in favour, although 425 of the 556 abstentions came from the London district where there was clearly some unease at the arrangement.[47]

To avoid splitting the anti-Tory vote, the CPGB reduced the number of its 1945 parliamentary candidates from 52 to 22, later 21, even though the Labour Party had refused an electoral agreement with the 'progressive forces' which the CPGB felt was essential if Labour was to be victorious.[48] In the general election of July 1945 the Labour Party won 393 seats out of the 640 in Parliament, a majority of 146 arising from its winning 47.8 per cent of the poll. The Communist Party did not share in this landslide victory and only two of its candidates – William Gallacher for West Fife and Phil Piratin for Mile End – were returned. Pollitt was narrowly defeated in East Rhondda as was Johnny Campbell in Greenock.[49] This threw the Party into confusion between August and October 1945 in the run up to the Party congress, at which the Party's support for a coalition government, possibly including Tories, came under attack.

Notwithstanding its own disappointments, the CPGB took heart from Labour's landslide victory and pledged its wholehearted support to the government in bringing an early victory in the war against Japan and in carrying out the great social changes and the policy of international co-operation 'for which the people voted with such decision and confidence'. It also called for 'the fullest co-operation' of the whole Labour movement in fighting against the Tories, declaring that 'the Communist Party will do its utmost to develop this unity and to strengthen the organizations of the Labour Movement and their active support of the Labour Government'.[50]

In this climate the 1945 CPGB congress renewed its efforts to gain affiliation to Labour. Pollitt sent a letter to Morgan Phillips, Secretary of the Labour Party, on 21

January 1946 asking for the application to be put before the annual conference. The NEC opposed the application, the Communist Party mounted a campaign and the *Daily Herald* condemned the Communist Party's action.

In calling for Labour to take the lead in forming a coalition government after the war, and campaigning within the labour movement to reverse Labour's policy of standing independently at the 1945 general election, the CPGB had prepared a powerful case for its own rejection when it made its final attempt to affiliate to the Labour Party. None the less, the CPGB still wished to affiliate. The Labour Party's archives reveal the considerable pressure that it was placed under by its own members in 1945 and 1946 to try to force it to allow the Communist Party to affiliate. Howdenshire Labour Party called for 'working-class unity in the country by allowing the Common Wealth, the ILP and the Communist Parties to affiliate with the National Labour Party'.[51] Many other district parties and trade unions followed suit.

Yet there was never a realistic prospect that Labour would allow the CPGB to affiliate and about one month before the Labour Conference in 1946, the NEC issued a pamphlet by Harold Laski entitled *The Secret Battalion*; it launched a devastating attack upon the CPGB's political opportunism and class collaboration policy which, the pamphlet said, sought to compromise the political independence of the Labour Party. Morgan Phillips, who was determined to oppose any such moves, replied in discouraging terms to the advocates of the affiliation of the CPGB and prepared detailed reports on how to counter the Communist campaign. The arguments presented were almost a mirror image of those put forward in the interwar years and focused upon the differences between the Labour Party and the CPGB. Phillips argued that while the Labour Party stood for democratic socialism and wished to use the full powers of Parliament and local government, 'the aims of the Communist Party are different. They aim at what they call the "Dictatorship of the Proletariat". This in practice does not mean the Dictatorship of the Proletariat at all. It means a Dictatorship over the Proletariat, exercised by the Communist Party bureaucracy.' The stark contrast was posed between democracy and tyranny and it was further maintained that the British people had voted against tyranny at the general election, and in any case the CPGB was operated by Moscow and had no independence of action. Phillips maintained that: 'If the Communist affiliation was foolishly granted the position would be intolerable. There would be within our Party another highly organised Party working for its own supremacy. Every local Labour Party would become a battle ground for democratic socialism versus communism.'[52]

In due course, the Labour Party's annual conference rejected the motion for affiliation by 468,000 votes to 2,675,000 in June 1946 – a larger margin than in 1943 and 1936, possibly because of the CPGB's class collaboration policy that had called for the continuation of the coalition government. At the same conference, a resolution was passed preventing any organization with its own rules and constitution that was not affiliated to Labour by 1 January 1946, from ever affiliating. That brought to an end the CPGB's attempts at affiliation. Emilé Burns reflected that 'several Trade Unions that formerly supported us have now, by considerable majorities, turned against us. Divisional Labour parties which welcome our aid in elections and were full of goodwill are today bitter opponents.'[53] Where was the CPGB to go from here?

The End of the War and the Future

The Big Three Meeting in Teheran from November to December 1943, attended by Roosevelt, Churchill and Stalin, anticipated the end of the war, and the Yalta Communiqués of February 1945 suggested to the CPGB that the causes of military conflict would also be brought to an end in the postwar world. Pollitt thus began to look to the future. The Party had begun to show interest in the shape of the postwar world with the publication of the Beveridge Report in December 1942. Indeed, in 1943 Pollitt encouraged the Party to set up six major sub-committees, including a foreign relations body and an organization committee.[54] The CPGB's *Britain for the People: Proposals for Post-War Policy*, published in May 1944, also demanded that the wartime gains, resulting particularly from full employment, should be maintained in the postwar world. In particular it stressed the need for full employment, social security, housing, good wages, a comprehensive national health service, a lasting peace settlement and a wider-based democracy. In order to achieve these objectives it was felt that state controls should be maintained and that vital sectors of the economy should be taken into public ownership on the way to creating a socialist society.

This document also signalled a fundamental change in the attitude of the CPGB towards Parliament. In *For Soviet Britain* (1935), it had been argued that socialism could not be achieved through Parliament because there would be resistance in the Houses from the ruling class and also because socialism required a different political system. *Britain for the People*, in contrast, suggested that while extra-parliamentary action was needed Parliament, particularly if reformed through a system of proportional representation based upon a single transferable vote arrangement, could be used to bring about a socialist society.[55] The final version of *Britain for the People* was accepted at the seventeenth Congress of the CPGB held at Shoreditch Town Hall, London, in October 1944.

There is no doubt that the CPGB had abandoned its commitment to revolutionary objectives, just as the dissolution of the Comintern in 1943 had effectively ended the goal of world revolution. By October 1944 the CPGB was using the terminology of Marxism–Leninism to support reformist policies which were a departure from genuine Marxist ideas. Undoubtedly this abandonment of Marxist-Leninist ideas came because the meetings between Roosevelt, Stalin and Churchill at Teheran, Moscow, the Crimea (Yalta) and Potsdam seemed to augur well for a postwar world of peaceful coexistence between the capitalist world and the first workers' state based in the USSR. It explains the CPGB's commitment to a wartime national or coalition government and the reassessment of the value of Parliament. It also explains why the Party did not officially criticize Earl Browder, General Secretary of the Communist Party of the USA, for his move towards a more moderate policy in relation to capitalism which saw the American Communist Party dissolve itself to become a 'political association'. It makes clear why the CPGB was initially committed to working with and through the Labour Party and Clement Attlee's postwar Labour government.

Relations with the Labour Party – Government and Politics 1945–51

The CPGB aimed to work closely with Attlee's government. Indeed, Pollitt wrote that 'the spread of Marxist thought is so essential for the carrying through of Labour's General Election programme' and called for another attempt at Communist affiliation to the Labour Party, which, as noted, failed.[56] Robin Page Arnot endorsed this view, noting the vital nature of cooperation during the Second World War[57] and Pollitt saw the Labour government as offering a transitional period in the journey to socialism. The Party continued to support Labour candidates in parliamentary by-elections and, as late as September 1947, was opposed to industrial action in the Yorkshire coalfields. The CPGB also focused upon the need for rapidly increasing production in order to meet the fuel crisis, housing crisis, balance of payment crisis and the periods of dependence upon the American dollar between 1947 and 1949. Pollitt was so concerned with production that he encouraged the East European model of the 'great weekend volunteer brigades' to help out British industries. In other words, he was convinced of the need for postwar production to rebuild Britain's economy. The Party also supported Labour's welfare state programme and the National Hospital Campaign in April 1946.[58]

The political honeymoon with Labour soon ceased. Churchill's 'Iron Curtain' speech at Fulton, Missouri, in 1946, the increasing dependence of Britain upon American finance and the final rejection of Communist affiliation by Labour undermined the confidence of the CPGB in both the Labour Party and the Labour government. As the Cold War between the communist and capitalist worlds progressed and as the Labour government became increasingly dependent upon the United States and hostile to communism, Pollitt and the CPGB became more critical of the Labour Party. The Communists continued to stress the need for international peace and recognized the problems of operating within the British political system. There was still a slavish loyalty to Stalin, at least until the late 1950s. Indeed, the Party accepted the Cominform criticism of Tito and Yugoslavia after the Stalin–Tito split in July 1948, denouncing the Yugoslav leader's 'arrogant rejection of self-criticism'; in other words they were not prepared to be dictated to by the CPSU.[59] The Party also supported the show trials of old communists in Hungary, Bulgaria and Czechoslovakia between 1949 and 1952. By now, however, it was evident that the Labour government was a disappointment to the CPGB.

By 1948 the CPGB was openly criticizing the shortcomings of Attlee's Labour government. It had 'failed to attack the class distinction which is still the outstanding feature of our educational system. It has failed even to provide for material conditions to allow of an advance in standards within our existing system.'[60] The Communists began to put forward more election candidates, returning sixty-four for various elected urban district council and rural district council seats in 1948.[61] In the autumn of 1948 it put Peter Kerrigan into the Gorbals parliamentary by-election against the Labour candidate, noting that Labour ran a 'scurrilous anti-social and anti-Communist campaign' in defeating Kerrigan.[62]

By the 1950 General Election the CPGB was openly hostile to the Labour Party and maintained that it differed from the other political parties in that it associated the parliamentary struggle with the mass struggle of the workers and constantly reiterated that its 'historic mission is to lead the workers in the victory over Capitalism, to destroy Capitalism and replace it with the power of the working class'.[63]

Against a backcloth of an intensification of the Cold War and irritated by the perceived failures of the Labour government the CPGB decided to put forward 100 candidates at the February 1950 general election, regardless of the fact that this might allow Tory candidates to defeat Labour ones. There had, in fact, been a discussion of this policy in *World News and Views* after which the Political Committee of the Party produced its reply committing the Party to 100 candidates.[64] In the end, the policy was a disaster for the Party which lost the two seats gained in 1945 and found ninety-seven of its candidates losing their deposits. Indeed, the 100 candidates received 91,815 votes compared to the 102,780 votes received by the Party's 21 candidates in 1945. Mick Bennett, of the Yorkshire District Council, was one of many who suggested that Pollitt should be more critical and make the Executive Committee aware that the policy was mistaken.[65] Partly as a result of this fiasco, and the threat that it could help create a Tory Britain, the CPGB decided to reduce the number of candidates from the initial list of twenty-five candidates[66] to a mere ten for the 1951 general election.[67] All ten failed to get 12.5 per cent of the votes cast and lost their deposits. The electoral and parliamentary performance of the CPGB had been disastrous and the industrial and trade union policy of the Party did not fare much better.

Industrial Policy, 1945–51

There were two major industrial problems facing the CPGB in the Attlee years. The first was its concern about the economic relationship with the United States, which led it to demand more nationalization and a drive for industrial production within Britain. The second was its worsening relationship with the TUC and the trade union leadership.

In the immediate postwar years, while still favouring Attlee's administration, the Party had encouraged nationalization as a way of increasing the efficiency of the economy. However, with Britain's rising financial difficulties, the fuel crisis of the winter of 1947 and the economic crisis of 1947, Britain became dependent upon the American loan. The CPGB felt that this was unfortunate and that the dollar gap could not be bridged.[68] Part of the deal by which Britain obtained American credit was the importation of American goods. The CPGB felt that this would be disastrous for the British economy and James Klugmann, later to become one of the historians of the CPGB, wrote that:

> the subjection of British to American imports would mean catastrophe for the British people. . . . The British ruling class, and its spokesmen the Labour Government, like their counterparts in other Western European countries, are selling out to Wall Street the national independence of their country in order to preserve their own class position and privilege.[69]

Pollitt also wrote of the need for Britain to be independent economically of the USA.[70] Such concerns were to shape the critical attitude of CPGB to the Labour government's foreign policy, dominated as it was by the military policies of the United States.

The second industrial consideration was the relationship of the CPGB to the trade union movement. There is no doubt that the Communist Party had extended its influence over the trade unions during the war years. Indeed, after the war the Party could point to significant successes, but it also faced a mounting campaign against its activities by the TUC, which appeared to be acting in concert with the Labour Party in rooting out Communist influence. There is no doubt that the CPGB's industrial work continued apace in engineering. Len Powell, a Communist, was full-time General Secretary of the Engineering and Allied Trades Shop Stewards' National Council. Its monthly organ, *The New Propeller*, became *The Metal Worker* and reached a circulation of 94,000.

Immediately after the war there was optimism for the future, particularly in view of Labour's victory in 1945, but problems began to occur with the switch over from war to peace production and the end of Essential Work Order in 1946. By the summer of 1946 there were reports in *The Metal Worker* of victimization and lock-outs and the firm of Shardlow's, in Sheffield, saw a strike by 1,100 workers after the dismissal of Communist convenor Bill Longdon – ultimately, the stoppage led to his reinstatement. In 1946 the Communist-led Shop Steward's National Council conference decided to start a campaign for a 40-hour week in place of the prevailing 47-hour week. By the autumn the Engineering Employers' Federation had agreed to a 44-hour week, with some firms introducing even shorter hours.[71] It is clear that some of the successes in the industrial field were partly the result of Communist pressure, although they have to be fitted into the wider context of issues which arose naturally out of trade unionism and it is impossible to measure precise proportions of influence. There were similar situations in the building trades. Frank Jackson, a full-time worker in the industrial department of the Communist Party, helped launch the *New Builders' Leader* in 1935. This journal became the focus for a formative pressure group in favour of the ultimately unsuccessful prewar and postwar attempts to create one union for the building industry.[72]

Through *The New Propeller* the Party also participated in the campaigns to get equal pay for women, and favoured worker representation on the board running the coal industry, although trade union leaders were ultimately reluctant to act in this capacity when the 1946 Coal Industry Act set up the National Coal Board with two of its members nominated by the TUC.[73] The CPGB complained of the lack of rank-and-file trade union involvement in the running of the coal industry, and feared that the trade union leaders might become cut off from their members.[74]

The CPGB's frustration with the Labour government led it to criticize the obvious failures in Labour's industrial policy. The Nineteenth Congress of the CPGB, held at Seymour Hall in Marylebone, London, on 22 February 1947, demanded that Labour stop compromising with big business. It argued that there was a severe manpower shortage, that men should be withdrawn from the army and that there should be equal pay for women. It also urged immediate nationalization of other industries. There was also concern about victimization of shop stewards and Pollitt urged delegates 'that joint production machinery – national, regional, local and factory – should be set up without delay' to help boost industrial production in a clear attempt to retain Britain's independence as a nation.[75] Eric Heffer, later a prominent figure on the Labour left, did not agree and felt that the economic crisis must be used for the overthrow of capitalism.[76] However, the Party's pressure upon industry and the Labour government failed and at the Twentieth Congress on 1 February 1948 that much was admitted. Not surprisingly, by 1949 Dutt, still a prominent figure in the CPGB and editor of *Labour Monthly*, was attacking the Labour Party's industrial policy and referring to the nationalized industries as 'capitalist pseudo-nationalisation'.[77]

Increasingly, the problem was that the CPGB was being isolated from the wider British labour movement. Morgan Phillips launched a campaign on 21 December 1947 to reduce CPGB influence in the Labour Party and the trade unions through a circular suggesting that it was a slavish supporter of the Cominform. It also suggested that Communists had infiltrated the trade unions by back-door methods, when in fact Communists continued to win seats on trades councils and trade unions in an open manner.[78] Indeed, in January 1948 all five Communist members of the executive committee of the South Wales area National Union of Mineworkers were re-elected after a secret ballot. Walter Stevens, communist, was elected General Secretary of the Electrical Trade Union.[79] Two communists were voted on to the London regional council of the National Federation of Building Operatives. Les Ambrose topped the poll to be the Amalgamated Engineering Union organizer and Walter Hannington was also returned to the AEU's executive.[80] Eight communists were also returned to the general executive council of the Transport & General Workers' Union, including Bert Papworth of the London busworkers.[81] Ten members were also elected to the Scottish NUM Executive in 1948.[82]

The CPGB felt that Phillips' attack was provoked by the Labour government's decision to impose wage restraint. Ever since the financial crisis of 1947 the threat to wages had been on the agenda. On 6 August 1947, Attlee asked the workers and the TUC not to demand wage increases and on 4 February 1948 the government issued a White Paper (Cmnd 7321) outlining the need for wage restraint.

The possibility of a wage freeze was at the centre of discussion at the Twentieth Congress of CPGB in February 1948. In opposition to the projected freeze, Congress called for measures to keep profits down, to increase taxes on the rich, and to modernize industry. Pollitt noted that 'the Government had put increased production as their principal method of solving the crisis, in order to cover up their anti-working-class policy as a whole'.[83] The CPGB felt that the workers had fought hard for the nation and could not be expected to respond to the government's request for a wage freeze.[84]

The General Council of the TUC accepted the wage restraint measures of government on 24 March 1948, although Communist trade union leaders such as Abe Moffatt and Arthur Horner stood against it. A motion opposing wage restraint was lost by 5.2 million votes to 2.1 million. As a result, wages rose 6 per cent over the following year at a time when prices rose by about 10 per cent. Faced with falling real wages, the number of industrial disputes, many of them unofficial, increased.

One such dispute occurred in mid-June 1948, when there was an unofficial strike over 'dirty cargo money' at the Regent Canal dock in London. This resulted in the suspension of eleven dockers for two weeks and their loss of attendance money for thirteen weeks. In response 1,100 men went on strike and other dockers, including some from Liverpool, came out in support. A tribunal cut the thirteen weeks penalty to two weeks but 31,000 dockworkers remained out on strike until the end of the month. The government proclaimed a state of emergency and brought troops into the docks.

Eventually, on 29 June 1948, a mass meeting at London's Victoria Docks saw 6,000 dockers return to work on the recommendation of the strike committee.[85]

The strike was attacked in the press as being part of a 'communist plot', even though the strike committee of forty included nineteen Labour Party members and only five communists. The strike had been opposed by Arthur Deakin, General Secretary of the Transport & General Workers' Union, whose members were out on strike. The *Daily Worker*'s industrial correspondent reacted to the 'communist plot' allegation on 3 July 1948, stating that three of the communist activists had been born in dockland and had served their time in dockland trade unionism. They had not joined the union to cause trouble as the press and Attlee implied.

At the 1948 TUC conference its president Florence Hancock attacked the CPGB for 'fomenting unofficial strikes' and 'undermining' the authority of union officials. A Congress resolution called for 'determination to expose and defeat those elements'. Following this there was an anti-communist campaign by the TUC leadership which issued the 'Warning to Trade Unionists' on 27 October 1948 and urged the unions to take energetic steps to 'stop communist activity'.[86] On 29 October 1948 the *Daily Worker* claimed that the latest 'heresy hunt' was motivated by the desire to remove communist opposition to wage restraint. The TUC replied with the pamphlet *Defend Democracy*, which attacked Communist disruption. In March 1949 this was followed by another pamphlet entitled *The Tactics of Disruption* in which it was argued that the Communists never regarded unions as a means for the 'protection of workers or to improve their standard of living', a statement which the Party was quick to deny.[87]

Several trade unions rejected moves to ban Communist activists from holding office, including the Fire Brigades' Union, the Electrical Trade Union, the Tobacco Workers and the Foundry Workers, though most did not. The Transport & General Workers' Union, at its biennial conference, voted by more than two to one against allowing Communists to hold any office in the union; this ruling lasted from January 1950 to 1968. In September 1950, Deakin also moved further in favour of encouraging the government to pass legislation banning the Communist Party.[88] The TUC Conference of 1949 also endorsed anti-Communist action by 6,746,000 to 760,000.[89]

The CPGB found itself increasingly isolated by the late 1940s. The policy of encouraging industrial production to establish Britain's economic independence from the United States lacked economic reality and its influence upon the trade union movement was being challenged by the TUC. The failure to develop led to some frustration within Communist ranks. Indeed, Mollie Guiart launched a determined attack upon the failure of these policies noting that the Party had made no single and decisive statement in favour of any strike since 1945 and criticizing the way in which the political letter of February 1949 and the extended executive committee meeting of the same month had played down the importance of nationalization in order to increase industrial efficiency.[90] In some respect these criticisms were justified. The fact is that the CPGB was often torn between claiming influence and denying that its actions were 'communist plots'. Perhaps it was coming to accept that a party struggling to keep only 40,000 members could do little more than contribute to events. Whatever the views of the Labour government and the right-wing press, it is clear that the CPGB's industrial and trade union policies were marginal in shaping events. In some respects its problem was that it had expanded its membership rapidly between the mid-1930s and mid-1940s and faced serious organizational difficulties in keeping the Party focused upon its main objectives.

Organization Commission

The Party had a mere 3,000 members in the early 1930s but membership had risen to over 56,000 by 1942. Despite some decline in the late 1940s, membership still hovered around 40,000. This presented organizational difficulties, most notably in providing the best system to retain members and in establishing the most effective way to ensure that the opinions of the Party membership were properly represented on the Central Committee/Executive Committee – the body that was intended to be the representative forum for the Party. Both issues were hotly discussed in the 1940s, only to re-emerge as major points of discussion later, particularly in 1956 when E.P. Thompson and John Saville challenged the representative nature of the Party through *The Reasoner* debate. The issue of inner party structure and representation was thus seen as vital to the continued attractiveness, efficiency and well-being of the Party.

The volatility of membership figures encouraged the Party to examine the possibility of new arrangements. An organization committee was set up at the Seventeenth Congress of the Party in October 1944 and reported to the Executive Committee on 17 December 1944, suggesting that all members of a branch should be resident in the branch area. Committees were to be elected by people working in factories. The new structure kept the branch as the focus of organization, as it had been since 1936, but no longer allowed people working but not living in the area to be members. The plans were confirmed at the Eighteenth Party Congress in November 1945 but there remained problems in the collection of dues and, as a result, a commission was set up to examine and modify the functions of the various bodies in the Party.[91]

This organization commission reported to the Executive Committee on 10 September 1946, subject to an amendment already made by the EC. Set up under the chairmanship of Peter Kerrigan, the commission had consisted of five EC members and six members taken from a cross-section of districts. It met on five occasions and recommended that the leadership of the Party should give more guidance and be more helpful, and that industrial leadership should be increasingly organized through district industrial committees which would keep a list of those prominently placed in trade unions and co-ordinate the work of factory committees. It argued that the Party should build up its strength in new areas by the districts improving connections with individual members and organizing weekend meetings. It was also suggested that Party cadres should circulate around the branches and that there should be 'more checking on decisions and self-criticism'.[92]

Yet, despite the various recommendations made since 1944, the Party still faced difficulties in collecting membership dues. As a result it was finally deemed expedient that factory committees could be set up wherever possible in order to improve the organization and without the stringent requirement that members both live and work within the area.[93] The powerful London district acted quickly and set up seventeen new factory branches with 677 members in a few months.[94] The new move was endorsed by a change of rules at the Twentieth Congress in February 1948 under which branches consisted of 'members living, or in some cases working, within a defined area'. There had been a return to the old system.

The Twentieth Congress also introduced changes in the methods of electing the Party's Executive Committee in order to improve Party democracy. Between 1929 and 1943, the Central Committee had been elected by a panel system, under which a commission, consisting mainly of appointees from the districts, was appointed to go through the nominations made by districts and branches. Delegates could propose additions to the list and then it was voted upon at Congress. In 1943, the panel system was abandoned. The Seventeenth Congress in 1944 decided that the new Executive Committee would be elected by a ballot of all those nominated, without a recommended list. This arrangement was used at both the Seventeenth and Eighteenth congresses. However, there was some dissatisfaction that the system favoured the high-profile activists at the expense of the hard-working, less well-known Party members and, therefore, after the 1945 Congress the Executive Committee of thirty co-opted six other representatives. A commission was also set up to examine the situation and endorsed the revival of a recommended list although delegates would be able to nominate others. This arrangement was approved by the Nineteenth Congress in 1947.

The success of these minor amendments is far from certain. On 8 March 1948 it was reported that the Party had 38,833 members compared with 38,579 in June 1947, and it was hoped that this figure would be raised to 43,500 by 1949. Within three months 4,240 new members were recruited by the new members campaign.[95] However, there were losses of existing members and concern was constantly expressed that it was difficult to get the membership figure to 40,000.[96] Indeed, the London District Committee reported in June 1950 that 'our overall position is that of barely holding our ground. While 1,500 new members were made in 1949 and 600 in the General

Election [1950], our total membership remains what it was a year ago'.[97] Indeed, the early 1950s saw a dramatic decline of Party membership with numbers falling from about 38,000 in 1950 to about 27,000 in 1957. The problems of Party organization obviously led to some membership decline but the situation was also exacerbated by the development of the Cold War and the foreign policy of the Party.

Foreign Policy and the Cold War, 1945–51

The CPGB was committed to world peace and the development of friendship between Britain, Europe and the Soviet Union in order to prevent war between the USA and Soviet Russia. This stance was maintained throughout the late 1940s, even though the Cold War made it difficult to sustain.

The CPGB, referring to the Cold War policy of the United States and Britain, opposed the 'exclusive Anglo-American Alliance with its dangers of new wars',[98] and maintained 'the need for class co-operation between Britain, the USA and the Soviet Union as the main foundation for the success United Nations.'[99] Indeed, by November 1948 Pollitt was warning that Labour's leaders had now become the 'principal instruments through which the imperialists are organizing for actual war against the Soviet Union'.[100] The point was amplified further by John Gollan when he stated pithily that 'the only possible policy open to us is genuine Three-Power co-operation, with the USSR and the USA'.[101]

Yet the CPGB believed that this three-power cooperation depended upon Britain acting independently of the United States by virtue of her rapid increase in industrial output. Thus Pollitt objected strongly to the Marshall Plan of economic aid for Europe being applied to Britain for it meant Britain taking tobacco, dried eggs and limitations upon building up her shipbuilding industry.[102] To Pollitt the Marshall Plan was not simply an attack on 'hunger, poverty, desperation and chaos' but had political implications and he supported the alternative Molotov Proposals against American aid to Eastern Europe.

Churchill's 'Iron Curtain' speech in 1946 paved the way for the Cold War. By the time of the formation of the Communist Information Bureau or Cominform, the new forum of European communism, in September 1947, it is clear that the world had been divided into the two main armed camps of communism and capitalism. From then onwards, the basic elements of the CPGB's attitude to the Cold War were evident: anti-American Imperialism, anti-colonialism, peace campaigns and the fight to win trade union support.

The move in 1948 to form the Western Union, out of which NATO emerged, worried the CPGB. Willie Rust complained that it was 'an essential part of the war preparations of the Anglo-American Powers' throughout 1948. Both the Political

Committee and the Executive Committee of the CPGB agreed to help organize a peace movement and to work with the National Peace Council.[103] In a more concerted attack upon the Cold War and the growth of American dominance, the Party argued that Britain needed to operate political and economic independence from the United States which, it was felt, intended to use 'Britain as one of its main bases in the event of war'.[104] There was also a tirade against the Labour government for its abandonment of socialism and for allowing a decline in the standard of living of the British working class. The CPGB launched its campaign for peace with the press statement 'Stop the Drift to War', which argued that the 'lives and liberty of the British people are in danger' as a result of the Atlantic Pact and domination by the Americans.[105] Such concerns and demands for lasting peace and democracy continued throughout 1950.[106] A peace congress was held on 22 and 23 July.[107]

The formation of NATO had provoked the Party into determined action to prevent war but it was the issue of the hydrogen bomb and the outbreak of the Korean War that drew most of its attention in 1950. The American development of the hydrogen bomb provoked a movement against nuclear weapons by the Permanent Committee of the World Peace Congress in Stockholm in March 1950. The British Peace Committee started a campaign for signatures entitled the 'peace petition', aimed at getting people to sign and become active in the movement. By September 1950 more than 1 million had signed.[108] The Labour Party listed the British Peace Commission as a proscribed organization and the *Daily Herald* recorded expulsions of BPC members from Labour from August 1950 onwards. The TUC also circulated local trades councils, informing them that the British Peace Committee was a subsidiary of the Communist Party and instructing them not to participate in its activities. At the September 1950 TUC Conference the motion to ban atomic weapons was defeated by 5.6 million to 1.9 million votes.

On 23 September 1950 the British Peace Committee, with which the CPGB was closely associated, announced that it planned to hold the Second World Peace Congress in Sheffield City Hall, on 13–19 November – the first Congress having been held in Paris in 1949. Yet Attlee, the Prime Minister who had talked of the need for mass democratic rights just two months before, denounced the BPC on 1 November and refused to address the Sheffield Conference. Chuter Ede, Home Secretary, also reported that 215 of 561 applications for British entry visas for delegates had been rejected.[109] Even those granted visas were interviewed and sometimes forbidden entry; 65 of the 196 delegates from non-visa countries were barred. Indeed, two-thirds of all foreign delegates were also forbidden entry and on 13 November the Conference decided to transfer to Warsaw.

The outbreak of the Korean War made the need for peace even more pressing. In June 1950, the North Koreans crossed the border into South Korea. and the USA entered the war on the side of the South Koreans. At the end of the Second World War, the Soviet Army, which released North Korea from Japanese domination, and the US Army, which had done the same for South Korea, agreed that the demarcation line between North and South Korea would be the thirty-eighth parallel. Gradually both armies withdrew and left Kim-Il Sung in charge of the North and Syngman Rhee in control of the South. When the North invaded the South the United States called for the United Nations to condemn this action and called for member nations to help the South. This was done and Britain came to the support of the United States, deciding to send land troops to Korea on 25 July 1950. British forces were in Korea by mid-August and the American troops invaded North Korea on 9 October.

The CPGB instantly attacked what it saw as naked colonial aggression. Alan Winnington, writing for the *Daily Worker*, gave reports from the North and the South as he travelled with the northern troops and produced a pamphlet on 26 September 1950 entitled *I Saw the Truth in Korea*. The cabinet and legal authorities discussed the possibility of the publication being banned and Winnington being placed on trial for treason – ultimately the issue was dropped since it was felt that no jury would impose the death penalty, the only penalty available for treason.

In the end China entered the war and forced the Americans back to the thirty-eighth parallel. Gradually a peace settlement was brokered. Yet the war had exerted a major impact in Britain where the length of duty for national service was extended to two years and an enormous extra defence burden was imposed upon the British people, which led to new austerity measures and cuts in food rations. Emilé Burns, and others, wrote extensively on the war and the need to bring about a speedy peace[110] and the Party gathered 330,000 signatures for the Peace Petition against the Korean War on 4 June 1951.[111] The fact is that despite the creation of NATO and the Korean War, the CPGB foreign policy was still directed towards the peace that it felt was essential to prevent world war and improve relations between the United States and the Soviet Union. The Party, still closely associated with the Soviet Union, appeared less overtly so than it had once been. The new moderation was to be found on the domestic front as well.

The British Road to Socialism

It was probably the Popular Front strategy of the mid-1930s, and its continuation after 1941, that drove the CPGB in a parliamentary direction. However, there were also more immediate considerations leading the way. Throughout the Second World War Pollitt was convinced that there would be a continuation of an arrangement with capitalism in the postwar world. Stalin appeared to be moving in that direction and it seemed sensible for the CPGB to follow. Before 1939 the Party felt that capitalism was a fetter to production: Soviet entry into the war changed its attitude. With wartime cooperation Pollitt became convinced that socialism/Marxism was now possible without class conflict – even though the possibility of conflict could never be ruled out. The Comintern had been disbanded in 1943 along with the revolutionary concepts that had brought it into being. Pollitt now posited the idea of a nation's working class advancing ever more determinedly towards a greater say in the nation's affairs, participating in parliamentary democracy through its own democratic organizations.

The new strategy brought a dramatic change of line. In 1935 the Party had advocated that a socialist society could never be achieved through parliamentary legislation and that the only alternative was to abolish Parliament and to replace it with a system of workers' councils and soviets. By May 1944 the idea that Parliaments should be discarded had been abandoned. The CPGB now aimed to democratize Parliament and the existing political system. The 'British Road to Socialism' proposals advocated a change to proportional representation in the form of a single transferable vote, a measure which Willie Gallacher had advocated in the House of Commons on 18 February 1944. No longer concerned about the Second Front, the Party turned its attention to its new programme at the Seventeenth Congress held at Shoreditch Town Hall in October 1944. It envisaged the idea that postwar domestic policies could not be separated from international policy and that there would be some element of continued class collaboration after the war. Such views had previously been put forward by Earl Browder, general secretary of the Communist Party of the United States, and seemed to be accepted by the CPGB. Indeed, it was not until August 1945 that Browder's ideas were seriously challenged because they went too far in suggesting the winding up of the Communist Party of the United States.[112] In actual fact the American Communist Party was dissolved and formed into a political association instead.

Any attempt to block the new political line was opposed by Pollitt. Indeed, when Walter Hannington objected to it Pollitt described his objections as 'the policy of 1928 – Class Against Class.[113] However, this episode did not end with the usual acceptance of the leadership's view but led to a discussion of the issues in the Party's weekly *World News and Views* and extensive discussion at the Eighteenth Party Congress in November 1945. There were further complaints that the Party was not democratically run but Pollitt maintained that the CPGB was 'the most democratically run political organization in the world' and he would not budge from the Yalta standpoint regarding the spheres of influence of the Three Great Powers, which meant that he accepted the Attlee position and the possibility of peaceful coexistence in the postwar world.

Despite the influence of Stalin and the changed international position there is no disguising the fact that the CPGB was invariably concerned about its declining membership at this stage and that this was a force behind the progress to The British Road to Socialism. The Party's decline had been explained in many different ways but sectarianism and narrowness of perception were factors which Pollitt highlighted. According to him: 'The Party wants to be a narrow Party, it wants to be a Party of exclusive Marxists'.[114] His attack seems to have been directed against Willie Rust, a party functionary constantly opposed to Pollitt, in whom, according to Kevin Morgan, there were few redeeming features.[115] It is clear that Pollitt's initial support for the Attlee government was countered by Rust's opposition to such moves but by and large the majority of the Party's leading functionaries – Campbell, Kerrigan, Gallacher, Bramley and Gollan – favoured Pollitt rather than Rust.

The new line developed over the next two years and was put forward by Kitty Cornforth in an article entitled 'British Road to Socialism', which looked to ways in which socialism could be reconstructed in Britain.[116] At the same time, in August 1947, Pollitt published a lengthy pamphlet entitled *Looking Ahead*. The sixth chapter, 'The British Road to Socialism' stated that:

> Marxists have never maintained that the Road to Socialism in any country is neatly mapped out and time-tabled, that each country will pass to Socialism in the same way and at the same speed, with similar forms of state organization. . . . Communists have never said that the Russian Revolution of October, 1917, is a model which has exactly to be copied. Indeed, the whole work of Marx and Engels, Lenin and Stalin . . . has been to explain to the people how to recognise the deep laws of development of society, and to show how the working class and the people can decide on correct slogans and correct programmes based on a study of the economic and social forces at a given time. Communists have always said, on the other hand, that the study of the Russian Revolution and of all previous revolutions . . . is pregnant with meaning and lessons for the working class. But this does not mean that these lessons must be learnt by heart, or initiated mechanically, or applied at different times and under different conditions.
>
> The progress of democratic and Socialist forces throughout the world has opened out the new possibilities of transition to Socialism by other paths than those followed by the Russian Revolution.[117]

Pollitt's views on a peaceful transition to socialism/Marxism were to be affected by the Cold War but by 1951 his underlying commitment to a peaceful and parliamentary transition to socialism/Marxism was to survive in the CPGB's new long-term programme, *The British Road to Socialism*.[118] This ground-breaking document claimed to offer a conception of democracy that had emerged from the 'people's war' and that gave Pollitt's agenda for Britain a distinctively parliamentary slant. The main break with earlier Marxist thought lay in the claim that it was now possible for the working class to win control over the capitalist state in Britain by constitutional means, and then to transform the capitalist state into one that met the needs of the working class. In other words, the idea of the parliamentary *cul-de-sac* was abandoned and the parliamentary road to socialism took the place of the proletarian dictatorship as advocated by Marx, Engels and Lenin.

The immediate reason for the production of this document seems to have been Pollitt's visit to Stalin in the summer of 1950 to discuss the British political situation. Stalin suggested the need for a long-term perspective after discussing the disastrous general election results of 1950. Pollitt presented his report of the meeting to the EC on 8 July 1950. So began the Party's final moves towards *The British Road to Socialism*.

Despite intense argument while it was being drafted in 1950, the document was accepted under the title *The British Road to Socialism* by the Executive Committee and issued for discussion in January 1951. It opened with the suggestion that the Labour governments had been failures, introducing capitalistic nationalization, and had allied themselves to the United States against the Soviet Union and China. It suggested the need for socialistic nationalization of all large-scale industries. Capitalist monopoly would be ended, and so would capitalist exploitation and profit. In order to achieve this, capitalist democracy had to be replaced with a people's democracy. This involved 'transforming Parliament, the product of Britain's historic struggle for democracy, into the democratic instrument of the will of the vast majority of the people'. The working class, along with sections of the middle class, it was felt, would be more than sufficient to return a majority representing the interests of the British people to Parliament and would be able to remove the rich and establish a people's government. This government would introduce a planned economy based upon socialist principles and democratic electoral reform. Proportional representation would be introduced and the voting age would be reduced to eighteen. The House of Commons would be made the sole national authority and the House of Lords would be abolished.

In an attempt to counter widespread misconceptions about the CPGB and its objectives the new programme emphasized that Britain had no need to fear aggression from socialist states, that bloody revolution was not inevitable and that there was no wish to abolish Parliament. The new programme was issued as a 3*d* pamphlet and sold about 200,000 copies. The *Communist Review* also discussed the various aspects of the new programme throughout 1951. Through its pages, Pollitt attempted to respond to the 'unfair criticism' of the Party.[119] Emilé Burns discussed the people's democracy idea, suggesting that it meant a new form of democracy in which trade unions and other working-class bodies would take their part: 'Such are some of the principal points of *The British Road to Socialism*, as put forward in the programme, drawing both on our own traditions and the institutions and on the experience of the People's Democracies, as well as the whole world situation.'[120] James Klugmann emphasized that the programme was aimed at the whole labour movement, not just CPGB members, and that it provided an opportunity to study the finer points of Marxist-Leninist principles.[121]

In the spring of 1952 the policy was finally adopted at the Twenty-Second Congress of the CPGB. Although it was partly redrafted in 1957, to include the term 'socialist government' in the place of 'people's government', and further redrafted on later occasions, this document remained the programme of the Party until it was replaced in the late 1980s and early 1990s by the *Manifesto for New Times*, with its more 'pick-and-mix' type of policies for the 'Marxist' activist.

Conclusion

What, then, was the position of the CPGB in the late 1940s? On the one hand, it was still dominated by its uncritical support of the Soviet Union and the policies of Cominform and had failed to develop policies responsive to the needs and demands of the British workers – instead, the CPGB always took its political cue from the requirements of Soviet state policy. On the other hand, it did achieve some success in building up workplace organization in many industries, campaigned for equal pay for women and fought, with the wider labour movement, to regain trade union rights through the abolition of Order 1305, which had suspended strike rights during the war.

The CPGB had moved a long way since 1941. Its commitment to the war effort and the possibility of domestic and international cooperation between communism and capitalism in the postwar world had tempered its commitment to revolutionary change and proletarian dictatorship, thus paving the way for a commitment to the parliamentary route to socialism. This was despite the fact that neither the Labour Party nor the Western Union/NATO was friendly towards the CPGB and communism between 1946 and 1951 once the wartime 'political honeymoon' was over. Declining membership and rejection by both the political and industrial labour movements in the 'Cold War' climate had helped to create this change in a situation where a third world war seemed a possibility. The next forty years saw the 'revisionism' represented by *The British Road to Socialism* develop to such an extent that the Party was almost completely divorced from its proletarian dictatorship, prewar days as Eurocommunists and broad-based pragmatic communists created a situation whereby British communists could practically create their own agenda from green, anti-racist and social issues.

V

British Communism: 'Intellectual Immorality', Division and Decline, 1951–91

The final forty years of the CPGB were marked by deep conflicts and intense dissension, often sparked off by some major event that had convulsed international Marxism. Such conflict was evident with Khrushchev's criticism of Stalin at the Twentieth Congress of the CPSU in early 1956, along with the suppression of the Hungarian Revolution in October and November 1956, and provided the context for *The Reasoner* debate and the demand for Inner Party Democracy. This debate led to the temporary expulsion, and eventual resignation, of E.P. Thompson and John Saville from the Party, and the departure of about 7,000 members who were both appalled at the Hungarian invasion and the lack of open discussion within the Party. Another major international crisis for Marxism was the Soviet invasion of Czechoslovakia in 1968, an event that provoked CPGB criticism of the Soviet Union. However, given the financial contributions made by the Soviet Union to the leadership of the CPGB between 1957 and 1979, the importance of this disagreement should not be exaggerated. There were also other major disputes throughout the period that were connected with the conflict between the Soviet Union and Maoism in the late 1950s and early 1960s, the rivalry of international socialism and orthodox communism in the 1960s, the conflict between Stalinists and Eurocommunists in the 1980s (incorporating the conflict between the Party leadership and *Morning Star*), and the rise of the more pragmatic Marxism of the 1980s and 1990s, where the emphasis was placed upon broad-based socialism, anti-racism, pro-Green politics and the rejection of the democratic centralism and the class politics of the old Marxist-Leninists. Stalinist and Marxist-Leninist orthodoxy was thus in conflict with revisionism throughout the last forty years of the Party's existence, and was intensified by the problems of international Marxism.

These intermittent convulsions occurred during the period 1951 to 1991 when Party membership fell from 38,000 to 4,750 – back to levels of the late 1920s and the early 1930s when the Party was a small sectarian body. If anything, however, there was less excuse for this later decline for the Party was now far more broad-based in its policies. However, the declining membership followed no rapid downward trajectory – at least not until the 1970s and 1980s. There was a volatility about membership figures, the loss of 7,000 or so of 33,000 members in 1956 being offset by a rise to more than 34,000 members by 1964. By the mid-1970s, however, the membership was declining rapidly as the Party was wracked by conflict between those who supported the Soviet Union, and the Eurocommunists who did not. The history of the CPGB after 1951 was thus one of the related issues of political dissension and declining membership.

The central question in this period is – why did the CPGB decline and disappear? The obvious answer is that its demise was made inevitable by the collapse of the Stalinist régime in Poland as a result of the victory of Solidarity in the national assembly elections of July 1989, the end of other Stalinist régimes in Eastern Europe between October and December 1989 and similar developments leading to the dissolving of the Warsaw Pact in July 1991 and the USSR in December 1991. Not surprisingly, the CPGB expired just before the collapse of the Soviet Union. Yet even before the collapse of international Stalinism the CPGB was becoming convinced of the need to abandon Marxist ideas and to develop new, broader and more personalized socialist agendas. Indeed, there is a possibility that the CPGB would have disappeared even if Stalinism had survived in Eastern Europe, although one has to recognize that the decline of the Soviet bloc clearly fashioned debates in Britain.

1951–6: the CPGB in Transition

The British Road to Socialism did not arrest the declining membership of the Party, which fell from 38,000 in 1951 to about 33,000 in 1956. Indicative of the concern about this reduction in numbers was the continued tinkering with the Party structure in the hope of attracting new members. Residential-based branches, with some allowance for factory members, continued and the Party constantly played with the voting system for returning members to the Executive Committee in the early 1950s. After experimenting with a more open style of government in the early 1950s the Party reverted to the panel system for electing its leading area committees. The ballot system was also discontinued in the early 1950s and the Congress once again voted for a show of hands on the complete panel as presented, although the ballot was brought back again in 1954.[1] There was always going to be a tension between the demands for greater democracy within the Party and the democratic centralist view with the emphasis it placed upon higher committees taking decisions after discussions.

After the Second World War the CPGB was still very much under the influence of Stalin and the *Daily Worker* gave wholehearted support to the new show trials of communists in Hungary, Czechoslovakia and Bulgaria in the late 1940s and the break with Tito and Yugoslavia in 1948. There was also little criticism of the Red Army's bloody repression of the general strike movement which spread through East Germany in June 1953. However, the 1952 trials of Communists in Czechoslovakia created real tension since John Gollan, later to become General Secretary of the CPGB, had been a personal friend of Rudolf Slansky, the Czech General Secretary. This did not stop James Klugmann writing in his 'Lessons of the Prague Trial' that the developments in Czechoslovakia had shown the dangers of Trotskyism and bourgeois nationalism.[2]

There were, however, some minor political successes to offset the difficulties of international Marxism. The Party put 162 candidates up in municipal contests in 1952, gaining 49,983 votes, which was much more impressive than the performance in 1951 when 220 candidates obtained only 37,443 votes.[3] However, other indicators were suggesting a decline in support for the Party. The circulation figures of the *Daily Worker* fell from 120,000 in 1945 to 91,000 in June 1950 and to 79,000 in 1955, before recovering to 93,000 in December 1956 following a major circulation campaign. Sales in Yorkshire had fallen from 5,706 in April 1951 to 3,727 in April 1956, and in London, for the same dates, from 37,696 to 25,281.[4]

Communist activity throughout the British Empire/Commonwealth did little to widen the popularity of the CPGB. The Party faced public hostility after attacking the British government's actions in dealing with the Malayan guerrilla war crisis in the early 1950s and there was significant Party criticism of the way in which the government dealt with independence movements in Kenya, British Guiana and Cyprus in the early 1950s. The CPGB's constant reference to the need for colonial states to be independent did not carry much weight with British public opinion given that it emerged from an organization so clearly subject to the authority of the Soviet Union. Such hostility to the CPGB's position was fuelled further by the anti-Soviet revolt in Berlin in June 1953.

Nevertheless, the death of Stalin in March 1953, followed shortly afterwards by the execution of Laurenti Beria, his acolyte and security chief, did much to raise the prospects of an easing of the Cold War tensions. Also, in 1955, Khrushchev and Bulganin journeyed to Belgrade and repudiated publicly all the Cominform charges against Tito, the Cominform itself being wound up later the same year. Changes were afoot in international communism, although it was some time before their impact came to be accepted by the CPGB.

The Party's continued political isolation still reflected in its poor showing in both the 1955 general election and municipal elections. Thus, the Twenty-Fourth Congress of CPGB met in March 1956 with the intention of reconnecting the CPGB with the

Labour Party. In fact this resulted in very little action and the continued failure to attract support was reflected in a report from the north-east district of the CPGB presented to the Political Committee of the CPGB in October 1956, which stated that:

> . . . in the eyes of the people of the North East we are still seen as a Party of distressed times, and we have not convinced people of our role and policy at the present time as a Party fighting for and capable of defending and preserving 'full employment'. Another point raised is that we are also seen by many as not a British Party.
>
> This brings very clearly the need to do more in our work in taking *The British Road to Socialism* to the North East.[5]

The British Road to Socialism was in fact being revised at this time, with greatest emphasis being placed upon national independence for all the peoples of the Empire.[6] But other events were encouraging its redrafting.

The Twentieth Congress of the Communist Party of the Soviet Union, and Freedom of Expression within the Party

Although more than 200,000 copies of *The British Road to Socialism* had been sold the new programme was not to be the basis of a revivified Party. At the 1956 Party Congress Pollitt kept alive the hope that the Party would be more than a 'ginger group' but he resigned as General Secretary in May 1956 and withdrew in favour of John Gollan. The Stalinist ideas he had supported all his political life were challenged by Khrushchev at the Twentieth Congress of the Communist Party of the Soviet Union in February 1956; Khrushchev's secret speech was released for public consumption in the West by the US State Department in early June 1956 and was first published in Britain by the *Observer* shortly afterwards.[7] According to Harry Evans, a journalist to whom Pollitt often confided, this attack was the final straw: 'For Harry thought it despicable to kick the corpse of Stalin' and 'Harry found that he was too old to go into reverse and denigrate the man whom he had admired above all others for more than a quarter of a century'.[8] Pollitt was at the Twentieth Congress of the CPSU but was not present at the secret session on 25 February 1956 when Khrushchev provided a damning indictment of Stalin's tyranny. Pollitt commented, 'I was being conducted around a French-letter factory. At my age, I suppose that it was a compliment.'[9] Nevertheless, he must have been aware of the debates and discussions about the 'cult of personality' which Khrushchev had attacked.

At first, Pollitt was reluctant to report on the details of Khrushchev's criticism of Stalin in the *Daily Worker* and J.R. Campbell, the editor, quickly declared, on 12

March 1956, that no more letters would be published on the matter. On 17 March Laszlo Rajk, chief victim of the 1949 purge trial in Hungary, was officially rehabilitated, although the CPGB made little of this development at its Twenty-Fourth Congress in March 1956. However, new, younger, members were beginning to voice their concerns about Party democracy and would not be deflected by Pollitt's constant assertion that the CPGB should not be afraid to proclaim that it had exercised democratic rights. Harry Evans noted that the younger members of the Party sneered at Pollitt's work and it is clear that his pugnacious response – 'if you have got a headache you should take an aspirin' – did little to endear him to them.[10] Soon after the Twenty-Fourth Congress Pollitt resigned as General Secretary, ostensibly on grounds of ill-health. He remained an active member of the Party until his death on 27 June 1960.

The Reasoner Debate

The slowness and reluctance of the CPGB leadership to respond to the criticism of Stalin and the more critical stance of international communism created serious tensions within the Party at this time and produced several organized groups of opposition. One of the most important was that which gathered around Edward P. Thompson and John Saville in *The Reasoner* debate.[11] Thompson, an extra-mural lecturer at the University of Leeds, was already challenging the Party leadership over its interpretation of British labour history at the time of the attacks upon Stalin. These criticisms of the lack of flexibility within the Party soon turned into the more serious debate about the publication of *The Reasoner*, which was initiated by both Thompson and John Saville, a lecturer at the University of Hull.

Thompson had already been in conflict with the Party leadership for some months before the publication of the first issue of *The Reasoner*, in July 1956. He objected to the way in which a work school on Marxism was being organized. From February 1956 his correspondence with James Klugmann and other Party officials became increasingly irascible as he sensed an attempt to impose restrictions on the form of teaching and discussion that was to occur.[12] Thompson was concerned that the Party leadership was more intent on offering lectures on the French Revolution than on the British domestic working-class tradition, which Party officials felt was a bourgeois, rather than a working-class, experience. He later recalled:

Recently I was invited to take part in the National School on the History of our Labour Movement. I suggested that one of the twelve sessions might be called, 'The Free-Born Englishman', a discussion on the illusions and realities of our democratic tradition. Several letters were exchanged. At length it was decided that there was no room for such a session in the formal syllabus – but that provisionally an extra, optional, session would be put in on the last afternoon for those not shopping or at the sea.[13]

The whole purpose of Thompson's letters was to attack the old style of CPGB operation where democratic centralism – freedom of discussion, unity of action – effectively meant the endorsement of the views of the CPGB leadership and stifled opposition. Thompson praised Khrushchev's 'different roads to socialism' approach and asked 'Why is the *Daily Worker* the bleakest and least inspired paper in Labour History?'[14] Thompson's views on the leadership were clear: 'I think that the leadership of our Party is opportunist and lacking in socialist principles: de-classed, remote from the working class, and even from the rank and file of the Party; contemptuous of theory.'[15] Indeed, Thompson was attempting to provoke the Party leadership and admitted to Klugmann that 'I have written letters to you containing deliberately provocative statements but have received neither reply or comment upon them.'[16] That was not entirely true for just previous to this particular letter Klugmann had written to Thompson that 'You seem to be rather cross with King Street [the headquarters of the CPGB], and take it for granted that all Communist officials are a bit dim, dull, dusty and doctrinaire.'[17] Thompson was indeed rather cross with King Street and, in a letter to Bert Ramelson, of the Yorkshire District Committee, complained of the lack of self-criticism within the Party, reflecting that 'All I can say is, thank God there is no chance of the EC ever having power in Britain; it would destroy in a month every liberty of thought, concern and expression, which it has taken the British people over 300 odd years to win.'[18] It was just after this that Thompson's article submitted to *World News and Views*, 'Winter Wheat in Omsk', was reduced from 1,700 words to 1,000 words in a process which he regarded as censorship.[19] Indeed it was so, since the article was passed on to the Political Committee which discussed it critically on 7 June 1956 and objected to Thompson's statement that:

Comrade John Saville, in a recent letter, referred to the weakening tradition of controversy in the Party in recent years. This is true. How often has the routine of the unanimous vote, the common front against the class enemy, the search 'for the correct formulation', inhibited the development of sharp controversy.

Year after year the Monolith, from its cave somewhere inside *For a Lasting Peace, For a People's Democracy*, has droned on in a dogmatic monotone, without individual variation, without moral inflexion, without native dialect.

'We do not see' (wrote Milton), 'that while we still affect by all means a rigid external formality, we may soon fall . . . into a gross conforming stupidity, a stark and dead congealment of wood and hay and stubble, forced and frozen together.'[20]

Thompson asked that the Party adopt argument, debate and polemic in order to bring about a rebirth of controversy in the place of dogma and opportunism; to take up the tradition of Lilburne, Winstanley, Cobbett, Oastler, Ernest Jones and the Chartists, and to remember that 'the propaganda of Morris and of the early ILP was imbued with this passionate moral protest against capitalism. Tom Mann illustrated his thundering speeches with passages from the Sermon on the Mount.' His point was that such a view was not moral guff. However, neither the editor of *World News and Views* nor the CPGB leadership warmed to the article and conflict proved inevitable.

Saville and Thompson began their wider campaign against the blocking of discussions within the Party by issuing their own journal, *The Reasoner*, in July 1956. It was to be 'A Journal of Discussion' and was headed by a quote from Marx: 'To leave error unrefuted is to encourage intellectual immorality.' The first editorial declared that there was deep disagreement over the meaning of 'Marxism'. The purpose of the journal was to 'perform a practical service in loosening up the constricted forms within which discussion between Communists has taken place in recent years'. It wished to get rid of the Party's procedures which, it was felt, had limited sharp criticism and had prevented the development of new ideas and the development of theory.[21]

The first issue of *The Reasoner* contained an article by Ken Alexander which suggested that democratic centralism, the basis of the CPGB's organization, should be replaced by the 'concept of democratic control and initiative'. It effectively attacked the development of the CPGB as a bureaucratic centralist organization that paid little more than lip-service to consultation throughout the Party.

In response the CPGB leadership felt that the rules of democratic centralism had been flouted. These stressed that after the fullest discussion throughout the Party the agreed policy determined by the Party collectively, usually at a congress, must be adhered to by its members whether they agreed with the decision or not. The principles of democratic centralism were encapsulated in the slogan 'freedom of discussion, unity of action'. Both Saville and Thompson denied that there were any such rules. The CPGB leadership did not immediately expel the dissidents, as it would have done in the past, but called them to attend the Executive Committee meeting of 8–9 September, where they were told to desist from publishing *The Reasoner*, a second copy of which had been produced on 7 September. The Executive Committee reported: 'It regrets that the comrades refused to agree to the request of the Yorkshire District Committee and the Political Committee to give an undertaking not to produce any further issues of *The Reasoner*.'[22] It then appealed to Thompson and Saville to relent. Only two months previously the Party leadership had acknowledged that there had been 'serious mistakes and grave abuses' under Stalin and agreed to a special conference, without decision-making powers, which had the right to appoint a commission with dissidents upon it to examine the issue of Inner Party Democracy.[23] Despite these concessions, both Saville and Thompson decided to publish a third issue of *The Reasoner*, for which they might be disciplined: 'As soon as we left [the EC meeting], we both decided the right course would be to resign and carry on the journal.'[24] After that they intended to cease publication, return to the Party and fight within it for change. However, the armed uprising against Stalinist rule in Hungary began at the end of October 1956 and its suppression by Soviet military forces at the beginning of November transformed the situation.

The third issue of *The Reasoner* appeared on 4 November and, in an article on 'The Smoke of Budapest', which began with the statement that 'STALINISM has sown the wind, and now the whirlwind centres on Hungary', Thompson demanded that the CPGB leadership publicly condemn the Soviet action. The editorial made much the same point, stressing that while the recent British invasion of Egypt was cynical imperialism, the Soviet invasion of Hungary must also be condemned especially since the working people and students of Budapest 'were demonstrating against an oppressive machine which gave them no adequate democratic channels for expressing the popular will'. They called for the Executive Committee to dissociate itself from Soviet action, to demand the withdrawal of Soviet troops and to declare solidarity with the Polish people, also under the threat of Soviet invasion. For this action, Saville and Thompson were suspended from the Party for three months but they then concluded that the Party was unreformable and resigned on 14 November 1956.[25] In a letter to Howard Hill (a member of the Executive Committee of the Party), dated 9 November, Thompson admitted 'this Hungary is the last straw' and said that he could not see how he could 'stay within the party beyond the coming weekend' if the Executive Committee did not change its position. He hoped that a Yorkshire group of dissident communists would keep together for 'scores of people are leaving already; if the Party can't be changed from inside it will have to be changed from outside'.[26] Indeed, within the Leeds CPGB there was a group of Party members, led by Jim Roche who had been area secretary in the late 1940s, which developed links with the Fife Socialist League which had arisen out of a split with the Scottish CPGB over the events of 1956.[27]

The Reasoner debate was further discussed by the Executive Committee on 10 and 11 November 1956 where it was noted that the third issue had been published.[28] By that time Party condemnation meant nothing to Saville and Thompson as they contemplated resignation. Yet the Party was conscious that it was losing members over the issues raised by *The Reasoner* as well as because of its stance on the Soviet invasion of Hungary. Party files indicate deep divisions within Communist ranks, although about two-thirds of the branches supported the Executive Committee over *The Reasoner* debate and Hungary.[29] The West Yorkshire district, firmly under the control of Bert Ramelson, ignored the appeal of John Saville and condemned the publication of *The*

Reasoner.[30] Many others did the same in a collection of resolutions presented to the Executive Committee on 15 December 1956. Nevertheless, the Writers' Group, in a letter with thirteen signatures attached, attacked the EC's handling of the dispute: 'EC prepared to resist uprooting last vestiges of Stalinism – prefers journalistic discussion or discipline – against full discussion and free publication.'[31] Not surprisingly, since Thompson lived in Halifax, the Halifax branch of the CPGB 'wholeheartedly supported' the publication of *The Reasoner*.[32] Indeed, five members of the Halifax CPGB branch resigned from the Party immediately after Thompson.[33] The whole episode, of course, was given added impetus by the fact that the Hungarian rising had occurred at the crucial moment in the Party democracy debate.

There is an interesting postscript to this debate in the fact that at the beginning of 1957 the Political Committee discussed a report on 'Some Thoughts About Intellectuals', probably written by John Gollan, which stated that 'I think middle-class intellectuals who join the Communist Party and continue to live the lives of middle-class intellectuals are bound to create certain problems both for the Party and themselves, and that it is only realistic to recognize this.' There then followed comments about how intellectuals were often out of touch with reality and that they were putting themselves at the head of a petty-bourgeois attempt to take over the Party.[34] This was one way of saying that the Party would not change. Indeed, there was little concession to democracy within the Party until the 1960s and the discussions on Inner Party Democracy. The events in Hungary were, of course, crucial to this decision not to change.

The Hungarian Revolution of 1956

The Hungarian rising occurred against the background of the general strike movement that developed in Poland during the summer of 1956. Soviet intervention in Poland was only narrowly averted in October 1956, but when Hungary rebelled against Stalinist rule in favour of 'communism with a human face' and 'a degree of national sovereignty', the Russian army was sent to crush the revolution. Soviet troops were called in on the night of 23 October only to be withdrawn on 30 October as sections defected to the revolution. These were replaced by troops from Siberia, who believed that they had been sent to Berlin to fight German fascism, and whose second invasion on 4 November crushed the Hungarian rising at the cost of over 20,000 casualties.[35]

The *Daily Worker* admitted that the Hungarian rebellion had a popular basis but began to ignore articles written to this effect by its own journalists and posed the accusation that the revolt in Hungary was inspired by the USA. John Gollan, the new General Secretary of the Party, was equally adamant, noting that 'there is the greatest danger that reaction can obtain victory in Hungary'.[36] With the leadership and the organ of the Party determined to support the Soviet position on Hungary, despite genuine widespread popular unrest amongst the workers, it was clear that the central mechanisms of the CPGB would simply close ranks to endorse the line of its pro-Soviet Stalinist leadership.

A special Executive Committee meeting on 3 November 1956 decided to support the Soviet intervention.[37] Gollan discussed the problems of the Soviet Union and the 'cult of the individual' which had blighted communism but asserted that the Hungarian events had been the product of a reactionary force and related to the history of prewar Hungarian fascism. Nevertheless, despite the denials of George Matthews, a member of the Executive Committee, there was significant dissent. Howard Hill opposed the use of the Red Army in Hungary and felt that 'its threatened use in Poland [is] a violation of Socialist principles'. He also claimed that a majority of those present at the meeting were opposed to the PC.[38] At this meeting he was supported by a range of people, including Peter Kerrigan, Industrial Organizer of the Party at this time. However, the hand-written notes on the meeting suggest that the majority favoured Gollan's report, which justified the Soviet action, and were concerned at the way in which the Twentieth Congress of the CPSU had been handled. Arnold Kettle, Phil Piratin, Idris Cox and many others did not object to the use of Russian troops, although some EC members felt that their use in Hungary was a blunder.[39] As Idris Cox suggested, 'What is at stake is the whole future of Socialism in this country', and it was this thought which probably brought unity into a deeply divided Party. Klugmann paid tribute to the Party for giving one of 'the finest demonstrations of loyalty . . . that has ever take place'.[40] Yet the lengthy draft resolution which emerged from that meeting attempted to keep both sides happy with both an endorsement of the necessity of Soviet invasion and an admission that the Nagy government had been responsible for 'mistakes and wrong practices, utterly contrary to Socialist and Communist principles'. The Party declared that it was uncertain whether the Hungarian government should have called in Soviet troops but that 'the Soviet Union was absolutely correct to respond to the call when it was made'. However, it should be pointed out that the short-lived Nagy government of 27 October–4 November had not called in the Russian troops. Indeed, on 2 November the Hungarian government renounced the Warsaw Pact treaty and appealed to the United Nations for support against Russian intervention. Khrushchev sent in the Red Army following the failure of the Nagy government to bring an end to the uprising by peaceful means.[41] Such details did not concern the Executive Committee of the Party which then turned its attention towards the British Conservative government's recent intervention in Egypt to secure the Suez Canal.[42]

The Political Committee of the Party, dominated by Gollan and the leading officials, was also resolute in its attempt to keep the Communists behind the Soviet Union. It was admitted, probably by Bert Ramelson, that 'those open to conviction have in the main tended to stiffen up. But some will go out. But also some v[ery] good have been sh[a]ken to the core.'[43] M. Bennett also suggested, rather accurately as it turned out, that there was 70 per cent rather than 90 per cent support for the Executive Committee. At a meeting on 15 November, J.R. Campbell felt that the Party should not pin too much faith on the Janos Kadar government that had now taken power in Hungary.[44] It is not surprising that Gollan should reflect that 'It is certainly no easy job to be in the leadership of the Communist Party during these days.'[45] Indeed, he seems to have spent a substantial amount of his time writing outlines of the events of Hungary and Poland, justifying Soviet action by pointing to the fact that the Nagy government had called in Soviet troops while attempting to deflect criticism of the Soviet Union by focusing attention upon the Suez affair.[46]

The Hungarian tragedy, along with *The Reasoner* debate, led to the loss of 7,000 members between 1956 and 1957, including academics such as Saville, Thompson and many trade union leaders such as John Horner, General Secretary of the Fire Brigades' Union and Alex Moffat of the Scottish NUM executive, although he later returned. Moffat wrote a letter to Gollan indicating that he was 'no longer convinced that a party of our type is a necessary condition to achieve socialism here' and that 'I have had doubts over the past six months and Hungary was the culmination'.[47] More than a third of the staff of the *Daily Worker* resigned because of the Party line on the Hungarian revolution.

The Party monitored changes in membership closely. Indeed, at the Executive Committee meeting of 10 and 11 November 1956, Arnold Kettle stated that no one was under any illusions about the gravity of the situation. There was clearly widespread disillusionment within the CPGB. The University of Sheffield branch voted 7 to 3 against the Executive Committee's statement on the presence of Soviet troops in Hungary and there had been numerous other protests in the seventy or so meetings that were held on the matter.[48] A letter from the Manchester University graduates branch of the CPGB also included a resolution passed on 5 November 1956 which suggested that 'In placing sole reliance on Moscow's report . . . the CPGB is opening itself to complete and irredeemable isolation' and called for the reversal of the Party line.[49] There was also a spate of resolutions from branches, with Stoke Newington condemning the Hungarian and Soviet parties, Colne CPGB criticizing the CPSU's behaviour in Hungary, and Bristol South dismissing the dependence upon the Russian account of events.[50] Many members left these branches in protest. A.A. Willis, Secretary of the East and West Riding area of the Electrical Trades Union, resigned from the Bradford branch of the CPGB along with a dozen others, since 'I could no longer accept the Communist road to Socialism, or the operation of Socialism under Communist administration. I have come to the conclusion that Communism is not the dictatorship of the proletariat but the dictatorship of a well-organized and well-disciplined minority imposing its will upon the majority.'[51]

Such losses led those remaining within the Party to unite in a defensive reaction. Indeed, when, in December, a number of dissidents published a letter (previously refused by the *Daily Worker*) in *Tribune* and the *New Statesman*, John Gollan stated that Party members going outside the Party to criticize the Party would not be tolerated in future.[52] Centralism, once more, was being invoked. The internal criticism continued, though, with a letter to Matthews and the Political Committee suggesting that 'we should improve the situation and repair some of the damage'.[53]

Party discussions revealed that the EC had a clear majority on Hungary and of 332 branches making a report 240 supported it, 69 opposed it and 232 were undecided. In 188 branch meetings where votes were held, 2,095 members voted for the EC position, 745 against and 301 abstained. Area aggregate meetings returned votes of 1,029 for, 295 against and 80 abstentions.[54] Throughout the country the majority of Party members supported the leadership but there was no hiding the fact that many members were worried at the unthinking support the Party leaders had given to the Soviet action. Geoff Hodgson, an active member of the Leeds branch of the CPGB, admitted that he was a little critical of the policy adopted by the Soviet Union but did believe that 'there had been a counter-revolutionary movement in Hungary with Cardinal Mindszenty of the Roman Catholic Church and the former landowners backed by the United States and all the reactionary forces worldwide. That said I was not too happy about the fate meted out to Rajk by Rakovsi and his cohorts. I felt that 1956 allowed the past errors to be put forward.'[55] However, the leadership took this majority support to be an endorsement of the old Party practices and was reluctant to make any positive concessions to those demanding more democratic procedures.

This reluctance quickly became evident in the discussions that took place over Inner Party Democracy. In December 1956 the Executive Committee elevated the status of the National Conference to that of a Special Congress for Easter 1957. It was supposed to discuss a redraft of *The British Road to Socialism* prepared in December 1956, as well as Inner Party Democracy. The former was relatively uncontentious when compared with the latter issue, since the Inner Party Democracy commission contained some well-known dissidents, although ten of its fifteen members were central and district full-time officials and thus Party faithfuls.

The commission on Inner Party Democracy took no evidence and focused upon general principles rather than the realities of the situation within the Party. Betty Reid of the Organization Department acted as secretary and John Mahon, a member of the London District and of the Political Committee, was chairman. Malcolm MacEwan, who had been included as a dissident and had resigned as the *Daily Worker*'s Features Editor, later wrote that Mahon 'did not see his role as leading an investigation: he saw it as securing the defeat of the "revisionists" who were critical of democratic centralism'.[56]

Christopher Hill and Peter Cadogan, two other dissidents, were also critical of the way in which the Party had been induced to follow the Cominform line of criticizing Tito and Yugoslavia, and the way in which the British communist press had been controlled since the Twentieth Congress of the CPSU. With Malcolm MacEwan, they challenged the CPGB's tight control of the ten members who were committed to democratic centralism and the two 'neutral' members, Kevin Halpen and Joe Cheek. Outnumbered, the three dissidents wrote a minority report that challenged the majority report's belief in democratic centralism. Written mainly by MacEwan, it suggested that the commission had failed to discharge the task it had been given, argued that democratic centralism was certainly not democracy and maintained that it was foolish to compel members to fight for policies in which they had no confidence.

The 'Report to the Executive Committee of the Communist Party on Inner Party Democracy' endorsed the majority report in most areas. It stated that:

We consider that our Party should now correct what we believe to have been a serious error – too general an emphasis on centralism and an insufficient emphasis on democracy. The tendency to consider a strong centralised leadership as sufficient has resulted in not enough being done to bring the membership into the discussion of Party problems and in failure to take sufficient practical measures to build strong Party branches.[57]

The National Conference of Easter 1957, the 'Special' Twenty-Fifth Congress of the CPGB, accepted the majority report when it met between 19 and 22 April at Hammersmith Town Hall. It was chaired impartially by Pollitt, but the Party leadership, nevertheless, ensured that the dissidents would be defeated. Gollan was unbalanced in his address, in which he declared of Hungary that 'it was a tragedy these events could take place. It would have been a bigger tragedy if reaction had won.' On Stalin, he stated that 'the actual form in which the distortions of Socialism arose was due to Stalin's personal character' but 'political power was in the hands of the people' and 'we must also see his great services to the revolution'. Revisionism was considered to be the principal problem and danger for the CPGB and was to be repudiated 'in the first place to achieve the course of development for the British working class put in this report'. Gollan maintained that the dissidents would never flourish as Marxists outside the party because 'historical circumstances have created the party organizations of the British working class. There is no such thing as Marxism without the Communist Party.' He therefore called for the rejection of the minority report in what appeared to be a Stalinist reflex. Mahon, the chairman of the commission, compounded the obvious bias of the commission by barely addressing the vital issues but demanding the retention of Marxist-Leninist ideals. Christopher Hill spoke for the minority report but Congress voted by over 20 to 1 for the majority view. Democratic centralism was advocated and the dissident representation was excluded from the new EC that was about to be elected. The Party had not learned the lessons of 1956 and was unwilling to respond to the issues raised by *The Reasoner* debate. Hill and many other intellectuals left the Party, although some, such as Eric Hobsbawm and Maurice Dobb, remained.

Driven closer to Moscow, Gollan arranged that considerable sums of money, up to £100,000 on some occasions, should be sent through the Soviet Embassy for the next twenty-one years to finance the *Daily Worker* (the *Morning Star* from 1966), although only Gollan, Reuben Falber, the Assistant Secretary, and Party official David Ainley, seem to have known about this until it became public knowledge in 1991.[58]

The Moscow link was thus endorsed, albeit secretly, and the Party continued to stifle criticism of Soviet action by restricting the opportunities for democratic debate that Thompson and Saville had promoted. The Party was slow to change and only did so when a continuing crisis in falling membership forced it to change tack from the mid-1960s onwards.

The Expansion and Division of Marxism in the late 1950s and the 1960s

The Party membership declined considerably in the wake of the events of 1956 – a situation not helped by the ongoing world economic boom of that period which meant the Conservative government was not an easy target for criticism. Given this situation there was a tendency to look to alliances with bodies outside the Party in order to strengthen Communist influence.

Having once rejected the Campaign for Nuclear Disarmament (CND) as an unnecessary distraction, in 1960 the Party decided to support its cause. Efforts were made to establish other alliances and Party fortunes were improved by Khrushchev who, having privately denounced Stalin at the Twentieth Congress of the CPSU in 1956, publicly denounced him at the Twenty-Second Congress. In this new climate membership began to increase and rose from 27,500 in 1961 to more than 34,000 in 1964. YCL membership also rose from just under 3,000 to nearly 4,700 between 1957 and 1963. The CPGB was enjoying an Indian summer.

However, the Party had changed little since 1956 and the leaders of 1956–7 were still in charge. Gollan remained General Secretary, George Matthews continued to edit the *Daily Worker*, Peter Kerrigan still presided over the Industrial Department and Dutt still influenced national and international thinking through *Labour Monthly*.

James Klugmann edited the new theoretical journal *Marxism Today*. The Party also continued to practise the bureaucratic centralism of the past, which had helped to create the crisis of 1956. Not surprisingly, the Party claimed to be the sole embodiment and defence of the working class, at the same time as it decided to enter the mainstream of British politics: 'It moves together *with*, although it *leads*, the working class and the mass of the people.'[59]

Nevertheless, continuity and propaganda brought little significant improvement in the Party's membership and the immediate objective of winning 100,000, later reduced to 50,000, members remained a pipe dream, although membership did recover to its 1956 level of 33,000 to 34,000 by 1964. The Party fought election campaigns to raise its profile, sought to widen its trade union base and conducted educational work, publishing the translated Soviet work *Fundamentals of Marxism–Leninism*. The CPGB had limited success. It was unable to win a seat in the 1959 general election and appears to have lost ground in its trade union activities. Indeed, in the latter sphere it faced a serious setback with the controversy that surrounded its activities within the Electrical Trade Union (ETU).

The ETU had been dominated by the Communist Party for some years but when Les Cannon resigned from the Party over Hungary he was removed from his post at the union's training college. At that moment, anti-Communists began to support John Byrne, the Glasgow district secretary, and they secured the election of anti-Communists, including Frank Chapple, to the union executive. This campaign led to a press attack upon the union's Communist leadership, and particularly against Frank Foulkes, the president, and Frank Haxell, the secretary. When Haxell defeated Byrne for the secretaryship in early 1960 there were allegations of ballot-rigging. This resulted in a lawsuit which, in June 1961, culminated in Communist union officials being found guilty of conspiracy to prevent Byrne's election by disqualifying the vote of branches who supported Byrne and by stuffing ballot boxes in others. The court ordered that Byrne should replace Haxell as secretary and the TUC demanded that Foulkes should re-submit himself for election. When Foulkes refused the union was expelled from the TUC. But the Communists on the union executive were soon routed; Byrne, Cannon and Chapple secured control of the union and sought, and gained, readmission to the TUC.

Throughout these events the Party supported the Communist defendants in the trial but after the verdict it sought to distance itself from such corrupt leadership. Peter Kerrigan reported to the CPGB's 1963 congress that:

> We have declared that the ballot rigging in the Electrical Trade Union was a complete violation of the principles on which Communists have worked for over forty years, and took place without our Party leadership being aware of it . . .

The conduct of the election at the Head Office of the ETU gravely compromised our Party and all those progressive forces in the trade union movement who, for a number of years, defended the ETU against attacks of the reactionaries. Our Party have taken steps to ensure that Communist Party members will never again be involved in such an affair.[60]

The ETU affair brought home to the Party the reality that its trade union base was precarious even in unions dominated by its members. From that time onwards it began to recognize that it would have to share power with other progressive forces, a fact which was accepted at the Twenty-Eighth Congress of the Party in 1963. The 'broad left' strategy was beginning to emerge.

Such national events were fought against a background of turmoil within the international communist community. The Chinese communist 'Great Leap Forward' in 1958, which had sought to encourage everyone within every community to be jointly involved in both agricultural and industrial output, cut across the Soviet emphasis upon heavy industrial development to speed up the growth of communist economic power. This divergence of economic priorities aroused controversy in the late 1950s, leading to fewer Soviet experts being sent to China. By the early 1960s the split between the Soviet and the Maoist approaches was becoming even more marked and led, by the mid- and late 1960s, to boundary disputes between the Soviet Union and China along the Amur river. With two rival international centres for Marxism clashing, the world's communist countries began to divide between support for China and support for the Soviet Union, and any disputes, such as that between the Soviet Union and Albania in 1961, led the participants to identify with one of the alternative powers and approaches. The split became more open in late 1963 when the Chinese accused Khrushchev, and the Soviets, of revisionism.

The Party remained loyally Soviet in its approach on any matter that divided Moscow from Peking, a relationship galvanized further during the Cuban missile crisis of 1962. It also supported the Soviet Union in its erection of the Berlin Wall in August 1961. The *Daily Worker* commented that it was the warmongering activities of the United States 'playing with fire at the most explosive point in Europe, which have made it necessary for the government of the GDR, at the request of the Warsaw Treaty Powers, to take new steps to control the West Berlin border'.[61] The Executive Committee of the CPGB acknowledged the divisions between Moscow and Peking in January 1963 and published a statement entitled *Restore the Unity of the International Communist Movement*, calling for unity to avoid a disastrous split. This theme was continued in *Marxism Today* when Palme Dutt and James Klugmann made further appeals for unity.[62] The Party, not entirely unreservedly, sided with the Soviet Union when it came to the crunch.

There was a small Maoist movement led by Michael McCreery, from New Zealand, which gained the support of a couple of London branches and a few individuals. In 1963 McCreery formed the Committee to Defeat Revisionism for Communist Unity, which produced the monthly paper *Vanguard* for a short time. He also published several pamphlets, the most famous being *Destroy the Old to Build the New* in which he attacked *The British Road to Socialism* and the notion that the working class could win control over the capitalist state in Britain by constitutional means. He sought to prove that the armed forces would take control of the decaying capitalist state in order to prevent it being taken over by Marxists and socialists, adding:

How is this threat to be countered? By mobilising the 'political and industrial strength' of the people. But political parties and trade unions cannot stand against an army. There is no escaping the need at some stage of the revolution, for *armed strength* to back the political and industrial strength of the people. Only *the people in arms* can counter a putsch of the army. To ignore that fact is to ensure the defeat of the revolution. But it is ignored in *The British Road to Socialism*.[63]

The split between the Soviets and the Maoists was of limited significance within Britain. The Party supported the Soviet Union and kept behind *The British Road to Socialism*, continuing to press for its wider acceptance. To keep in touch with political changes, though, the Party partly redrafted *The British Road to Socialism* in 1957–8, 1968 and 1977.[64] Yet the Party achieved little political success. Indeed, in the late 1950s it was stated that the immediate aim of the CPGB was to defeat the Tory government and return a Labour government pledged to a new policy of peace and social advance.[65] But it did not work and the Party failed to win a parliamentary seat in 1959.

In municipal politics there was also failure and humiliation. Lawrence Daly, a promising party activist in Scotland based in Ballingray, Fife, a member of the Scottish District Committee and secretary of a miners' trade union branch, announced his departure from the CPGB in March 1957. He then formed the Fife Socialist League as a new political party, argued that the CPGB was subservient to the CPSU and criticized the CPGB's failure to reform itself in the light of Khrushchev's revelations about Stalin and the Hungarian rising. His organization beat Communists in local union elections and won seats against sitting Communist councillors.[66] The municipal performance of the Party nationally was steadily getting worse. In 1945 it had more than 200 local authority seats but was reduced to about twenty in the mid-1960s. There was a major test of the new electoral strategy to defeat the Tories and return a Labour government in April 1964 with the first contests for the newly created Greater London Council, where the Party decided to contest all thirty-two divisions. Great claims were made about the opportunities this provided but in the end the Party obtained only 93,000 votes, rather fewer than it had expected.[67] Notwithstanding this, Gollan and the Party pressed ahead with the electoral campaign with an article entitled 'Now the Future Depends on Us and our Campaign', which suggested, rather optimistically, that the likely improvement of the political situation depended upon the CPGB's growth and campaigning.[68]

The fact is that such Party statements were just not tenable on the basis of its performance. In order to achieve some success, Gollan informed the Party Congress of 1965, now held in the autumn, that he was willing to join with non-Communist forces. Yet even this was to little avail. In the general election of 1966 not one of the CPGB's fifty-seven candidates was returned and its five-minute television slot proved to be a waste of time since its overall vote was only 62,000. This represented a 38 per cent drop in the vote for the fourteen constituencies which had been contested continually since 1955. This was followed by further failures in the Greater London Council elections, worse than in 1964, although one or two council seats were won in Scotland.

The electoral failures of the CPGB contrasted with the success of the new reformist and anti-Communist Labour government which came into office in 1964. Harold Wilson, the new Prime Minister, was indeed positively hostile to the CPGB and most markedly so in dealing with industrial and trade union policies. The trade union activities of the CPGB had fallen foul of the TUC in 1960. They now fell foul of the Wilson Labour government. This was most evident when Wilson informed the House of Commons on Monday 20 June 1966 that a small number of Communists had been able to influence the decisions of the National Union of Seamen in a strike that had lasted about five weeks. The next day this charge was denied by William Hogarth, the seamen's leader, who argued that there was not one Communist on the 48-member executive of the union.[69] George Woodcock, the General Secretary of the TUC, noted that Wilson had not consulted the TUC before making his statement and added that 'the fact that the Communist Party has shown an interest in the strike is to me something to spend a lot of time not bothering about'.[70] Gollan, writing in The *Star*, 25 June 1966, felt that this suggestion was an insult to the seamen: 'The Communist Party has declared its position openly and clearly. It supports the seaman's struggle and their just demands. . . . Tens of thousands of Labour Party members have done the same.' The seamen produced their own defence of their demands in a thirty-page pamphlet written by Charles Hodgson and John Prescott, later Deputy Prime Minister in the Labour government elected in 1997.

The seamen's strike did provoke the Party to a more aggressive reaction against the new Labour government's incomes policy. The 'lobby organizing committee', which had existed among rank-and-file organizations, principally in London, during the 1960s, held a meeting with the shop stewards' coordinating committees on Clydeside in September 1966 and decided to campaign through mass meetings and deputations.

In February 1967 they formed the Liaison Committee for the Defence of Trade Unions whose main task was to organize a major campaign against the wage freeze being imposed by the Labour government. Thus the grass roots of the Party were being given an added political dimension and the Political Committee of the Party noted that 'the strike of municipal busmen due to start on August 12th is the clearest indication that the incomes policy is state interference with the collective agreement'.[71]

The Party felt that any attempt at wage restraint would lead to a fall in workers' living standards. Although the Donovan Commission examining industrial relations did not want state wage restraint it wanted some voluntary restraint and therefore came in for a hostile reception from the CPGB, which conducted considerable agitation against government policies. In the Lancashire and Cheshire district of the CPGB it was noted that 'the fight against the Wage Freeze, Redundancy, legislation on Trade Unions, against American Methods of Industry, etc., as well as support for Peace in Vietnam have all figured in the industrial action and activity of Trade Unions, the Shop Steward and Rank and File movement'.[72]

Yet there was still a feeling that the Party needed to be better organized in its industrial activities. The EC was concerned to improve factory organization and Kerrigan talked of the creation of twenty-four new factory branches.[73] The Political Committee also raised the issue of factory branch life and produced a draft report in October 1968 to encourage greater participation, the broadening of the struggle, and the raising of the profile of *The British Road to Socialism* since the 'overall situation of our factory branches is unsatisfactory' and 'the majority don't meet regularly, don't have a factory Branch Committee, don't have a place of work or a clear perception of their work'.[74]

The Party did reasonably well out of the revolt against the wage freeze in the late 1960s and opposed Barbara Castle's White Paper *In Place of Strife* when it was published in 1969, since it proposed wage controls. However, ultimately the industrial policy of the Party was little more successful than its electoral policy. The Party now attempted to broaden its approach in order to gain a greater degree of support.

The Broad-based Approach and the Students

The mid- and late 1960s provided many opportunities for the CPGB to latch on to popular unrest connected with anti-racism,[75] nuclear disarmament and the Vietnam War. The Labour Party had opposed the construction of nuclear-armed submarines in 1964 but was in office when the first one was commissioned in 1969. The Campaign for Nuclear Disarmament, which had been declining since 1962, linked up with the CPGB to protest against the action of the Labour government in commissioning nuclear submarines. The Party also campaigned against the Labour government's support of the mass bombing of Vietnam by the Americans and called for 'Peace in Vietnam'. Such policies attracted much support among students.

The formation of many new universities in the early and mid-1960s swelled the number of students at a time when student unrest in Britain, France and the United States was at its height. The CPGB placed great emphasis upon student support, employed a full-time National Student Organizer, formed a National Student Committee and held an annual student conference. The success of this strategy was evident when Digby Jack, a Communist, became the President of the National Union of Students in 1971.

Fergus Nicholson, the National Student Organizer for the Party, was largely responsible for its success among students and was behind the formation of the Communist University of London in 1969, with its week-long seminar. However, the CPGB was only one of many socialist groups active among students at this time. Most of these organizations were more left, or ultra-left, wing and some still called upon the older Marxist-Leninist traditions that many felt the CPGB had dropped as a result of *The British Road to Socialism*. The CPGB simply regarded these bodies as Trotskyist. There had been a re-grouping of the left following the failure of the New Left and the Bevanites in the 1950s. The new student groups that emerged were encouraged by the national and international issues of the day, such as Vietnam and the student riots in France in 1968. In this atmosphere 'Trotskyist' groups did well, as did the 'Maoists'. They seized the initiative from the CPGB and mobilized 100,000 people to demonstrate in London in October 1968 as part of the Vietnam Solidarity Campaign.

There was a bewildering array of between eighty and ninety socialist parties, groupings, movements and papers active during the mid-1960s. These included the ILP (which had left the Labour Party in 1932 and did not rejoin until 1975), Keep Left, the Britain-Vietnam Solidarity Front, the Vietnam Solidarity Campaign, the Committee to Defeat Revisionism for Communist Unity (which had splintered on the death of Michael McCreery), two versions of the Fourth International, the Anarchist Federation of Great Britain and the Hands off Vietnam Committees. The pro-Chinese contingent included the New Era Publishing Group, Reg Birch's Communist Party of Britain (formed at Easter 1968), *The Marxist* group, the London Workers' Committee, the Workers' Party of Scotland, the Finsbury Communist Association and the *Red Front*. All these bodies, and others, frequently split and reorganized themselves into new alignments.

The four dominant organizations were based upon the Trotskyist tradition supporting the Russian Revolution and the Soviet state as it existed under the leadership of Lenin and Trotsky, while opposing the subsequent bureaucratic 'Stalinist' degeneration of both the modern Soviet Union and the CPGB. Three of the organizations had common origins in the Revolutionary Communist Party that united the majority of British Trotskyists between 1944 and 1947. When Labour was elected in 1945 and began to introduce basic socialist measures, the need for an independent Trotskyist party was challenged by many of the RCP's own leaders, including Gerry Healy and Tony Cliff who proposed entering the Labour Party.

In 1947 Gerry Healy led the majority of the RCP into the Labour Party and in 1956–7 his supporters formed the Socialist Labour League (SLL). They were joined by Communist Party defectors such as Cliff Slaughter, Peter Fryer, Michael Banda (editor of *Newsletter*), Tom Kemp (a Hull lecturer) and Geoffrey Pilling (a Sheffield lecturer). SLL members later captured the leadership of the Labour Party's Young Socialists but were expelled in 1965, after publicly criticizing Wilson in the midst of the 1964 general election campaign. The SLL then set up its own misleadingly titled Young Socialists. Its adult membership was only a few hundred in 1967 and 1968 but it claimed 30,000 members in the Young Socialists. The organization had widespread support at universities such as Bristol, Exeter and Sheffield and its anti-Stalinist policies drove it to support the Chinese Cultural Revolution of the mid- and late 1960s, to criticize Castro and to support Black Power.

Secondly, there were the International Socialists (IS) founded by Tony Cliff. Unlike Gerry Healy, he believed that the postwar Soviet Union was no longer a bureaucratically deformed workers' state but a form of state capitalism. The IS rejected both international blocs in their slogan 'Neither Washington nor Moscow' and campaigned in tenant struggles and in defence of trade union rights. Because of its broad-based policies it attracted many young left-wing students and lecturers at universities. Among the IS leaders were John Palmer, William Fancy, Raymond Challinor, Paul Foot, Nicholas Hood, Peter Sedgewick and Alistair Macintyre. The membership was a mere 360 in 1967, but had risen to between 600 and 800 by 1968. This growth was assisted by the fact that, after the exclusion of the SLL from the Labour Party Young Socialists the IS inherited the leadership of the LPYS. The IS claimed to be operating thirty-five clubs in its own right in 1968 but was intent upon working through the Labour Party, which had not proscribed it. This policy was reversed after the Labour government sent troops to Northern Ireland in 1969, the IS later withdrawing from the Labour Party and organizing independently as the Socialist Workers' Party.

Thirdly, there was the Militant Tendency, organized around the *Militant* newspaper (launched in October 1964) and led by Ted Grant. Grant had led those in the RCP who had resisted the move into the Labour Party in the late 1940s. As a result, his supporters had lost ground and the Militant Tendency was rather obscure in the mid-1960s, though it gathered considerable support at the University of Sussex and its members entered the Labour Party. After the withdrawal of IS, it became the dominant grouping within the Labour Party Young Socialists, with the opportunity for enhanced recruiting this presented.

In 1964, the Fourth International urged the Militant Tendency to fuse with a fourth body, the International Group (IG). The IG was based in Nottingham; it was led by Tony Topham, Ken Coates and Alan Rooney and produced a journal called *The Week*. Fusion took place in 1965 but only lasted a few months. The Fourth International held the Militant Tendency responsible for this failure and in 1967 the Militant Tendency was replaced as the British section of the Fourth International by the IG, which altered its name to the International Marxist Group (IMG) and attracted figures such as Tariq Ali, a leading Marxist student activist.[76]

These organizations, and others, challenged the CPGB control of the radical student body and were therefore watched closely. Considered sectarian and ultra-leftist, they were mentioned in a duplicated listing which was circulated in March 1964 under the title *The Attack upon the Party from the So-called 'Extreme Left'*, and an article connected with it was written by Betty Reid and published in *Marxism Today*.[77] It stated that they 'are out to destroy the party and to weaken and confuse the British Labour Movement'.[78] The list was updated in 1968 when Reid produced a catalogue of eighty-eight socialist parties, groups, newspapers and journals of the ultra-left, with brief outlines of their history and fragmentation.[79]

James Klugmann, who added to this list in 1968, suggested to the Party that there were some organizations that should be encouraged. In particular he favoured those groups who gathered around *New Left Review* and the New Left May Day Manifesto Group, which published its first draft of the May Day Manifesto on 1 May 1967. This was issued as a Penguin publication in May 1968. The Group included in their ranks people such as leading Marxist and socialist intellectuals Raymond Williams, Edward Thompson and Stuart Hall. The views of these leaders were represented, by one report, in the following way:

> Very many people are now ready to combine into a purposeful extra-Parliamentary opposition, a socialist movement that is not limited to elections and industrial conflict, in which all groups can participate openly and sincerely in effective work about 'extra-Parliamentary opposition' to emphasise the features of different local groups on partial issues (rent, education, racialism, housing, etc.).[80]

To many of the leaders, then, the May Day Group was to be an alliance of socialist groups that would take up a broad range of social issues.

Agreement ended there, for within the May Day Group there were deep divisions between those who wished to form a new socialist party and those who wished to remain linked to the Labour Party. Williams and Thompson wished the group to maintain the connection with the Labour Party while others, most obviously Tony Cliff and the IS faction, wanted to create a new socialist party.

The CPGB, still wishing to operate within the Labour Party to extend its influence, followed the events of the May Day Manifesto Conference in April 1968 with great interest. It noted the absence of the main leaders, and criticized Tony Cliff, who made a 'wild and damaging speech', and his IS supporters who wanted to form a new independent socialist party. However, it supported the ideas of Stephen Yeo, a Labour Party candidate for Haringey in 1966 and an academic historian, who demanded a 'loosely structured organization' and opposed very strongly a 'great declaration of the need for a new movement'. In the end, the conference agreed by 65 votes to 35 to condemn the Labour Party as a capitalist party, and decided upon a systematic approach to implementing the 'May Day Manifesto, 1968' and to the holding of a National Convention in the autumn of 1968.

Despite the Party's determined efforts to encourage student membership, and its commitment to working through the Labour Party, its overall membership did not increase. It acquired some student support, though much less than its opposing student-based socialist societies, but its overall membership fell away as a result of its association with the construction of a monstrous police state in Russia, which had operated against democratic forms of socialism in Hungary and was to do so again in Czechoslovakia. Its overall membership continued to decline from 1964 onwards. The Yorkshire district fell from 2,512 members in 1966 to 2,294 in 1968 (Sheffield rose from 805 to 815 but Leeds fell from 646 to 606 in the respective years).[81] A similar pattern of slow seepage was evident in the London district which had 6,770 members in February 1967 and 5,935 in June 1968. Its main branches at Haringey and Islington had fallen from 748 to 648 and 640 to 512 respectively between those dates. The Young Communist League membership in London also fell rather dramatically from 1,507 in February 1967 to 1,023 in February 1968, before recovering slightly to 1,044 in April 1968.[82] In contrast, the membership of the Party in the Lancashire and Cheshire district showed a slight increase from 3,880 members in February 1967 to 4,013 in July 1968.[83] On balance, however, the Party was losing support and had begun its inexorable decline.

Nevertheless, by 1968, in the heyday of student action, the feeling was that the Party was progressing. There was optimism that student membership would enable the Party to get back on course and a letter to the Political Committee stated: 'If we could make only one appeal to militant and socialist students it would be this: Don't ignore or underestimate the power and vitality of the existing organizations of the working class in Britain.'[84] However, the Soviet invasion of Czechoslovakia undermined the Party's cause.

The Invasion of Czechoslovakia, 1968

In 1967 the Party endorsed the view that all communist and socialist countries should be allowed to develop socialism in their own way. This meant that socialist nations should not invade other socialist nations. The Soviet invasion of Czechoslovakia in 1968 challenged this approach.

In January 1968 Anton Novotny was dismissed as President by the Czech Communist Party leadership, an action which was followed by the liberalization of the 'Prague Spring'. The *Morning Star* supported these development and compared them with *The British Road to Socialism*, welcoming the 'positive steps taken to tackle the wrongs of the past and strengthen socialist democracy'.[85] Although there were many in the Party who disagreed with this view, it openly criticized the Warsaw Pact invasion when it eventually occurred on 21 August.

Throughout the spring and summer of 1968 Eastern Europe was at the forefront of discussions within the Party[86] and a draft statement was made on Czechoslovakia which noted that 'Respect for the autonomy of each Communist Party is the only real base on which to build working-class internationalism.'[87] By 8 August the Party was emphasizing the point and hoping that the talks, in Bratislava, on 3 August between the Soviets and Alexander Dubcek, General Secretary of the Czechoslovakian Communist Party, and Svoboda, a leading Czech Communist, would be successful.[88] They did not prove so and the Soviets invaded.

Before and during the invasion, there were numerous CPGB expressions of concern at the Soviet threats and actions. Deanne Lubelski, secretary of the Middlesbrough branch, referred to the branch support for the Czechs, as did several others. On the other hand, the Bexley branch condemned the Political Committee for its open anti-Sovietism, a view supported by Sid French of the Surrey district committee.[89] In condemning the Soviet invasion the CPGB was in line with public opinion and the EC criticized the Soviet invasion on 24 August. The Political Committee of the Party discussed the situation on 29 August 1968 and referred to the moving speech made by Dubcek, noting that 'Both he [Dubcek] and President Svoboda stated that there is no going back to pre-January days'.[90] In September a draft statement by the PC, which outlined developments, angrily rejected the statement of the Central Committee of the CPSU that the majority of the Presidium of the Czechoslovak Communist Party and Government had asked the Soviets for immediate help:

> It is now clear to us that this statement is not true, that there was no majority, neither in the Presidium nor in the Government, which appealed for entry of the troops. We must register the strongest objection to your attempt to mislead us in this way. Mutual trust between Brother Parties must be based on honest and principled behaviour.[91]

Later that month the EC made a statement 'deploring the intervention of the Warsaw Pact troops into Czechoslovakia'.[92] It wished for a quick settlement to the dispute and welcomed the Moscow meeting between the Soviet and Czech leaders as a basis for settlement. In the meantime: 'In our view the quickest possible withdrawal of troops is needed so that the Czechoslovak working people, the Communist Party and the Government, can act with complete sovereignty, to develop their Socialist system in accordance with their own decisions.'[93] The mutual cooperation of socialist states had become the principal driving force of CPGB actions.

The Young Communist League Executive Committee issued its own condemnation of Soviet action on 3 October, criticizing both the illegal imprisonment of Czech leaders and the presence of 600,000 Soviet troops in Czechoslovakia.[94] The London District Congress, held on 16–17 November, also deplored the invasion of the Warsaw Pact troops which it characterized as a 'tragic mistake', but rejected the 'anti-Soviet policies of the capitalist press' and the 'aggressive policies of NATO' which were 'the main danger to peace in Europe'.[95]

The Soviet invasion of Czechoslovakia damaged the CPGB, despite its condemnation of Soviet action, and membership continued to decline from nearly 33,000 in 1967 to just under 29,000 in 1971. It fluctuated around that level throughout the early 1970s as the CPGB gained some support for its condemnation of the industrial and trade union policy of Edward Heath's Conservative government, most particularly the Industrial Relations Act of 1971 that created an Industrial Relations Court with powers to impose fines upon unions to compensate employers where unfair industrial practice had taken place. The Party helped in the release of the Pentonville dockers, who had been imprisoned for picketing in defiance of restrictions imposed by the 1971 Act. Such support that the CPGB gained was, of course, undermined once Eurocommunism developed by internal wranglings between the pro-Soviets and the reformers.

Eurocommunism and Splits, 1970s

In the early and mid-1970s communist parties began to reassess the way in which communism could achieve power. The CPGB had already worked out a programme, *The British Road to Socialism*, which envisaged a peaceful transition to socialism through parliamentary activity and pluralistic democratic socialism.[96] By 1976 the French, Spanish, Italian and several other communist parties had developed this strategy further. They stressed the need to extend democratic liberties and human rights and to win an electoral mandate to achieve socialism, thus relating their approach to the conditions of 'advanced capitalism'. They also pointed to the need to diverge from the communism of Moscow.[97] They decided to delete the phrase 'dictatorship of the proletariat' from their phraseology; the words had referred to

Marx's democratic state ruled by the representatives of the working class based upon the principle of democratic centralism, bridging the interval between the overthrow of bourgeois rule and the establishment of a society of abundance which would have no need for a state of any sort – 'rule over men' would be replaced by the 'administration of things'. To Lenin the dictatorship of the proletariat and democratic centralism were the twin principles of the state of society before the arrival of full communism. Eurocommunism emerged to challenge these Leninist ideas with the belief that a Communist Party could define its own brand of socialism, participate with whichever capitalist enterprises it wished, work with whatever foreign groups it desired, and criticize other communist parties, including that in the Soviet Union.[98] Eurocommunism thus came to mean that any communist party could pursue whatever policies seemed appropriate for the creation of a communist state. The primacy of the Soviet Union, and the 'dictatorship of the proletariat' were no longer to be defining qualities for communism. Those who supported Eurocommunism often referred to the Gramscian ideas of gaining political hegemony through alliances, compromises and the gradual parliamentary extension of communist ideals.[99]

Many of the older members of the Party and faithful supporters of the Soviet Union disagreed with the new Eurocommunist ideas which they saw as being unfairly critical of the Soviet Union and the abandonment of the class struggle. Indeed, in 1977 Marion Slug complained of the CPGB's criticism of the USSR over Czechoslovakia. In Reuben Falber's reply on 16 March he stated that 'people who have different points of view in the development of socialism from that of the Czechoslovak authorities are denied any means of expressing it'.[100] Indeed this, and other letters, referred to the fact that eighteen countries had signed Charter 77 supporting the Czechoslovakian people against the Soviet Union's intervention in that country.

The *Morning Star*, with Tony Chater as its editor, also acted as a conduit for this type of criticism of the CPGB, particularly between February and July 1977.[101] This paper, which was called the *Daily Worker* until 1966, enjoyed its Fiftieth anniversary on 15 June 1980.[102] From 1977 onwards, it and Tony Chater led the so-called Stalinist backlash to the Eurocommunism that was beginning to dominate the CPGB. However, there was also criticism of the Party from Sid French, full-time secretary of the Surrey district of the CPGB. French felt that the Party was wasting its opportunities by attempting to become the fourth party of British politics[103] and was wrong in condemning the Soviet Union. He had already revealed his credentials in this respect in 1967 when during the discussions connected with the redrafting of *The British Road to Socialism*, he had written: 'We are seen to be equivocating in our attitude to the world communist movement and concerned to be disassociating ourselves from the Russians to the point of absurdity.'[104] Ten years later with the arrival of Eurocommunism in 1977, he was determined to challenge the new leadership at the

Congress. However, in the event on 17 July he and his supporters left the Party and formed the New Communist Party. About 700 CPGB members joined it, mainly from Surrey and Sussex but with some from Yorkshire and Lancashire.[105] This meant that the new version of *The British Road to Socialism* was passed at the 1977 congress with little opposition.

By this stage, however, the CPGB was declining rapidly. In May 1978 *Comment* noted that 'Between the 34th and 35th Congresses our membership fell from 28,501 to 25,293'.[106] 'We have to date issued only 21,145 members with their 1978 cards and the position of the YCL is even more serious with only 1,942 cards issued.'[107] Letters to its columns expressed alarm at the decline of membership, one noting 'The harsh reality is that we are suffering from a loss of 7,000 members in 4 years, almost the same as at the time of the Hungarian events'.[108] Thus membership fell by about a quarter in the mid-1970s, and trade union leaders such as Jimmy Reid left the Party. Even more alarming was the fact that this had occurred against a background of bitter industrial unrest, which had brought down Edward Heath's Conservative government in 1974, and the rising conflict that had occurred in reaction to the 'social contract' and the spending cuts of the Labour government of 1974–9. This was also a period which saw the growth of the Bennite Left – supporters of Tony Benn – and the demand for the greater accountability of MPs. Indeed, there were moves in the early 1980s to force the Labour leadership to accept democratic reforms within the party, such as the mandatory reselection contests for MPs, events which almost led to Tony Benn being elected as deputy leader of the Labour Party in 1981.

Why, given these developments within the Labour Party and the wider labour movement, had the CPGB lost members? There may be two reasons. Firstly, labour politics elsewhere were rather more lively and attractive. Secondly, it may be that some members were alarmed and disillusioned at the increasing rightward drift within the Party, whose 1977/8 version of *The British Road to Socialism* had declared of a future Labour government that 'It would not be a socialist government carrying out a socialist revolution, but one which, in close relationship with the mass struggle outside Parliament, would begin to carry out a major democratic transformation of British society'.[109] In other words, there was to be class collaboration to establish a 'broad democratic alliance': 'There is therefore an objective basis for an alliance between the working class and many in those sections of the capitalist class against the main enemy – the big British and international capitalists.'[110] In effect the CPGB appeared to be a smaller version of the non-revolutionary Bennite Left and it may have been that the Bennite Left operating within the Labour Party proved a stronger pole of attraction. In the meantime the Party was splitting.

The CPGB leadership had responded quickly to the formation of the New Communist Party. A letter from Reuben Falber to the EC on 18 July 1977 informed it of the breakaway, indicating that the rumours of a split had now become reality and that two of the five members of the Surrey committee remaining in the Party were intent upon organizing an aggregate meeting the coming weekend 'to re-constitute our organization in Surrey'.[111]

The 'Eurocommunist' approach gathered pace within the Party because of the disillusionment with the Soviet model of communism and with the move from an industrial base to the Party to one increasingly dominated by intellectuals who had come through the student movement. Not surprisingly, showing a haughty disregard for the working class, Martin Jacques commented that 'without the left intellectuals, the labour movement cannot emerge as a leading force'. The domination by left-wing academics was particularly evident with the holding of a Communist University in 1979. With up to 280 speakers attempting to broaden the appeal of the Party, Sue Slipman suggested to the EC in March 1979 that industrial action, a feature of old communist practices, was isolating workers from each other: 'The building of the Broad Democratic Alliance is the mechanics for democratic political change. . . . At the moment we are tail-ending those involved in wage struggle, unable to intervene in a process which may be politically disastrous.'[112] The point was that the anti-capitalist alliances and strikes were leading the workers into conflict with their political allies in the Labour Party. In effect, the Eurocommunists within the Party were attempting to abandon completely the class approach to politics. No longer was the Party geared to becoming the mass party of the working class which it had adopted as its goal at its founding convention in 1920. Only the old Stalinists clung to the 1920 goal, still orienting themselves towards the organized working class.

At the EC of March 1979, Mick Costello, the Industrial Organizer, presented a report suggesting that Communist representatives were in the highest ranks of the TUC, on the General Council, and noting the existence of publications such as *Broad Left*: 'The broad left is an essential ingredient in the fight for the implementation of left policies.' Nevertheless, he admitted that the neglect of workplace organization was responsible for the failure of Party campaigning as a whole – there had been a workplace conference in 1967 but no further conferences until 1976. This was not entirely accurate since the Party had been involved in protesting against the Industrial Relations Act of 1971, had fought for the release of the five dockers who had been imprisoned because of the legislation and had revived the Liaison Committee for the Defence of Trade Unions. It had fought with others (successfully, as it emerged) to ensure that the Upper Clyde Shipbuilders, which was threatened with closure, would continue to receive government help. It had also worked through Mick McGahey to support the successful national miners' strike in 1972.

Faced with the Costello report and others of a similar nature, the Party began to renew its efforts to widen the appeal of its policies. There was further discussion on democracy within the Party and an Inner Party Democracy report was produced in

October 1979, calling for a re-examination of the Party structure which was still based upon democratic centralism.[113] This renewed discussion suggested the need for more self-criticism, the importance of the vitality of branch life, and the need for a subcommittee to be formed in order to update the organization and modify the democratic centralist approach of the Party.

The issue was taken further in 1980 in a 46-page document which presented this 'Broad Left' approach. It suggested that democratic centralism, which 'combined the democratic participation of the membership in centralized leadership capable of directing the entire Party', was what *The British Road to Socialism* was about and was justified. Democratic centralism allowed for the election of all leading committees and for the higher committee to impose its will upon the lower committees, as long as this was not in conflict with the wish of the Congress. Lower committees were, however, encouraged to express their views. This report restated the rules of the Party and reiterated the right of some to hold opinions contrary to those of the Party but felt that proper discussions within the Party should eliminate factionalism. It suggested that the higher committee should encourage and elevate the role of lower committees and implement the constant review of the work of the full-time workers within the Party. What this meant was that the report wished to make democratic centralism more responsive to the needs of Party members in the hope of avoiding future damaging splits.

Unfortunately, the report's objective of greater discussions to root out factionalism did not work. Instead, the CPGB rules and democratic centralism were used by the Eurocommunists in the 1980s to root out the opposition of the old Stalinist and pro-Moscow type of communists, much as the latter had rooted out the dissidents in the 1950s.

The tensions between the two sides began to mount in 1980. At the very moment when there were discussions about Inner Party Democracy, there was an internal policy review in which, in a clear reference to Russian intervention in Afghanistan, it was stated that 'The battle for peaceful co-existence and for the application of the principle of non-interference in the internal affairs of other countries is a base class position.'[114] Later in the document there was an explicit reference to the EC objecting to Soviet intervention in Afghanistan.[115] This was at a time when the Party was no longer receiving secret financial contributions from Moscow and when its financial position was becoming increasingly embarrassing. Indeed, the situation worsened year on year. Income in 1979 was £165,299 and expenditure £198,468, leaving a deficit of £33,169. This compared badly with 1978, when income had been £189,726 and the expenditure £166,877, leaving a surplus of £22,849.[116]

The bitter 'Stalinist *v* Eurocommunist' debate of the 1980s thus began against a background of a Party whose membership had fallen to 21,145 in 1978, and whose finances were in a poor condition.[117] Such conflict could only be disastrous for the Party in both the short and the long run.

'Stalinists' *v* Eurocommunists in the 1980s

Edmund and Ruth Frow, Party members and labour historians, produced a pamphlet shortly before Edmund's death in 1997 entitled *The Liquidation of the Communist Party of Great Britain*.[118] Their main contention was that the CPGB was eventually liquidated because the leadership of the Party colluded with *Marxism Today* in the 1980s to abandon scientific socialism, as outlined by Karl Marx and Frederick Engels in *The Communist Manifesto*. The abandonment of revolutionary Marxism:

> was promoted in the pages of *Marxism Today* under Martin Jacques' editorship. Non-Party academics and journalists were invited to contribute. Their main line of attack was on the decline of the working class, the autonomy of the State and the need for Labour Party members to distance themselves from their traditional basis. The article which made the position abundantly clear was a vicious attack on shop stewards by Tony Lane in a September, 1982 issue.[119]

In the Tony Lane article the shop stewards were portrayed not as hard-working men who were vulnerable to victimization because of their activities but as foremen and managers in waiting. Lane wrote:

> Here we are simply observing the creation of a new working-class élite which has the opportunity (and too often takes it) of sharing in the expense accounts syndrome: the franchise of perks and fiddles which has often been widened.
>
> Shop stewards and full-time officers have had other opportunities. Some stewards have used their position as a stepping stone to promotion to charge-hand and foreman. A favoured few, usually convenors and full-time officers, have gone on to become personnel managers and even industrial relations directors. Such routes of progression, to say the very least, induce a mixture of cynicism and resentment among the rank and file. Other stewards have simply used the role as a means of an easy life, an opportunity to get off the job and out of the plant with spurious excuses of 'union business'.[120]

To their criticism the Frows added a concern about the security services: they believed that Harry Newton, a Communist who was an agent of MI5, and many others were operating to undermine the unity and principles of the CPGB. This had led to false accusations that there was a red plot to encourage strike activity and that the 'liquidators' had, in a deliberate move, acted to expel in a most undemocratic and dictatorial manner many of those members who still believed in Marxist-Leninist ideas. The end product of this was that 'At the 43rd Congress of the CPGB held in November 1991, the Eurocommunist majority formed the Democratic Left which abandoned the theoretical basis and principles on which the CPGB had been formed. It became a loose, amorphous organisation functioning as a pressure group.'[121] The basic story that the Frows presented was, of course, correct, although it was in fact much more complex than they suggested, and it is clear that they were looking at developments with the passion of those who clung to the old party views and were dubbed, inaccurately, 'Stalinists' by their opponents. Also, they did not recognize that the Popular Front of 1935 had effectively abandoned Marxism–Leninism as a revolutionary tool and that *The British Road to Socialism* had re-emphasized this in 1951.

The fact is that the continued decline of the CPGB's membership allowed for the ascendancy of other groups, often referred to as Eurocommunist, who suggested that there was not one model, the Soviet model, for communism but several different ones according to local circumstances. Building upon the ground prepared by E.P. Thompson in the 1950s and European communist parties in the 1970s, Eurocommunism began to emerge most effectively in Britain in the late 1970s and early 1980s.

This development was not welcomed by the *Morning Star*, which remained strongly pro-Soviet. It therefore came under the scrutiny of a critical Eurocommunist-dominated Party leadership which wished to control its views. The *Morning Star* was run by a cooperative society registered as the People's Printing Press Society (PPPS), which had been formed in 1946 and included CPGB representatives. Glimpses of the tensions between the Party and paper could be seen in the late 1970s. Both the *Morning Star* and the PPPS came under severe criticism at the Party's congress in 1977 and a subcommittee was set up to examine the whole question of its content. However, revealing that the Eurocommunist influence was not yet totally dominant, the subcommittee reported that the paper was doing a good job with limited resources in the face of falling circulation. The Draft Report, written by Dave Cook, despaired of the fall in circulation and asked, 'Is the political situation and capacity of the Party such that we cannot reverse the downward trend in circulation?'[122] The report noted, however, that the CPGB and the *Morning Star* were separate units and that it would be wise for it not to be run by the King Street headquarters of the Party.[123]

This was a view challenged in 1981 by two *Morning Star* journalists who wrote to the *Guardian* suggesting that the PPPS was a 'Communist Front' and attacking the increasing Party control of the paper. On 6 February 1981, however, the *Guardian* carried a report from a CPGB spokesmen suggesting that this was not the case although its representatives at PPPS meetings might express their own, undirected, communist views to the paper. In effect, then, the Party did not own the *Morning Star* but was attempting to increase its influence through its representatives at a time when both the paper and the Party were diverging on the issue of the Soviet model for communism.

The tension between the Party leadership and the *Morning Star* became more pronounced when the former criticized the latter at the 1981 Party congress. Tony Chater, the editor of the *Morning Star*, felt betrayed by criticism to the effect that the Party believed that the *Morning Star* should become more commercial in its approach, a view which rankled with Chater who saw it as a pure labour paper and not a capitalist venture. The situation worsened in December 1981 when the *Morning Star* was critical of the EC's condemnation of the Soviet-inspired takeover of Poland and the suppression of the Solidarity movement. The *Morning Star* suggested that the Soviet actions were correct because the Polish people had forgotten their class destiny.

By this stage the conflict between the Eurocommunists and the CPGB's old Stalinist section was overt. On the Party's Political Committee, Mick Costello, the Industrial Organizer, was almost alone as a sceptic of Eurocommunism for he felt that it played down the importance of the Party's industrial role. He worked closely with Tony Chater, editor of the *Morning Star*. At the same time some members of the *Star* were Eurocommunist party loyalists, including journalists Chris Myant and Frank Chalmers. These divisions and realignments were fully exposed in August 1982 just before Tony Lane's brief article on trade unionism appeared in the September issue of *Marxism Today*.[124] As already indicated, Lane, a sociologist from Liverpool University, examined the growing isolation of the trade union movement in British society and referred to the petty corruption and expenses fiddles in which lower levels of unions officials and shop stewards sometimes indulged. This led Mick Costello to criticize Lane in an article which appeared on the front page of the *Morning Star* on 26 August 1982, claiming that the Lane article was an insult to trade unionism and a 'gross slander on the labour movement' and noting that it had been picked up by the anti-left *Daily Mirror* and was providing comfort to the class enemies of the Party. However, Willie Thompson suggests that Costello had arranged for this revelation through his journalistic contacts, a fact that Costello does not appear to have denied in subsequent correspondence.[125] Tony Lane responded by complaining about the Costello article in a letter written to the EC on 26 August, maintaining that the issue of perks and fiddles had been mentioned in a gentle way and that 'I hope it will not seem immodest if I say that I think the article in question is one of the best analytical pieces I have written and raises a host of serious questions.'[126]

When the EC of the Party met on 12 September it gave a mild rebuke to Martin Jacques, editor of *Marxism Today*,[127] for printing the Lane article without fuller consultation. However, it stated that 'the executive committee does not accept that it was a gross slander on the labour movement', while it did believe in the importance and integrity of the shop steward movement.[128] It was more critical of Chater, Costello and the *Morning Star*'s deputy editor David Whitfield for forming a cabal to attack another Party journal and to use the Party's name without reference to the EC. It was thus clear that the CPGB was dominated by the Eurocommunists and that those who opposed the dilution of 'class politics' had received a rebuff. Chater did, however, take an extended trip to Moscow, where Leonid Brezhnev was still in charge, and appears to have brokered some arrangement whereby the press in the Soviet bloc became less critical of the *Morning Star*.

The Executive Committee files contain about eighty letters expressing various concerns about this conflict. They were more or less evenly divided between those favouring Lane, Jacques and *Marxism Today* and those favouring Costello and Chater. The Hastings CPGB branch attacked Costello and asked for self-criticism within the trade union movement, and Willie Thompson expressed the view that Martin Jacques had done a good job and made *Marxism Today* 'an asset to our Party'. On the other hand, the Sheffield CPGB resented the 'Lane smear' and favoured the censure of the editorial board of *Marxism Today*, and the Newcastle City branch did not consider *Marxism Today* to be a Marxist journal.[129] Vic Allen, the famous Marxist Leeds University lecturer, wrote an article in the *Morning Star* stressing that Eurocommunism in the CPGB had gone too far in shaping foreign policy and thus welcoming Mick Costello's intervention.[130]

Relations between the increasingly Eurocommunist-dominated Party and the pro-Soviet *Morning Star* began to worsen as the PC of the Party attempted to secure Chater's removal as editor. The Party continued to work with the *Morning Star* and helped it out in its January 1983 campaign to increase its daily circulation, but relations became more difficult since Costello, according to the Frows, appears to have resigned as Industrial Organizer of the CPGB to become the Industrial Correspondent of the *Morning Star* in November 1982. According to Willie Thompson, however, Costello resigned as Industrial Organizer in November 1982 and was appointed as Industrial Correspondent of the *Morning Star* seven weeks later.[131]

As the *Morning Star*'s circulation campaign failed each side blamed the other and relations worsened still further. Gordon McLennan, the General Secretary of the Party after Gollan's departure in 1976, offered to meet Chater to resolve differences but nothing happened. The Party could not sack Chater, Costello or Whitfield from their posts on the *Morning Star* because the PPPS was a self-governing body. Nevertheless, it bitterly complained that these individuals had been appointed to the *Morning Star* without the EC being in a position to express its opinion and decided to put forward a recommended list of candidates for the forthcoming election of six representatives to the management committee in 1983.[132] The list included George Matthews, a former editor, Bert Pearce, the Welsh District Secretary, David Priscott, the Yorkshire District Secretary and, for decency's sake, Tony Chater, the errant editor. Yet matters got worse when the *Morning Star* complained in June 1983 that a 'powerful outside body' was attempting to take over the paper. It was not immediately obvious to many Party members that this meant the Party itself. Despite the offence this created the Chaterite candidates defeated the EC nominees in the AGM elections for the *Morning Star*.

The movement was now deeply divided between the Party and the *Morning Star*. The Party was supported by Eurocommunists, pragmatic traditionalists and the rank-and-file loyalists who resented Chater's action in hijacking the *Morning Star*. Chater and his supporters appealed to those on the left, including the 'Straight-Leftists', who wished to protect the Party's working-class heritage. Chater and Costello attempted to present the Eurocommunists, the Party leaders and *Marxism Today* as both anti-trade unionist and anti-working class. They claimed to represent working-class interests and to be defending the Party and movement against dangerous revisionism. It was this type of action that led Beatrix Campbell to write a letter of criticism to the *Morning Star*, which appeared in *City Limits*, and to send a copy to the Executive Committee of the Party.[133]

The Party leadership emphasized that the development of political consciousness required compromise and realignment if the historic mission of the Party, the securing of working-class power, was to be achieved. To underline this point, *Marxism Today* stressed the need for the Labour left to review its policies while the *Morning Star* contained articles admiring the achievements of the Soviet bloc. The Party continued to favour *Marxism Today* in this situation, reporting favourably upon its development and noting its increase of sales from 4,500 in 1978 to 11,500 in 1983. Indeed, Martin Jacques was praised for taking up the key political issues of the day in this monthly journal.[134]

The Straight Left faction, named after the journal *Straight Left* which appeared in 1979, also entered the debate with a 34-page pamphlet entitled *The Crisis in Our Communist Party: Cause, Effect and Cure*, allegedly written by Charlie Woods, an 83-year-old retired miner but possibly written by Fergus Nicholson or Brian Filling. It attacked the existing leadership and the *Morning Star* and called for 'a new leadership with new principles.'

The conflict of opinion between all three factions spilled into the communist press, including the monthly bulletin *Communist Focus*, where Mick Costello placed a critical article in anticipation of the Thirty-Eighth Congress, held in November 1983. Despite the serious Chaterite challenge at the congress the Executive Committee of the Party remained firmly in the hands of Eurocommunists. The Chaterites and the Straight Leftists, although antagonistic towards one another, produced a clandestine recommended list for the Executive Committee, and the Straight Leftists also produced a personalized bulletin called *Congress Truth*, which attacked both the EC and the Chaterites. In the end, the EC got congress to condemn the actions of the opposition groups. Congress also censured Chater and Whitfield and removed them, and most of their supporters, from the EC. There was also criticism of the fact that four members of the Election Preparation Committee were involved in putting forward a 'Political Alternative List'; Barry Johnson later withdrew his name from this list but

Brian Topping, Bruce Allen and Barbara O'Hare continued to assert that they had done nothing wrong.

The EC of the CPGB moved quickly to discipline and remove members who broke the rules. Its May 1984 meeting adopted two statements attacking the events of the Thirty-Eighth Congress. One, 'Factional & other Unprincipled Activity at the 38th Congress', condemned the Woods' pamphlet for factionalism and expelled him from the Party. On 17 July 1984 three of the four who had produced the 'Political Alternative List' were also expelled from the Party and Johnson was suspended for three months.[135] The Executive Committee's statement also noted that the PPPS was now facing an annual general meeting and declared that the Party was putting forward five candidates for the management committee – George Bolton, Tricia David, Ron Halverson, H. Mitchell and Chris Myant.

The disciplinary action of the EC drew widespread criticism. The East Midland district and the Carlisle branch both complained about the expulsions, the latter stating that 'The expulsions were in fact an attempt at stifling the widespread criticism within the party of the present leadership and its policies, by administrative methods.' This was seen to be an example of 'the retreat of the leadership of the party from the revolutionary Marxist-Leninist past and an open avowal of their revisionist socialist-democratic stance'.[136]

These conflicts were further fought out against the backdrop of the miners' strike of 1984/5, which produced deep industrial unrest throughout the country. During that strike *Marxism Today* publicly acknowledged that 'the Party is deeply divided and in crisis'.[137] The Party worked with support groups for the miners, yet it and *Marxism Today* were much criticized for their lukewarm attitude to industrial and class conflict, *Marxism Today* publishing only three articles on the miners' strike throughout 1984 and 1985. Indeed, the Party's condemnation of Arthur Scargill's tactics as the defeat of the miners became imminent,[138] was seen by some critics as evidence of the lack of support for the miners by the Eurocommunists. The *Morning Star*, on the other hand, supported the miners so strongly that Scargill commented, 'The *Morning Star* is guilty of one act, it supports working class politics and socialism'.[139] The divisions within the Party would simply not go away. The EC put forward candidates for election to the PPPS management committee in opposition to the Chater-supported candidate and called for the removal of Chater and Whitfield at the 1984 AGM. This AGM was scarred with conflict and when the votes were counted only two Party candidates – George Bolton (Mick McGahey's vice-president in the Scottish NUM) and Chris Myant – were returned.

The Chaterites then went on the offensive and attempted to work within the Party districts in an attempt to oust the Eurocommunists. They won some support, most obviously in London where the Chaterites and Straight Left presence was substantial.

But in November 1984 the London Secretary, Bill Dunn, died and the EC moved to appoint Ian McKay, the National Organizer, as Acting Secretary. He used previous allegations against the Hackney branch to forbid the London District Congress on 24 November 1984 to elect a new district committee on the grounds that there were at least ten delegates whose representation was questionable. When the Chaterites refused to accept the ruling, congress co-chairman McLennan declared the congress closed and walked out, accompanied by the loyal and the Straight Left delegates. However, the congress continued with Hicks in the chair.[140]

The action of the Chaterites, particularly in continuing the London District Congress, allowed the Party to discipline these members for breaking the rules. The result was that twenty-two of those who participated in the continued congress were summarily suspended from the Party at a Special Executive Committee meeting on 30 November 1984.[141] The Party also issued from this meeting a statement to *Unite the Party for the British Road: Defeat the Factionalists*.

The London leaders issued collective statements and refused to follow the Party line: the CPGB reacted by sacking the full-time organizers of the London district, co-opting a provisional London district of its own choosing and checking the membership returns of branches in places where there was opposition. At its January meeting in 1985 the EC expelled, along with Chater and Whitfield, the four most defiant of the London twenty-two (Mike Hicks, Tom Durkin, Roger Trask and Ian Beavis), continued the suspension of six others and barred the remainder from Party office. The EC also took control of the meetings of the north-west district committee, where it was alleged that there had been difficulties associated with the fact that the Party's recommended list of candidates had been largely ignored in the elections for the new district committee. Suspecting factional activity the EC appointed Gerry Pocock and Dave Priscott to attend the district committee meetings and to report on their proceedings to the EC.[142] In the face of stubborn resistance from the north-west district committee the EC of the CPGB dissolved it in July 1985 and imposed a provisional committee made up of its own candidates. Confident that it now had control, the EC organized a Special National Congress in May 1985.

Meanwhile, the Party demanded that the PPPS call a special general meeting to discuss the actions of Chater and Whitfield. Initially, Chater managed to stave off this effort. However, the EC moved stealthily to expel those who openly protested against the further dilution of Marxist-Leninist ideas and retained a belief in the dictatorship of the working classes. Indeed, from January 1985 the Party circulated the periodical *Focus*, which condemned such ideas, free to every member as part of its campaign of expulsions.

The London expulsions attracted most attention and the Party's Special Congress in May 1985 was organized in such a way as to give the 'right revisionists', or Eurocommunists, control. Indeed, Brent branch with 104 members and Clapham with 107, both active centres of opposition to the EC of the Party, were allowed to send only one delegate each while the more supportive Lewisham East, with forty-five members, was also allocated one member.[143] Monty Goldman, who had already been expelled by the Party, reflected: 'It means that the Congress is being packed by Executive delegates elected by the gerrymandering of the selection process.'[144] The result was that at the Congress there was a two to one majority in favour of the Eurocommunists. The Congress thus rejected the appeals of expelled London members, including the editor of the *Morning Star*, and endorsed the expulsions that had taken place in both London and the north-west. The Congress also elected a forty-five-strong Executive Committee that was formed largely of 'right revisionists'/Eurocommunists.[145]

In the north-west, the Party's actions went further. In November 1985 it set up a North-West Provisional Committee of twenty-three unelected members, ten representing Manchester, eight Merseyside and five from the counties.

Membership of the Party plummeted as a result of internal dissension, falling from 20,638 in 1978 to 12,711 by 1985.[146] The London district now had only 2,142 members, a fall of more than 400 since 1983. The Yorkshire district membership fell from 1,020 to 920. Therefore, in order to revive its flagging fortunes, the Party decided to produce a new weekly, *7 Days*, with Chris Myant as editor in October 1985. The PC also discussed plans to revive the Party fortunes in December 1984, the main focus being to arrange a meeting with forty-five trade union organizations in 1985.[147]

The Party's prospects were somewhat improved by the fact that in 1985 Mikhail Gorbachev rose to power in the Soviet Union. This forced the Straight Left and the Chaterites to support *perestroika*, *glasnost* and an altogether more reformist type of communism, even if only because they were committed to the Soviet Union.

However, membership continued its inexorable decline. The fact is that by this time Communists were even less radical than the Labour Party on some policies. This is revealed in the articles by John Grahl and Bob Rawthorne (the latter was a prominent Eurocommunist and on the Board of *Marxism Today*) in which they rejected the public ownership policies of the Labour Party in the 1983 general election as too radical. Abandoning the struggle for a socialist economic system, they argued that the Labour Party had to be realistic and had to aim for minor reforms within the realms of a capitalist economy: 'It means, of course, accepting the continued importance of capitalist enterprise in our economy, but there is really not much alternative.'[148]

Given this prevailing mood among leading Eurocommunists, many members felt that there was no point continuing with the CPGB. By 1987 there were only 10,350 members and this had fallen to 7,615 by 1989. Gordon McLennan, touring the UK in 1988, said, 'The more I travel round the country the more I am convinced that unless we fight for membership of the Communist Party with greater tenacity, perception, confidence and élan than at the present, the decline in membership will continue.'[149] The PC therefore discussed the need for a fundamental realignment of the Party in February 1987. There was intense disagreement at this meeting. Dave Priscott admitted that 'the ground had shifted from under our feet'. He said, 'My own position is a very simple one. As a Party of socialist revolution we may have hard times (nothing particularly new in that) but we can survive and fight our way forward. As a Party of radical democratic left reformism there is absolutely no future at all for us; that particular slot is already over full.'[150] Indeed, both Priscott and Monty Johnstone, who agreed with Priscott, were at odds with those members of the Party who were moving towards a democratic left perspective and Priscott eventually left the editorial board of *Marxism Today* as a result of the stance he adopted.

Nina Temple, the future General Secretary, gave her views at the Political Committee meeting on 14 February 1987 via a set of notes sent because of her absence due to illness and having to look after her baby. The previous year she had informed the EC that: 'First, of course, we are a Marxist Party. Not a Party of dogmatic, fossilized quotation-based Marxism, but a Party with a tradition of the creative development of the British Marxist tradition.'[151] The five pages of notes she sent to the 1987 meeting indicated that she had moved further towards democratic reform and broad socialist alliances and away from the socialist revolution she once proclaimed; these comments were a pointer to the future. Noting that Party membership had declined rapidly, that *7 Days'* circulation was down from 10,000 to 5,800 and that municipal results had been poor, Temple admitted that the old party had never become accepted as part of the mainstream of British politics but that it had an identity and militancy which made it attractive to British socialists. Indeed, she stated that:

In recent years we have embraced a wider political agenda, feminism, anti-racism, alliance politics, and largely through the success of *Marxism Today* have established ourselves as relevant to the thinking of the realigned left. But these developments have coincided with our glaring weakness in membership, electoral activity, trade unions, youth, & loss of *Star* which have greatly hindered our ability to conduct struggle.

She felt that the Party had to go forward with this fundamental realignment of its political orientation, particularly on issues such as feminism and anti-rascism, which it had recently rejected. Apparently, the recent political distractions and the need for greater accountability were the reasons for the Party's decline. In order to develop the Party she felt that there had to be vision and identity. A relevance to British politics had to be developed as well as an ability to affect events and develop an attractive Party life. She also listed a number of her personal interests and concerns, and emphasized the need for the leadership to work more closely together.[152] Thus even within the PC of the Party, a Party which had lost many of its pro-Soviet Union supporters, there remained divisions between those demanding socialist revolution and those who merely wanted radical democratic reform. Temple, a rising figure in the Party, was clearly veering to radical democratic reform and alliances with other labour and socialist groups.

The two main concerns at this stage were winning members and responding to the challenge of Thatcherism. The former could be seen in the moves to strengthen CPGB organization within student bodies, where the Party still had 508 members in March 1987.[153] The latter was evident in the Party's increasing hope that the Labour Party would replace the Tory government.

Outside the Party there were a number of Marxist groups who experienced some success in the 1980s. The most obvious example was the Militant Tendency which led the struggle of Liverpool City Council against ratecapping in 1984/5 and got three of its members elected as Labour MPs in the 1987 general elections – Pat Wall, Terry Fields and Dave Nellist.[154]

In contrast to the success of groups such as Militant, the membership of the CPGB continued to decline. Increasingly alarmed at this situation, the Party decided to hold a Special Emergency Executive Committee Meeting on 28 June 1987 to discuss the future of communism in Britain and there were many contributions to this debate. In particular, Nina Temple, following up her advice to the PC, suggested that the Party was still committed to removing social inequalities through *The British Road to Socialism* and the transformation of Parliament, and further stressed the importance of *Marxism Today* in countering and analysing Thatcherism even as the Party was 'consumed with inner divisions and disciplinary questions'.[155] There was also much discussion about the Broad Democratic Alliance, and the need to work with the Campaign for Nuclear Disarmament and similar protest organizations. At the same meeting Dave Cook, a committed reformer, suggested that even given the changes to *The British Road to Socialism* in 1977/8 it was now in need of an update. Others demanded more unity within the left.

There were no real fundamental differences of opinion at this meeting for it was recognized that the dominating view was Eurocommunism which was no longer sufficient. The only real differences were ones of emphasis. Dave Cook attacked the EC, dominated by Eurocommunists since 1977, for not allowing 'a more thoroughgoing transformation of the Party'. David Priscott, on the other hand, had modified his position over the previous six months and was less critical of the Eurocommunist-dominated EC, suggesting that 'our Party can learn from other CPs but for us there are no models, neither Socialist nor Euro-communist'. With the failure of Eurocommunism in Spain and other Western European countries, the term was in fact becoming redundant in the late 1980s. Pragmatism and broad-based socialism became the order of the day and this is what emerged from the Special Meeting. The Party decided that *The British Road to Socialism* would be redrafted and that henceforth the CPGB's approach would be to seek new alliances with the Greens, anti-racist bodies and students. The Party remained committed to democratic centralism but stressed the need for more democratic participation by the membership in Party life and an elected central leadership capable of directing the entire organization. These measures did not impress the external opponents of the leadership.

The *Morning Star* continued to react against the Party's approach and suggested that the 'Communist Party is being hijacked by a right-wing revisionist faction' which aimed to destroy 'the Marxist basis and class approach of the Communist Party'.[156] The Communist Campaign Group was also formed at this time to oppose revisionism within the Party and became particularly active in London, Brent being one of its major centres.[157] When the *Morning Star* kept reporting upon how the campaign group was breaching CPGB rules, the Party leadership became concerned and acted to meet and remove the challenge.[158]

In April 1988, many of those expelled in the CPGB reaction against the Communist Campaign Group formed the Communist Party of Britain as a mirror image of the Communist Party of Great Britain that had operated before the rise of Eurocommunism. It held its first Congress in November 1989 when it updated *The British Road to Socialism*, an admission of the fact that even this organization was much less radical than the CPGB of the 1930s and very much in line with the CPGB of the 1950s and 1960s.

Ignoring such opposition the CPGB meandered onwards towards political oblivion. It had lost much of its trade union support to Chater and the *Morning Star* faction and it is to be remembered that among those who left was Ken Gill, a trade union general secretary, a member of the TUC General Council and chair at the 1984 TUC Conference. Such a loss, and similar losses, could not be recovered easily. The CPGB failed in municipal elections, with the number of councillors coming down to single figures by the mid-1980s. In parliamentary politics the situation was even worse. Indeed, in March 1983 the Party put forward a candidate against Labour's Peter Tatchell at the Bermondsey by-election and received fewer votes than the Official Monster Raving Loony candidate.

In most respects, with perhaps the exception of the rising fortunes of *Marxism Today*, the Party faced one disaster after another in the 1980s. Indeed, *Marxism Today*'s sales success was something of a mixed blessing because its articles demolished many of the political icons of the CPGB and the labour movement. It attacked some of the institutions of trade unionism and undoubtedly lost the Party support. Increasingly it was read by non-communists, rather than communists, and by the time of the 1987 general election its broad and irreverent approach led it to suggest the need for an anti-Tory electoral pact – almost a popular front against Toryism. It became so prone to compromise that it accepted the importance of the European Economic Community for Britain and stressed that a socialist Britain could not cut contacts with capitalist nations. These moves by *Marxism Today*, which pushed the Party even further towards the right, won the day and were expressed through the redrafted version of *The British Road to Socialism* that became *Manifesto for New Times* at the November 1989 Congress. This *Manifesto* recognized the end of old forms of industrial and class conflict, addressed issues such as feminism, gay and green politics, and anticipated a remodelling of the Party.[159] However, the 1989 congress was a bad-tempered affair. Two resolutions were passed condemning *Marxism Today*, and the *Manifesto for New Times* was only passed by a narrow vote.

The 1989 congress also saw a change of Party leader. All tendencies within the Party had potential leadership candidates to replace Gordon McLennan. There was Ian McKay, the National Organizer, a Scot who embodied many of the old party virtues. Those in *Marxism Today* favoured Martin Jacques, its editor, and former Eurocommunists supported Nina Temple. Party members throughout the country were asked for their advice but Temple, thirty-three years of age, became General Secretary by default when the other two candidates elected to remain in their existing posts.

The End of the CPGB and the Forty-Third Congress, November 1991

McLennan handed over the general secretaryship of the Party to Temple in mid-January 1990.[160] He also handed over a Party of 7,625 members, much reduced from the 27,000 or so members he inherited in 1976. It was a Party which had shed many of the old Stalinist and pro-Soviet supporters but was further divided into two main tendencies. On the one hand, there were the *Marxism Today* supporters who were pragmatic, oriented towards 'consumerism', willing to explore a variety of political actions, and prepared to work alongside capitalism. On the other, there was the more inchoate tendency towards adopting a politically moralistic stand on such issues as Green politics, feminism and anti-racialism. The leading figures here were Nina Temple, formerly YCL National Secretary and Communist Party Press and Publicity Officer and now General Secretary, and London District Secretary Dave Green. Temple, in fact, was committed to a process of renewal and reconstruction within the Party aimed at transforming the landscape of left politics by reorganizing the Party and developing left alliances. Her views did not go quite as far as those of Tony McNally, though. He envisaged an eco-socialist movement based upon *Marxism Today*, *Manifesto for New Times*, the centrality of people's power, and the promotion of a new movement: it would be a group of associations rather than a Party, committed to uniting socialist and Green groupings in an alliance based upon 'ecologically sustainable development at home, democratized, decentralised, pluralist, non violent, multi-racial with a humanitarian internationalism'.[161]

Events in Eastern Europe, where neo-Stalinist régimes were collapsing in the face of demands for more democratic systems, began to challenge the Party to consider further its future role, especially as it had opposed popular domestic movements such as the mass campaign of non-payment organized by the All Britain Anti-Poll Tax Federation. The chairman of the Anti-Poll Tax Federation was Tommy Sheridan, a Glasgow councillor of Scottish Militant Labour, who played a leading role in the organization of the famous Trafalgar Square demonstration on 31 March 1991 of 150,000–200,000 people that led Thatcher eventually to abandon the charge. The CPGB could claim no success in this popular victory.

As a result of the poll tax, Eastern Europe and other circumstances, the EC threw open the debate about the Party's future at its January 1990 meeting. Three lines of argument were pursued. The old Eurocommunists, now gravitating towards the moralist standpoint of Nina Temple, wanted the Party to disband and its assets to go to a very different type of party based upon a more democratic approach and associated with broad left issues; this associationist line was supported by Martin Jacques and, ironically, the *Morning Star*. The traditionalists wished for any new organization to retain the name 'Communist' in its title, and some semblance of older values. The Straight Left, which had avoided separating from the Party as the Chaterites had done and had built up a base of support in London, attacked Stalinism even as communism was collapsing in Eastern Europe; its supporters saw no need for far-reaching changes.

In order to reconcile these three positions Temple suggested that there was a need to transform the Party while at the same time setting up a left-wing association to broaden the appeal of communism. However, the Party lacked the resources for this 'twin track' solution. Throughout the following year the traditionalists and Straight Leftists supported the idea of transforming the CPGB while keeping the basic beliefs of the past. However, Martin Jacques and the associationists wished simply to create a new and different organization, as they, Temple and others had proposed.[162] In this situation many members began to call for a special meeting to discuss the Party's future[163] and it was agreed that there would be a Special Congress in 1991. In the meantime, the crisis within the Party got even worse. Membership declined further and prominent activists, including the leading Welsh historian Hywel Francis, left. At the September 1990 Executive Committee it was also announced that John Peck, a long-time member of the Party and Eurocommunist who had built up a base of support in Nottingham, had left to join the Green Party.[164] The CPGB was simply falling apart. At the September EC meeting the largest single block of votes (thirteen) favoured dissolution but Nina Temple combined with the 'twin track' supporters and advocated both the reorganization of the Party and broad alliances – they defeated the dissolutionists with nineteen votes.

In this crisis the Special Congress, originally called for the spring of 1991, was brought forward to December 1990. It was now becoming clear that support for transformation was rapidly overtaking the idea of association. The key to Nina Temple getting her way on her 'twin track' proposal was the powerful Scottish section of the Party. She needed the Scots to agree that the 'association' proposal alone (which would end the Party) would not be accepted and that the 'twin track' proposal would be accepted with vague concessions to the 'association' proposal. It was also stressed that the restructured Party would be a federal organization with virtually complete autonomy for the Scottish and Welsh elements.

The congress of December 1990 convened in the TUC premises in Great Russell Street, to the accompaniment of shouting and chanting by Stalinists outside the building. It was here that the decision was taken to change the structure and politics of the Party, along the lines recommended by *Marxism Today*. Marxism–Leninism was finally rejected and so was the recommended list system for selecting candidates for the Executive Committee leaving the delegates free to decide matters at the next congress, including the name of the new party from a list of twenty-one different titles including the British Communist Federation, the Party of Democratic Socialism, the British Socialist Party and the Democratic Communist Party of Great Britain. There was also the possibility of keeping the existing name. A handful of Straight Leftists got elected to the new Executive Committee at the end of the congress but the majority were moderate traditionalists and old Eurocommunists willing to accept the compromise arrangements. In the wake of this meeting many pure 'association' advocates left the Party, including Brenda Kirsch, former Assistant Editor of *7 Days*, Sion Barrow, the editor of its more modest replacement, *Changes*, and Dave Green, the London District Secretary. Some had been members of the previous EC.

The new executive circulated its proposals for the 'transformed party' in March 1991. They amounted to little more than the rejected proposals of the previous year and it was suggested that the new party or organization – to be known as the Democratic Left – would be formed but left the decision up to the November 1991 Congress.

On 23 May 1991 the draft constitution for the new organization was circulated by the CPGB, from 6–9 Cynthia Street, London. It declared that the Party had decided to 'drop Marxism–Leninism and embrace a politics drawing from creative Marxism, feminism, anti-racism, ecology and other progressive traditions, and to replace democratic centralism with an open and democratic structure, involving the move towards federalism'.[165] It stated that its aim was:

to achieve a society in which people are free from oppression based on gender, race, age, sexuality and disability. We are committed to the transformation of society which will put power in the hands of people, enhancing their lives both on an individual and collective basis. Our ultimate goal is that of a classless society where all peoples are free and equal.

The old Marxist-Leninist views of class conflict, the dictatorship of the proletariat as an interim measure along the way to full communism, and ideas of democratic centralism were going to be swept away.

In September 1991 the Political Committee suggested the need for a sustained campaign to launch the Democratic Left and debated the procedures for setting up the Democratic Left after the Congress.[166] There were some objections to the title though, most obviously from David Priscott from Leeds, who suggested that the new name should be Democratic Socialist.[167]

At the Forty-Third Congress of the CPGB in November 1991, the old Euro-communist majority formed the Democratic Left. The theoretical base and principles of the CPGB were now abandoned. By a majority of about 2 to 1 it was decided to dismantle the existing Party structure and to replace it with a loosely organized federal body. About a third of the 220 delegates fought against the changes and applauded the recently revealed evidence that Moscow had provided money to the Party between 1957 and 1979. Voting on the name and rule book indicated that 72 delegates wanted the old CPGB rule book, 135 the new draft and 3 abstained. Bill Laughton from Glasgow, speaking in favour of the old constitution, argued that the Democratic Left added up to having 'an ideology you make up for yourself'. He wanted a Marxist party with 'communist ideological certainty to it'. Kate Hudson, of London, suggested that Democratic Left offered 'a travesty of effective organizational structure'. Steve Howell, of Sheffield, felt that the Democratic Left draft was full of 'bland platitudes that David Owen would be able to accept'. Pat Turnbull pointed out that 21 out of 108 branches who made returns had favoured the old and not the new draft. Yet, despite such hostility, the majority favoured the new pluralistic policies that had emerged.[168] The historic moment had arrived when the Communist Party of Great Britain had come to the end of its existence after just over seventy years. The Democratic Left was formed.

Conclusion

The last forty years of the Party's history had been years of decline. The CPGB had lost out in the Cold War atmosphere of the 1940s and 1950s. It had been slow to accept the implications of the Twentieth Congress of the CPSU in 1956 and lost support as many of its members demanded a more democratic and representative structure. However, the Party still retained some vestige of influence and was still attracted to the Soviet system. By the 1970s and the 1980s the situation had changed dramatically. The Party leadership had lurched to the right and was dominated increasingly by the Eurocommunists, who rejected the old traditions based upon support for the Soviet Union. As a result of the onslaught of Thatcherism, it was hurtling towards a broader-based type of socialism that owed less and less to the principles of Marxism and Leninism. This had seemed a necessary sacrifice for the CPGB leadership, which noted that the character of British society had changed, with the traditional industrial working class declining in number and influence at a time of increasing political diversification. In effect, the change from the CPGB to the Democratic Left, whether for good or ill, was a recognition that changes had occurred and that old-style Stalinism was now an anachronism that could not be saved even by the more moderate parliamentary approach towards achieving communism outlined in the various versions of *The British Road to Socialism*. In this respect Nina Temple's opening speech to the Forty-Third Congress seem apposite:

We must recognize that the era of Communist Parties is at an end. Our own party cannot be revived by nostalgia, discredited ideologies, rosy views of history or unaccountable command structures. Only an honest appraisal and a rupture with past undemocratic practices can take the best of our tradition forward with integrity.[169]

The Democratic Left, therefore, took up the mantle of the now defunct CPGB.

The Democratic Left has attracted little interest from the media and the public since it was formed in 1991. However, the old Marxist traditions and 'broad-based socialism' still survive. In Scotland the Marxist left and broad-based socialist tradition have come together in the Scottish Socialist Party, made up of Scottish Militant Labour and the Communist Party of Scotland, among others. In the elections to the new Scottish Parliament in May 1999 Tommy Sheridan was elected for the Scottish Socialist Party.

At the time of writing, in England and Wales, also, the Marxist/socialist left is coming together in socialist alliances that have resulted in electoral victories on a local scale, particularly the success of Dave Nellist, the ex-Militant MP, in May 1998. Within the trade unions too the Marxist/socialist left is coming together to provide an alternative to the policies of New Labour. Indeed, in the UNISON – public sector union – election for General Secretary in 1996, the Broad Left candidate Roger Bannister came second to Rodney Bickerstaffe with over 60,000 members supporting him, or 20 per cent of the vote. In May 1998, David Rix of the Socialist Labour Party, whose leader Arthur Scargill spent his youth in the CPGB, was elected General Secretary of the Amalgamated Society of Locomotive Engineers and Firemen.

There are signs that the Marxist-Leninist tradition and communism are not dead in Britain. Nevertheless, there is a long way to go before a meaningful and viable movement emerges again. At the present, like the CPGB for much of its history, Marxism is very marginal to British politics.

Epilogue and Conclusion

A news sheet produced by Kevin Morgan reported upon the Democratic Left Party Conference of 14 December 1996.[1] It referred to Steve Munby, the author of *Argument Towards a Democratic Left*, who was attempting to encourage the movement towards a more programmatic position. Munby's general argument was that communists in the 1980s must bear the responsibility for encouraging the rise of sectarianism within the Labour Party around Tony Benn – a development seen as an important factor in the split of the Social Democratic Party from the Labour Party in 1981 and Labour's crushing 1983 general election defeat. The general message was that the Democratic Left had to have programmes with a broad appeal and had to avoid the sectarianism of the past. This was a message that the CPGB would have appreciated since its past sectarianism had certainly contributed to its own failures in the twentieth century. Such sectarianism had continued among former members after the CPGB's dissolution in 1991 – the Scottish dissidents published their own bulletin entitled *Alert Scotland* and the Straight Leftists fragmented the new party. Yet sectarianism is just one of a number of possible explanations for the failure of Marxism in Britain and not necessarily the prime one, for the causes of that sectarianism have also to be explained. Any examination of the CPGB's failures must take into account the changing economic, social and political situation of Britain in the twentieth century, the collapse of communism in Eastern Europe and the Soviet Union and the opposition of the Labour Party and the trade unions.

Many historians have attempted to explain why people joined the CPGB. Some, such as Martin Crick, have seen it as a natural development of an association with Marxism while others, such as Walter Kendall, have referred to the appeal and influence of Lenin. Perhaps they were attracted by the prospect that the social order could be changed and the belief that the triumph of socialism over capitalism was inevitable. However, the real question is not why did people join but why did they not join?

There are some obvious explanations, partial though they may be. It is clear that the CPGB which emerged from a number of earlier Marxist bodies was never able to tap into the mainstream of British politics and remained sectarian and isolated. Indeed, these earlier Marxist bodies had often cut themselves off from the established routes to political power because of their expectation that they would be asked to lead the nation through a committee of public safety to establish a socialist society. It is equally likely that the political traditions of Britain made it difficult to carve out a niche. Hyndman's rejection of trade union influence meant that opportunities to win wider working-class support were missed at a vital moment in the 1890s and early 1900s and that this allowed the emerging Labour Party to seize the initiative. Clearly, there is much reason for speculation. However, none of these factors is sufficient explanation in its own right. Rather, it is likely that they worked together with other influences to ensure that Marxism would never be a major political force in British politics.

Certainly the economic and social climate of Britain, and the politics to which it gave rise were inhibiting to the CPGB. It was, after all, radical working men and MPs who initially supported the International Working Men's Association in London when it was formed by Marx in 1864. It was radical MPs and radical working men who initially formed the Democratic Federation in 1881. The tradition from which most of them emerged was the need to remove injustices and impediments to freedom rather than the implementation of the dictatorship of the proletariat *en route* to communism, although William Morris, Eleanor Marx, and Tom Mann all saw the need for the overthrow of capitalism. As this radical support disappeared, Marxism became just one small part of the socialist revival of the late nineteenth century. Soon overtaken by the more popular Independent Labour Party, the Social Democratic Federation sought its moment of compromise by affiliating to the Labour Representation Committee, which was formed in 1900. However, it left in 1901 although it affiliated again, as the British Socialist Party, in 1916. The decision of the SDF to leave the LRC was a fatal mistake brought about by Hyndman's sectarianism that isolated British Marxism from the Labour movement, following the failure to get the LRC to adopt a socialist clause in its constitution.

It would be difficult to see how the BSP (the former SDF) could have formed the basis of a revivified Marxist tradition had it not been for both the February and October revolutions of 1917 in Russia. It was these revolutions that gave impetus to its cause and, pressed on by the Comintern, led the BSP to push for the formation of the CPGB in 1920, and its reformation in 1921.

The problem with these developments is that the CPGB was always a small organization compared with its equivalents in Europe, where greater social upheavals, a stronger prewar Marxist tradition and greater divisions within socialist parties had occurred and led to the emergence of mass communist parties. It was thus heavily dependent upon the Soviet Union's foreign policy for its political direction and finance, perhaps to a greater degree than other communist parties. Indeed, it was financed by the Soviet Union throughout the interwar years, to the tune of £2,000 to £3,000 per month through Stockholm in the mid-1930s, and was heavily, though secretly, dependent upon the Soviet Union for finance between 1957 and 1979. Naturally, its policies were governed by Moscow with relation to Class Against Class, the United Front, the Popular Front, the Second World War and the Hungarian situation of 1956. It is true that there was much internal criticism of this relationship, that Pollitt and others often jibbed at the orders of Moscow and that the rank and file in both London and the provinces often went its own way, but in the end the Soviet line was normally accepted until at least the 1960s. Thereafter, even with the Party dependent upon Soviet money, there was more questioning of Soviet action, particularly after the invasion of Czechoslovakia in 1968. Many small Marxist groups emerged both within and outside the Party at this time but the most serious challenge was that presented by E.P. Thompson and later the Eurocommunists who doubted whether the Stalinist system, or any other for that matter, could be imposed upon Britain and sought other means to obtain influence, more broad-based and parliamentary in approach to win support for Marxism. Indeed, *The British Road to Socialism*, in all its forms, was effectively an acknowledgement of this fact.

Yet when the Party at last began to declare its independence from the Soviet Union, in the wake of the death and subsequent condemnation of Stalin, the British people were unwilling to respond. The membership of the Party declined rapidly from 56,000 in 1942 to just under 39,000 in 1950 and 4,742 in July 1991. It did not matter what was done because the Party's neglect of a broad-based socialist approach in the past had caught it up with it. The mass of the working class had been organized and won by the trade unions and through them was attached to the Labour Party, particularly through the interwar years. Even after 1951, when small nationalist parties were beginning to eat into the support of the two major political parties, the CPGB was making no inroads. Indeed, the support of some sections of the skilled working class was flowing to the Conservative Party, not the CPGB. At this point, the CPGB attempted to drop the sectarianism of the past but it was too late. Indeed, 'too little too late' would seem to sum up the history of the Party.

In the final analysis, pre-1914 Marxism in Britain had not taken advantage of the new political situation, eschewing both trade unionism and the emergent Labour Party, and the CPGB had come into existence after the realignment of British politics. The Party was never able to win a significant working-class base and was often too sectarian and too dependent upon Moscow as a result. When the collapse of the communist system in Eastern Europe and the Soviet Union occurred, the dissolving of this, now most reformist, party was inevitable. Effectively, early Marxist policies denied the CPGB more than a toehold in British politics and its adjustment to British conditions came too late. In other words, Marxist movements failed to take advantage of the opportunities that arose in the late nineteenth century, were too dependent upon the Soviet Union in the twentieth century, failed to capture the trade unions and working-class support, and were too slow to develop their own policies. In this situation, E.P. Thompson's article 'Winter Wheat in Omsk', which condemned the attempt to force the Stalinist model upon Britain through the CPGB, looks particularly apposite. Communists became 'The Lost Sheep' of British politics, as Morgan Phillips, General Secretary of the Labour Party in the 1940s and 1950s, would have us believe.[2]

The CPGB attempted to impose inappropriate policies on the British political tradition, which partly accounts for its failure to win the support of the mass of the workers who were tied into the trade unions and the Labour Party. It stood no chance of success, appearing, as it was, an anachronism in British politics once its forbears had missed its opportunities in the late nineteenth and early twentieth centuries. Nevertheless, one must acknowledge the sterling efforts made by communists such as Tom Mann, Ben Tillett, Will Thorne and Eleanor Marx in building up the unskilled unions, in the fight for independent Labour representation in Parliament, the efforts the CPGB made to defend the unemployed in the interwar years and the efforts that the rank and file, if not always the leadership, made to oppose Mosley in the 1930s. Clearly, there were some achievements to be proud of and at least the CPGB tried to improve and defend the position of the workers in British society.

BIOGRAPHICAL GLOSSARY

John Ross Campbell (1894–1969)
Campbell was a writer and socialist propagandist. He was assistant editor and then editor of the *Workers' Weekly* during the 1920s and of the *Daily Worker*, 1939 and again between 1949 and 1959. He was a member of the BSP, organizer of the Scottish Workers Committee between 1919 and 1921 and chairman of the National Workers' Committee movement between 1921 and 1922. He joined the CPGB in 1920 and served on its executive between 1923 and 1965.

Rajani Palme Dutt (1896–1974)
Dutt was one of the intellectuals of the Communist Party of Great Britain; he had gained a first class honours degree at Cambridge. He joined the CPGB in 1920, edited *Labour Monthly*, from 1921, and the *Workers' Weekly* from 1922 and, between 1936 and 1938 edited the *Daily Worker*. He was a dedicated Stalinist throughout most of his life, justifying every twist and turn of the Communist International's policy with an endless supply of quotes to justify any 'about turn'. He frequently represented the CPGB in Moscow, being present when the Seventh Congress of the Comintern (Communist International) declared in favour of a popular front against fascism in 1935. Between 1939 and 1941 he was General Secretary of the CPGB.

Frederick Engels (1820–95)
Engels was a German philosopher and collaborator with Karl Marx. Together, he and Marx, formulated the historical and dialectical materialism which formed the basis of Marxist philosophy. In 1842 he moved to Manchester where he began a lifelong involvement with the British Labour movement. His encouragement led Eleanor Marx, Marx's daughter, and William Morris to split away from the quasi-Marxist Social Democratic Federation to form the Socialist League in December 1884.

William Gallacher (1881–1965)
'Willie' Gallacher was Chairman of the Clyde Workers' Committee between 1915 and 1919, and was imprisoned four times for his political activities. He was also Communist MP for West Fife between 1935 and 1950. He remained an active Communist even after his departure from the House of Commons, often acting as chairman of the Communist Party of Great Britain until 1956 and president of the Party until 1963.

191

John Gollan (1911–77)

Gollan, who was born in Glasgow, joined the Communist Party of Great Britain in 1927 and became secretary of the Young Communist League and a member of the Central Committee of the CPGB in 1935. In 1940 he joined the Political Bureau of the CPGB and was regional secretary for Scotland until 1947. On the death of William Rust, in 1949, he became the Deputy Secretary of the Party and editor-in-chief of the *Daily Worker*. He succeeded Harry Pollitt in 1956, at a time when the now dead Stalin was being criticized by Krushchev and at the moment when the Soviet Union invaded Hungary. Subsequently, at the time of the Cuban Missile Crisis, he was active in editing *Marxism Today* and he wrote an article in this journal in 1976 which raised the issue of eurocommunism. He retired as general secretary of the Party in 1975.

Walter Hannington (1896–1966)

Hannington was National Organizer of the NUWM between 1922 and 1942, and was a communist trade union official. He was a founder member of the CPGB and served on its executive committee (Central Committee) for most of the interwar period. In 1942 he was elected National organizer for the Amalgamated Engineering Union.

Arthur Horner (1894–1968)

Horner was the first Communist to lead a major union, holding the office of President of the South Wales Miners' Federation from 1936 to 1946 and General Secretary of the National Union of Mineworkers between 1946 and 1959. A lifelong Communist, he joined the Communist Party of Great Britain in 1920, and played a leading role in the miners' rank-and-file movements up to 1936. His tendency to put trade union interests before those of the CPGB led, in the early 1930s and the early 1940, to the term 'Hornerism' being used.

Henry Mayers Hyndman (1842–1921)

Hyndman was the founder of the Social Democratic Federation in 1883, a radical body which had been originally formed as the Democratic Federation in 1881. The SDF was the first British political party to claim an adherence to Marxism. Hyndman led the SDF and its successors the Social Democratic Party and the British Socialist Party, but left the BSP in 1916 and formed the pro-war National Socialist Party. Hyndman was severely criticized by Engels and others for his social chauvinism and his inadequate grasp of Marxism.

Albert Inkpin (1884–1944)

Inkpin was Assistant Secretary of the SDF/BSP between 1907 and 1913, General Secretary of the BSP between 1913 and 1920 and General Secretary of the CPGB between 1920 and 1929. He played a prominent role in the unity negotiations that led to the founding of the

CPGB in 1920 and 1921. He served two long prison sentences, one in connection with the Incitement to Mutiny Act (1797), while CPGB General Secretary and in 1929 he was removed from his post and appointed Secretary of the Friends of the Soviet Union.

Tom Mann (1856–1941)

Mann was a member and eventual secretary of the Amalgamated Society of Engineers and a leading figure in the 'New Unionism' of the 1890s. During this time he was also a member of the SDF and the Independent Labour Party. After spending some time in Australia he returned to lead the syndicalist movement in Britain between 1909 and 1914. He was a founder member of the CPGB and played a prominent role in its ancillary organizations, being chairman of the British Bureau of the Red International of Labour Unions and Treasurer of the NUWM.

Gordon McLennan (1925–)

McLennan became General Secretary of the CPGB in 1976. He proved unable to halt the internecine conflict which accelerated the Party's disintegration in the 1980s and was replaced as Secretary by Nina Temple in January 1990.

William Morris (1834–96)

Morris was a poet, textile designer, stained-glass designer, writer and socialist propagandist. He joined the (Social) Democratic Federation in 1883 but, the following year, he left to form the Socialist League with Eleanor Marx and others who were frustrated at the leadership of Henry Mayers Hyndman. His political writings and novels condemned Victorian capitalism and outlined his vision of a utopian socialist society.

John Thomas Murphy (1888–1965)

A Roman Catholic, born in Manchester, Murphy rose to fame as the leader of the engineers in Sheffield during the First World War. Indeed, he was active in the shop stewards' movement and active in wartime strikes against dilution – the employment of women in the place of male engineers who might be sent to the front. He joined the Communist Party of Great Britain on its formation in 1920, spent much of his time in Russia in the 1920s, and was imprisoned, with other Communists, in 1925 under the 1797 Incitement to Mutiny Act. He resigned from the CPGB in 1932, joined the Socialist League and was its general secretary from 1934 until 1936.

Phil Piratin (1907–96)

Piratin became a leading member of the Communist Party of Great Britain in the 1930s, and represented the CPGB on Stepney Borough Council, London, between 1937 and 1949. He was particularly opposed to Oswald Mosley and fascism in Britain but rose to national fame when he represented the Mile End Division of Stepney as a Communist MP from 1945 to 1950.

Harry Pollitt (1890–1960)

Pollitt was General Secretary of the Communist Party of Great Britain from 1929 until ill-health forced his resignation in 1956, with a brief break between 1939 and 1941. Previously a member of the Independent Labour Party, a socialist organization committed to both municipal and parliamentary politics, and then of the British Socialist Party, he was also a leading figure in the shop stewards' movement during the First World War. He was a founding member of the Communist Party of Great Britain and one of its key industrial organizers during the 1920s. He was also a member of the three-man commission which, in 1922, advocated the reorganization of the CPGB on more Leninist and pro-active lines.

William Rust (1903–49)

Rust joined the Communist Party in 1920, becoming the first secretary of the Young Communist League. He joined the Executive Committee of the CPGB in 1927 and was a member of the Executive Committee of the Comintern (Communist International). He became the first editor of the *Daily Worker* when it was formed in 1930.

David F. Springhall (died in 1950s)

Springhall was a CPGB official and a Soviet spy. A founder member of the Party and secretary of its London District during the 1930s, he was appointed as the first political commissioner for the British battalion of the International Brigaders in December 1936. In 1942 he was sentenced to seven years imprisonment for passing military secrets on to the USSR, which led to his expulsion from the CPGB. On his release from prison he worked in China and died in Moscow sometime in the 1950s.

Nina Temple (1956–)

Temple joined the Young Communist League in 1969, later becoming its National Secretary. She then became the Party's press and publicity officer in 1982. She became General Secretary of the CPGB in January 1990 and was the first secretary of its successor, the Democratic Left.

Edward Palmer Thompson (1924–93)

Thompson was a socialist, political activist, poet, writer and historian. He is one of the most widely cited historians of the twentieth century and his most important historical works chronicled the emergence of the English working classes in the eighteenth and early nineteenth centuries. He led the opposition to Stalinism within the CPGB in 1956, along with John Saville, and resigned from the CPGB in November 1956.

Notes

The records of the Communist Party of Great Britain and many of the collections of its prominent leaders are to be found in the National Museum of Labour History, 103 Princess Street, Manchester.

Introduction

1. W. Thompson, *The Good Old Cause: British Communism 1920–1991* (London, Pluto Press, 1992), p. 218.
2. M. Crick, *The History of the Social Democratic Federation* (Keele, Ryburn Publishing, Keele University Press, 1994).
3. R.C. Challinor, *The Origins of British Bolshevism* (London, Croom Helm, 1977); W. Kendall, *The Revolutionary Movement in Britain 1900–1921* (London, Weidenfeld & Nicolson, 1969).
4. Thompson, *The Good Old Cause*, pp. 4–5; *Lenin On War and Peace: Three Articles* (Peking, Foreign Languages Press, 1970).
5. J. Callaghan, *Socialism in Britain* (Oxford, Blackwells, 1990); N. Fishman, *The British Communist Party and the Trade Unions: 1933–1945* (Aldershot, Scolar Press, 1995), last chapter; R. Stevens, 'Trades Councils in the East Midlands, 1929–1951; Trade Unionism and Politics in a "Traditionally Moderate Area"' (University of Nottingham, unpublished PhD, 1995).
6. Labour Party, *Stalin's men: about turn* (London, Labour Party, 1940), p.3.
7. J. Attfield and S. Williams, *1939: The Communist Party and the War* (London, Lawrence & Wishart, 1984), particularly pp. 54–5; Monty Johnstone, 'The CPGB, the Comintern and the War, 1939–41: Filling in the Blackspots', *Science and Society*, Special Issue on Communism, Britain and the British Empire, vol. 61, no. 1, (Spring 1997), 27–45.
8. PC/CENT/PC/02/03, Political Committee file, June 1956, E.P. Thompson, 'Winter Wheat in Omsk'.
9. K. Marx and F. Engels, *Selected Correspondence* (London, Progress Publishers, fourth edition, 1982), letters Engels to Sorge, 12 May 1894 and 10 November 1894, pp. 448–51.

Chapter I Beginnings: The Emergence of Marxism in Britain, *c.* 1894–1914

1. K. Marx, *Capital*, vol. 1 (London, Lawrence & Wishart, 1974), part 3, chapters 7–11, pp. 173–295.
2. Marx and Engels developed the concept of the dictatorship of the proletariat in response to the experience of the Paris Commune of 1871 which was crushed following France's defeat in the Franco-Prussian War. See Marx and Engels, *Selected Works in One Volume* (London, Lawrence & Wishart, 1970), pp. 258–9.
3. K. Marx, 'Critique of the Gotha Programme', in Marx and Engels, *Selected Works in One Volume*, (London, Lawrence & Wishart, 1973), p. 321.
4. S. Rigby, *Marxism and History: A Critical Introduction* (Manchester, Manchester University Press, 1987); D. McLellan, *Marx before Marxism* (London, Macmillan Papermac, second edition, 1980).

195

5. Marx and Engels, *Selected Correspondence*, letters 194, 215, 245, 256, 257, 258 deal with issues such as the sectarianism, pettiness and unreliability of the SDF.

6. Ibid., letter 221 from Engels to Sorge, 7 December 1889, on how a genuine Marxist (Eleanor Marx) had intervened in the gasworkers' struggle in 1889; letter 223 Engels to Schluter, 11 January 1890, on the type of craft unions not favoured by Marx and Engels and the type they supported.

7. McLellan, *Marx before Marxism*, pp. 163–4.

8. K. Marx, 'The Inaugural Address and Provisional Rules of the International Working Men's Association' (1864) in M. Kamenka (ed.), *The Portable Karl Marx* (London, Penguin, 1983), p. 355.

9. K. Marx and F. Engels, 'The Alleged Splits in the International', in *The First International and After* (London, Pelican Library, Penguin Books, 1974 edition), edited by David Fernbach, pp. 272–314.

10. R. Harrison, *Before the Socialists: Studies in Labour and Politics 1861–1881* (London, Routledge & Kegan Paul, 1965).

11. Ibid., p. 233.

12. K. Marx, 'The Civil War in France. Address of the General Council of the International Working Men's Association' (1871) and from the first draft of 'The Civil War in France', in Kamenka, *The Portable Karl Marx*, pp. 509–32.

13. Letter from Marx to Kugelmann, 12 April 1871, in F. Mehring, *Karl Marx: the Story of His Life* (University of Michigan, Ann Arbor Paperbacks, second printing, 1969), p. 448.

14. Mehring, *Karl Marx*, p. 451.

15. Engels letter to Sorge, 14 May 1884, Kendall, *Revolutionary Movement*, pp. 11–12.

16. Ibid., p. 5.

17. Letter from Engels to Bebel, 30 August 1883, Marx and Engels, *Selected Correspondence*, pp. 343–4.

18. Y. Kapp, *Eleanor Marx* (London, Lawrence & Wishart, 1976), vol. 2, p. 61.

19. A document on the 'Proposed Democratic Federation', British Library of Economic and Social Sciences.

20. Democratic Federation, 'Socialism Made Plain', in H. Pelling (ed.), *The Challenge of Socialism* (London, Black, 1954) p. 131.

21. H.W. Lee and E. Archbold, *Social Democracy in Britain, The Social-Democratic Federation* (London, 1935).

22. Kendall, *Revolutionary Movement*; C. Tsuzuki, *H.M. Hyndman and British Socialism* (London, Heinemann and Oxford University Press, 1961).

23. Crick, *Social Democratic Federation*.

24. Kendall, *Revolutionary Movement*, p. 19; Tsuzuki, *Hyndman*, pp. 189–90.

25. R.P. Arnot, *William Morris: A Vindication* (London, 1935), p. 6.

26. Tsuzuki, *Hyndman*.

27. E.J. Hobsbawm, *Labouring Men* (London, Weidenfeld & Nicolson, 1971), pp. 234, 237–8.

28. H. Collins, 'The Marxism of the SDF', in A. Briggs and J. Saville (eds), *Essays in Labour History* (London, Macmillan, 1971), p. 67.

29. S. Pierson, *Marxism and the Origins of British Socialism. The Struggle for a New Consciousness* (London, Cornell University Press, 1973), pp. 61, 273.

30. W. Wolfe, *From Radicalism to Socialism* (New Haven, Yale University Press, 1975), pp. 96, 99, 105.

31. M. Bevir, 'H.M. Hyndman: A Rereading and a Reassessment', *History of Political Thought*, XII, I (Spring 1991); M. Bevir. 'British Social Democratic Federation 1880–1885', *International Review of Social History*, XXXVII (1992), 207–29.

32. *Justice*, 19 January 1884.

33. Bevir, 'British Social Democratic Federation', pp. 225–6.

34. Ibid., p. 227.

35. Crick, *Social Democratic Federation*, p. 296.

36. Challinor, *Origins of British Bolshevism*, p. 18; Kendall, *Revolutionary Movement*, p. 6.

37. Kapp, *Eleanor Marx*, vol. 2, p. 60.

38. Ibid., p. 59.

39. Letter from Hyndman to Marx, 29 October 1881, quoted in Pierson, *Marxism and the Origins of British Socialism*, p. 67.

40. H.M. Hyndman, *Historical Basis*, quoted in Tsuzuki, *Hyndman*, pp. 55–6.

41. Bevir, 'British Social Democratic Federation', p. 228.

42. Letter from F. Engels to Laura Lafargue, 4 May 1891, quoted in Kapp, *Eleanor Marx*, vol. 2, p. 475.

43. T. Mann, *Memoirs* (London, Labour Publishing Company, 1923), p. 41.

44. Kendall, *Revolutionary Movement*, p. 321.

45. K. Marx and F. Engels, *Manifesto of the Communist Party* (Moscow, Progress Publishers, 1977), p. 45.

46. Letter 223 from Engels to Schluter, 11 January 1890, Marx and Engels, *Selected Correspondence*, pp. 388–9.

47. SDF, *Annual Conference Report*, 1894, pp. 28–31. Hyndman's views were rejected by Hunter Watts.

48. P. Thompson, *Socialists, Liberals and Labour: The Struggle for London 1885–1914* (London, Routledge & Kegan Paul, 1967), p. 122.

49. Quoted in Margaret Jones, 'William Morris – Revolutionary Socialist Pioneer', *Socialism Today*, issue 11 (September 1996), 23.

50. Tsuzuki, *Hyndman*, pp. 70–1.

51. Lee and Archbold, *Social-Democracy in Britain*, p. 109.

52. Bevir, 'British Social Democratic Federation 1880–1885', *International Review of Social History*, XXXVII (1992), 207–29.

53. Ibid., p. 217.

54. Arnot, *William Morris*; Collins, 'The Marxism of the SDF' in Briggs and Saville (eds), *Essays in Labour History*; Hobsbawm, *Labouring Men*.

55. Bevir, 'H.M. Hyndman: A Rereading and a Reassessment'; Bevir, 'British Social Democratic Federation 1880–1885'; Crick, *Social Democratic Federation*.

56. E.P. Thompson, *William Morris: Romantic to Revolutionary* (London, Merlin Press, 1977).

57. Ibid., pp. 125–6; *Justice*, 16 June 1894; *Political Writings of William Morris*, edited with an introduction by A.L. Morton (London, Lawrence & Wishart, 1973), p. 245.

58. R.P. Arnot, *William Morris: the man and the myth*, (London, Lawrence & Wishart, 1964, reprint of Arnot, *William Morris*), p. 15.

59. F. MacCarthy, *William Morris: A Life of Our Time* (London, Faber & Faber, 1994), p. xii.

60. Ibid., p. 64.

61. *Political Writings of William Morris*, Morton (ed.), p. 245.

62. Jones, 'Morris', pp. 21–4.

63. Kapp, *Eleanor Marx*, vol. 2, p. 61.

64. Ibid., pp. 63–4.

65. *News from Nowhere* is reproduced in *William Morris: Selected Writings and Designs*, edited by Asa Briggs (London, Penguin, 1973), pp. 183–301.

66. W. Morris, 'How I Became a Socialist', *Justice*, 16 June 1894.

67. Extract from *Commonweal*, 19 May and 17 August 1889, and quoted in Thompson, *William Morris: Romantic to Revolutionary*, p. 550; F. Boos (ed.), *William Morris' Socialist Diary* (London, Journeyman Press, 1985).

68. Jones, 'Morris', p. 23.

69. William Morris's statement on why he and his colleagues left the SDF, 13 January 1885, Morris correspondence, International Institute of Social History (IISH), Amsterdam.

70. Letter from William Morris to the Revd John Glasse, 23 May 1887, quoted in Thompson, *William Morris: Romantic to Revolutionary*, p. 45.

71. Letter from William Morris to J.L. Mahon, 17 May 1887, Morris correspondence, IISH.

72. Report of the Delegates of the Leeds Branch of the SDF, 8 February 1885 by J.L. Mahon, Socialist League Correspondence, International Institute of Social History, Amsterdam, 598. See also *Commonweal*, March 1885.

73. S. Yeo, 'A New Life: The Religion of Socialism in Britain 1883–1896', *History Workshop Journal*, 4 (1977), 5–56; *Manifesto* of the Socialist League.

74. Ibid., pp. 25, 31.

75. Crick, *Social Democratic Federation*, p. 198.

76. P.A. Watmough, 'The Membership of the Social Democratic Federation 1885–1902', *Bulletin of the Society for the Study of Labour History*, 34 (1977), 38; R. Barltrop, *The Monument: The Story of the Socialist Party of Great Britain* (London, Pluto Press, 1975); Challinor, *Origins of British Bolshevism*.

77. Crick, *Social Democratic Federation*, pp. 104, 168.

78. Tsuzuki, *Hyndman*, pp. 134–5; Kendall, *Revolutionary Movement*, p. 17.

79. Lee and Archbold, *Social-Democracy in Britain*, pp. 158–60; Crick, *Social Democratic Federation*, pp. 94–5.

80. Kendall, *Revolutionary Movement*, p. 328; BSP *Conference Report* 1914, pp. 15–16.

81. Quoted in B. Pierce and M. Woodhouse, *A History of Communism in Britain* (London, Bookmarks, 1995), p. 21.

82. Ibid., pp. 29–30.

83. *Justice*, 12 August 1893, 20 January 1894.

84. A.J. Kidd, 'The Social Democratic Federation and Popular Agitation amongst the Unemployed of Edwardian Manchester', *International Review of Social History*, 37 (1992), 336.

85. Francis Johnstone Collection, 1901/45, Rochdale, a letter from Shallard to J.K. Hardie, July 1901, in British Library of Political and Economic Science.

86. Crick, *Social Democratic Federation*, p. 330.

87. T.A. Jackson, *Solo Trumpet* (London, Lawrence & Wishart, 1953), p. 66.

88. *Justice*, 30 August 1902.

89. Challinor, *Origins of British Bolshevism*, p. 15.

90. Kendall, *Revolutionary Movement*, pp. 14–17; Challinor, *Origins of British Bolshevism*, pp. 9–23; Pierce and Woodhouse, *Communism in Britain*, pp. 24–5.

91. K. Laybourn, *A History of British Trade Unionism* (Stroud, Sutton, 1997), pp. 99–106.

92. Challinor, *Origins of British Bolshevism*, chapter on Lenin, pp. 33–4 and chapter 11.

93. Barltrop, *The Monument*.

94. T.A. Jackson, *Solo Trumpet* (London, Lawrence & Wishart, 1953) pp. 54–5.

95. D. Howell, *British Workers and the Independent Labour Party 1888–1906* (Manchester, Manchester University Press, 1983), pp. 389–97; Yeo, 'Religion of Socialism', pp. 5–56; M. Crick, '"A Call to Arms"; the Struggle for Socialist Unity in Britain, 1883–1914' in D. James, T. Jowitt and K. Laybourn (eds), *The*

Centennial History of the Independent Labour Party (Halifax, Ryburn, 1992) pp. 181–204; Crick, *Social Democratic Federation*, pp. 83–92, 238–60; K. Laybourn, 'The Failure of Socialist Unity in Britain *c*. 1893–1914', *Transactions of the Royal Historical Society*, 6th series, IV (1994), 153–75.

96. Howell, *British Workers and the ILP*, p. 389.
97. Ibid., pp. 393–7.
98. J. Hill, 'Social Democracy and the Labour Movement: the Social Democratic Federation in Lancashire', *North-West Labour History Society*, Bulletin 8 (1982–3).
99. *Clarion*, 4 August 1911.
100. Ibid., 11 August 1911.
101. Ibid., 6 October 1911.
102. *Justice*, 7 August 1897.
103. *ILP News*, August 1897.
104. ILP, *Annual Conference Report*, 1898.
105. *Justice*, 27 August 1898.
106. *Clarion*, 3 December 1898.
107. J. Hill, 'The ILP in Lancashire', in James, Jowitt and Laybourn (eds), 'The Centennial History of the ILP', p. 50.
108. *Bradford Labour Echo*, 11 April 1896.
109. Hill, 'Social Democracy', p. 53.
110. Lee and Archbold, *Social Democracy in Britain*, p. 159.
111. D. Howell, 'Was the Labour Party Inevitable?', *Bulletin of the North-West Labour History Society*, Bulletin 9 (1984), 17.
112. *Clarion*, 7 February 1902.
113. Kendall, *Revolutionary Movement*, p. 34.
114. V. Lenin, *British Labour and British Imperialism* (London, Lawrence & Wishart, 1969), pp. 93–8.
115. *Justice*, 17 October 1908.
116. Lenin, *British Labour and British Imperialism*, p. 98.
117. J.M. McLachlan and E. Hartley, *Should Socialists Join the Labour Party – a verbatim report of the debate* (1909).
118. *Clarion*, 7 July 1911.
119. Ibid., 13 October 1911.
120. K. Laybourn, '"A Story of Buried Talents and Wasted Opportunities": The Failure of the Socialist Unity Movement in Yorkshire 1911–1914', *Journal of Regional and Local Studies*, 7, 2 (1987), 15–31; D. Morris, 'The Origins of the British Socialist Party', *North-West Labour History Society*, Bulletin 8 (1982–3), 34–5.
121. Kendall, *Revolutionary Movement*, p. 38.
122. Crick, *Social Democratic Federation*, p. 198.
123. BSP, *Conference Report 1912*, p. 8.
124. Laybourn, 'A Story of Buried Talents and Wasted Opportunities', p. 25; A. Gardiner, Scrap Book.
125. BSP Papers 1910–1914 (Birmingham) in the British Library of Political and Economic Science, Coll. Misc. 155, M228, collected by H.B. Williams, particularly item 48/49/5, and item 46, the letter from Wintringham to Williams.
126. Z. Kahan, 'Peace and its Perils', *British Socialists*, I (1912), 56–68.
127. *Justice*, 8 February 1913; *Clarion*, 21 June 1913.
128. Ibid., 28 May 1914.
129. Yeo, 'Religion of Socialism', p. 31.

Chapter II The Emergence and Development of the Communist Party of Great Britain, 1914–32

1. K. Morgan, 'The CPGB and the Comintern Archives', *Journal of Socialist History* (1993), part 2, p. 14; Pierce and Woodhouse, *Communism in Britain*, p. 76.

2. Morgan, 'Comintern Archives', pp. 14–15; Pierce and Woodhouse, *Communism in Britain*, p. 76.

3. *Justice*, 13 August 1914.

4. Ibid., 17 September 1914.

5. Crick, *Social Democratic Federation*, pp. 268–9.

6. Tsuzuki, *Hyndman*, p. 243; *Justice*, 30 September 1915.

7. *Justice*, 24 June 1915.

8. Challinor, *Origins of British Bolshevism*, p. 162–3; Kendall, *Revolutionary Movement*, p. 98.

9. BSP, *Conference Report*, 1916, p. 3.

10. *Justice*, 8 June 1916.

11. N. Milton, *John Maclean* (London, Pluto Press, 1973).

12. Tsuzuki, *Hyndman*, p. 277.

13. J.M. Winter, *Socialism and the Challenge of War* (London, Routledge & Kegan Paul, 1974), pp. 253–5.

14. *Labour Leader*, 7 June 1917; K. Laybourn, *Philip Snowden* (Aldershot, Temple Smith/Gower/Wildwood, 1988), pp. 78–9.

15. S. White, 'Soviets in Britain: The Leeds Convention of 1917', *International Review of Social History*, XIX (1974), 192.

16. J. Slatter, 'Learning from Russia: The History of the Soviets in Britain', *Labour History Review*, 61.1, (Spring 1996), 16.

17. Ibid., p. 19.

18. Slatter, 'Learning from Russia', pp 15–20; Challinor, *Origins of British Bolshevism*, pp. 180–1.

19. *Yorkshire Factory Times*, 14 July 1917.

20. Slatter, 'Learning from Russia', p. 24; Challinor, *Origins of British Bolshevism*, p. 180.

21. BSP, *Conference Report*, 1918.

22. Dutt Papers, CP/IND/DUTT/01/01, the National Museum of Labour History, R.P. Dutt, 'Rough Draft on Some Experiences of the Communist International and the Period of Stalin's Leading Role', and also quoted in K. MacDermott and J. Agnew, *The Comintern. A History of International Communism from Lenin to Stalin* (London, Macmillan, 1996), pp. 55–6.

23. H. Pollitt, *Serving My Time* (London, Lawrence & Wishart, 1940), pp. 94–118.

24. Pollitt Papers, CP/IND/POLL/1/6, the 'Hands Off Russia' Conference report.

25. Pollitt Papers, CP/IND/POLL/1/8, *The Masses*, no. 1, vol. 1, February 1919.

26. Pollitt Papers, CP/IND/POLL/1/8, *Peace with Soviet Russia*.

27. Lenin, speeches of October 1920 in *Lenin on Britain* (London, Martin Lawrence, 1934), pp. 202–5; later republished as *British Labour and British Imperialism*.

28. Thompson, *The Good Old Cause*, p. 218.

29. J. Klugmann, *History of the Communist Party of Great Britain: Formation and Early Years, volume 1 1919–1924* (London, Lawrence & Wishart, 1968); Kendall, *Revolutionary Movement*; L.J. Macfarlane, *The British Communist Party: Its Origins and Development until 1929* (London, MacGibbon & Kee, 1966).

30. *Report of the 9th Annual Conference of the BSP*, 4–5 April 1920; *The Call*, 21 August 1919.

31. *The Call*, 9 October 1919 and *Report of the 9th Annual Conference of the BSP*, 4–5 April 1920.

32. *Workers' Dreadnought*, 21 December 1920.

33. *The Call*, 12 February 1920; *Workers' Dreadnought*, 21 February 1920.

34. *The Socialist*, 19 February 1920 quoted in Klugmann, *Communist Party 1919–1924*, p.33.

35. *The Call*, 1 April 1920.

36. Klugmann, *Communist Party 1919–1924*, pp. 34–5.

37. *The Call*, 22 July 1920.

38. *Official Report of the Unity Convention* (London, CPGB, September 1920).

39. V. Lenin, 'Speech on Affiliation to the British Labour Party delivered to the Second Congress of the Communist International, 6 August 1920', in V. Lenin, *Collected Works*, vol. 31, pp. 257–63.

40. Ibid., pp. 17–118.

41. Klugmann, *Communist Party 1919–1924*, p.63.

42. W. Gallacher, *Revolt on the Clyde* (London, 1936; London, Lawrence & Wishart, 1979), pp. 248–53, W. Gallacher, *Rolling of The Thunder* (London, Lawrence & Wishart, 1947), pp. 7–12.

43. *Workers' Dreadnought*, 2 October 1920.

44. *Communist*, 16 December 1920.

45. Ibid., 5 February 1921.

46. Crick, *Social Democratic Federation*, p. 287.

47. Kendall, *Revolutionary Movement*, pp. 196–302.

48. Challinor, *Origins of British Bolshevism*, chapters 10 and 11.

49. Trotsky, *Writings on Britain*, vols. 1 and 2; H. Dewar, *Communist Politics in Britain* (London, Pluto, 1976); R. Black, *Stalinism in Britain* (London, New Park, 1970); Pierce and Woodhouse, *Communism in Britain*, pp. 48–110, 142–53.

50. R. McKibbin, 'Why was there no Marxism in Britain?', *English Historical Review* (1984).

51. R. Martin, *Communism and British Trade Unions 1924–1933* (Oxford, Oxford University Press, 1969).

52. Callaghan, *Socialism in Britain*.

53. S. Macintyre, *A Proletarian Science: Marxism in Britain 1917–33* (Cambridge, Cambridge University Press, 1980); S. Macintyre, *Little Moscows: Communism and Working-Class Militancy in Inter-War Britain* (London, Croom Helm, 1980).

54. Challinor, *Origins of British Bolshevism*, pp. 214–56; Kendall, *Revolutionary Movement*, pp. 196–302.

55. K. Morgan, *Harry Pollitt* (Manchester, Manchester University Press, 1993), p. 61.

56. CP/IND/DUTT/01/01, Dutt, 'Rough Draft'.

57. Pollitt Papers, CP/IND/POLL/3/4, Letter from Dutt to Pollitt, 14 April 1931.

58. Pollitt in a letter to Salme Dutt, 1 July 1923, and located in the Working Class Movements Library, Manchester.

59. Morgan, *Pollitt*, p. 62.

60. Pollitt Papers, CP/IND/POLL/3/1, Letter from Dutt to Pollitt, 26 March 1928.

61. Ibid., Letter from Dutt to Pollitt, 8 April 1928.

62. Dutt Papers, CP/IND/DUTT/06/03, Letter from R.P. Dutt to D.A. Wilson (of Bradford), 10 December 1930.

63. *Communist Review* (January 1924).

64. Ibid., (February 1924).

65. J.T. Murphy, *New Horizons* (London, John Lane, 1941), p. 181.

66. J. Callaghan, *Rajani Palme Dutt: A Study in British Stalinism* (London, Lawrence & Wishart, 1993), pp. 47–8.

67. Macfarlane, *British Communist Party*, p. 103.

68. Klugmann, *Communist Party 1919–1924*, pp. 166–81 traces the moves made by the CPGB to gain affiliation to the Labour Party, and Labour's response, in immense detail.

69. Pollitt Papers, CP/IND/POLL/3/1, 'The New Phase in Britain and the Communist Party' (draft by R.P. Dutt), p. 29.

70. *Workers' Weekly*, 25 April 1924.

71. *Report of the Congress of the CPGB*, Salford, Manchester, 16–18 May 1924.

72. K. Morgan and R. Duncan, 'Loitering on the party line: The unpublished memoirs of J.T. Walton Newbold', *Labour History Review*, vol. 60, part 1 (1995), 35–51.

73. Phil Piratin, the CPGB's only other MP, was returned for Mile End, London, at the 1945 general election but defeated at the 1950 general election, when Gallacher also lost his parliamentary seat. Born on 15 May 1907, Piratin rose to fame when he joined the CPGB following the Olympia demonstration against fascism at which he was one of the protesters. He died on 10 December 1995.

74. Pollitt Papers, CP/IND/POLL/1/8, RILU, London Committee, reports and minutes.

75. Pollitt Papers, CP/IND/POLL/1/8, *The Docker* (Bulletin of Dockers' Unofficial Strike Committee), no. 1, 10 July 1923.

76. Pollitt Papers, CP/IND/POLL/1/8, H. Pollitt, 'The Only Way: Work Inside the Unions', *Worker* (presumably *Workers' Weekly*) 19 July 1924.

77. R. Martin, *Communism and British Trade Unionism 1924–1933* (Oxford, Clarendon Press, 1969), pp. 37–8.

78. *Report of the National Minority Movement Conference* (1924), p. 20.

79. Pollitt Papers, CP/IND/POLL/1/8.

80. *Final Agenda of the 4th Annual Conference of the Minority Movement* (1927).

81. W. Hannington, *The Insurgents in London* (London, NUWCM, 1923).

82. *Communist*, 11 March 1922.

83. Ibid., 8 October 1922, 26 November 1921.

84. *Amendments and Resolutions the First Annual Conference of the YCLGB held at Brotherhood Church Hall, London, 5–6 August 1922* (London. YCLGB, 1922).

85. *Workers' Weekly*, 12 September 1925.

86. *Communist Review* (October 1925).

87. Political Bureau (PB), Minutes, throughout 1930.

88. *Workers' Weekly*, 1 May 1926 provides a full listing of the participation of CPGB members on councils of action and strike committees.

89. J. Klugmann, 'Marxism, Reformism and the General Strike', in J. Skelley (ed.), *The General Strike 1926* (London, Lawrence & Wishart, 1976), p. 79.

90. Macfarlane, *British Communist Party*, pp. 167–9.

91. 'Workers' Bulletin', 13 May 1926.

92. Central Committee (CC), Minutes, 29-31 May 1926; *Workers' Weekly*, 4 June 1926; *Sunday Worker*, 13 June 1926.

93. Pierce and Woodhouse, *Communism in Britain*, pp. 107–8.

94. Trades Union Congress, *Report, 1927*, p. 320.

95. N. Branson, *History of the Communist Party of Great Britain 1927–1941* (London, Lawrence & Wishart, 1985), p. 12.

96. J. Reynolds and K. Laybourn, *Labour Heartland: A History of the Labour Party in West Yorkshire during the Inter-war Years 1918–1939* (Bradford, University of Bradford, 1987), p. 76.

97. Branson, *Communist Party 1927–1941*, p.5.

98. MacDermott and Agnew, *The Comintern*, p. 72.

99. Pollitt Papers, CP/IND/POLL/3/1, Letter from R.P. Dutt to Harry Pollitt, 23 January 1928.

100. Ibid., Letter from R. P. Dutt to Harry Pollitt, 13 February 1928.

101. 'Memorandum on the Theses of the Labour Party' accepted by the CC of the CPGB, 9 July 1928.

102. CC, Minutes, 18–19 November 1928. The vote was 13 to 4 in favour of suspending the NLWM.

103. Callaghan, *Socialism in Britain*, p. 102.

104. Morgan, *Pollitt*, p. 33.

105. Ibid., pp. 35–7; S. Dutt correspondence, Working Class Movements Library, Manchester.

106. R.P. Dutt letters, Working Class Movements Library, Manchester, Dutt to Pollitt, 8 July 1923.

107. Ibid., Dutt to Pollitt, 8 July 1923 and 21 July 1923.

108. Branson, *History of the Communist Party of Great Britain 1927–1941* (London, Lawrence & Wishart, 1985), p. 31; Thompson, *The Good Old Cause*, pp. 42–3.

109. Morgan, 'Comintern Archives', p. 19.

110. MacDermott and Agnew, *The Comintern*, pp. 74–5.

111. Ibid., p. 73.

112. Ibid., pp. 73–4.

113. Branson, *Communist Party 1927–1941*, p. 19; Thompson, *The Good Old Cause*, pp. 41–6.

114. CC, Minutes, 7–9 January 1928.

115. Pollitt Papers, CP/IND/POLL/3/1, Letter from Dutt to Pollitt 6 January 1928; also a letter from Dutt to Pollitt, 25 January 1928, for the main points of their alternative view.

116. Branson, *Communist Party 1927–1941*, p.23.

117. Pollitt Papers, CP/IND/POLL/3/1, R.P. Dutt, 'The New Phase in Britain and the Communist Party', p. 6.

118. Pollitt Papers, CP/IND/POLL/3/1, R.P. Dutt, Memorandum on the Theses of the Labour Party adopted by the Central Committee on 9 January 1928 and Alternative Proposals.

119. CC, Minutes, 17–18 March 1928; MacDermott and Agnew, *The Comintern*, pp. 76–8.

120. Branson, *Communist Party 1927–1941*, pp. 32–3.

121. Callaghan, *Palme Dutt*, chapter four. Callaghan particularly refers to J.T. Murphy's article, 'Socialism By Kind Permission', *Communist International*, 3, 2 (15 October 1926), 18; *Class Against Class*, pp. 9, 14, 17.

122. Pierce and Woodhouse, *Communism in Britain*, p. 194.

123. Morgan, *Pollitt*, pp. 64–5.

124. Pollitt, *Serving My Time*, p. 268.

125. Miscellaneous material on the 1995 Moscow Reel in the CPGB Archive.

126. S. Lerner, 'The History of the United Clothing Workers' Union' (unpublished PhD, University of London, 1956). For formation of the United Mineworkers of Scotland see Macfarlane, *British Communist Party*, pp. 265–74.

127. CPGB Secretariat meeting 8 December 1929.

128. *Communist Review* (January 1930), 4, an article by W.T.

129. Miscellaneous Material, 1995 Moscow Reel, CPGB, Secretariat meeting 18 December 1929. Also look at the December meetings of the Secretariat meetings on the same reel.

130. Morgan, *Pollitt*, pp. 67–8; M. Ferguson, 'Lessons of the Dawdon struggle', *Communist Review* (August 1929), 454–5.

131. Pollitt Papers, CP/IND/POLL/2/2, contain a collection of papers connected with the Dawdon Strike, including *The Dawdon Miner*, no. 1, 9 April 1929; no. 2, 14 April 1929; no. 9, 16 June 1929; *The Nack Miner* (Dawdon Vigilance Committee), no. 1, 26 April 1929; *The Miner*, 22 May 1929; CPGB, Tyneside District Party Committee circulars (undated); and a miscellaneous collection of other published material.

132. Morgan, 'The CPGB and the Comintern Archives', pp. 22-3.

133. Letter from Dutt to Pollitt, 14 August 1929, Pollitt Papers, CP/IND/POLL/3/2.

134. Ibid., Letter from Dutt to Pollitt, 7 November 1929.

135. Morgan, *Pollitt*, p. 68; Morgan, 'Comintern Archives', pp. 25–6.

136. 'One Hundred Per Cent Trade Unionism: Our Attitude', *Communist Review* (August 1930), 442–8.

137. Pierce and Woodhouse, *Communism in Britain*, p. 195.

138. Morgan, 'Comintern Archive', pp. 23–4.

139. W. Rust, *The Inside Story of the* Daily Worker: *Ten years of Working Class Journalism* (London, CPGB, 1940); *The Voice of the People* (London, CPGB, 1944).

140. CC, Minutes, 11–12 January 1930.

141. PB, Minutes, 15 January 1930.

142. Ibid., 12 February 1930.

143. Pollitt Papers, CP/IND/POLL/3/3, Letter from Dutt to Pollitt, 19 June 1930.

144. 'The Present Situation and the Task of the Party: Resolutions of the CC in March 1930', *Communist Review* (March 1930), 218–24.

145. H. Slater, 'The Charter Campaign: A Criticism', *Communist Review* (1932), 498–504.

146. PB, Minutes, 25 September 1930.

147. 'Our Party and the Workers' Charter Campaign', *Communist Review* (November 1930), 26.

148. Towards May Day, 1930', *Communist Review* (April 1930), 155.

149. R. Croucher, *We Refuse to Starve in Silence, A History of the National Unemployed Workers' Movement 1920–1940* (London, Lawrence & Wishart, 1987), p. 112.

150. PB, Minutes, 30 January 1930.

151. Pollitt Papers, CP/IND/POLL/3/3, Letter from Dutt to Pollitt, 15 August 1930.

152. CC, Minutes, 13 September 1930.

153. PB, Minutes, 9 April 1931; Central Committee, Minutes, 14–15 March 1931.

154. Ibid., 16 and 23 April 1931; the latter refers to the 'Open Letter of RILU to the Charter Convention'.

155. H. Pollitt, 'Towards the National Charter Convention', *Communist Review* (1931), 90.

156. Pollitt Papers, CP/IND/POLL/3/3, Letter from Dutt to Pollitt, Pollitt Papers, 1 November 1930.

157. Slater, 'Charter Campaign', pp. 498–504.

158. PB, Minutes, 23 April 1931.

159. Pollitt Papers, CP/IND/POLL/3/4, Letter from Dutt to Pollitt and Secretariat, 29 June 1931.

160. Ibid., Letters from Dutt to Pollitt and Secretariat, 7 and 14 July 1931.

161. Morgan, 'Comintern Archives', p. 25.

162. CC, Minutes, 11–12 January 1930.

163. PB, Minutes, 23 January 1930.

164. Morgan, 'Comintern Archives', p. 25.

165. PB, Minutes, 6 February 1930.

166. Morgan, 'Comintern Archives', p. 25.

167. E.H. Brown, 'The Struggle in the Woollen Industry', *Communist Review* (April 1930), 136–41.

168. PB, Minutes, 3 April 1930.

169. Ibid., 8 May 1930.

170. Ibid., 23 May 1930.

171. Ibid., 26 May 1930.

172. Ibid., 30 May 1930.

173. Ibid., 12 June 1930.

174. Ibid., 24 April 1930.

175. Ibid., 12 June 1930.

176. Reynolds and Laybourn, *Labour Heartland*, pp. 78, 98–100.

177. PB, Minutes, 6 November 1930.

178. Ibid., 13 November 1930.

179. W. Paynter, *My Generation* (London, 1972), p. 109.

180. PB, Minutes, 2 October 1930.

181. Branson, *Communist Party 1927–1941*, p. 86.

182. J. Clifford, 'Horner *v* Political Bureau' and Our Reply, *Communist Review* (1931), pp. 183–92.

183. *Daily Worker*, 26, 28, 29 January 1931; 3 February 1931.

184. PB, Minutes, 22 January 1931.

185. 'Political Bureau Statement re Arthur Horner, 27 February 1931', *Communist Review* (March 1931), 145–57.

186. Ibid., p. 146.

187. CC, Minutes, 14–15 March 1931.

188. PB, Minutes, 22 January 1931.

189. Ibid., 22–23 January 1931.

190. Ibid., 16 April 1931.

191. CC, Minutes, 30 May 1931.

192. Ibid., 20 September 1931.

193. Ibid., 4 May, 9 November 1931.

194. Ibid., 16 January 1932.

195. 'Immediate Tasks before the Party and the Working Class: Resolution of the Central Committee, CPGB, January 1932', *Communist Review* (February 1932), 55–69.

196. Ibid., pp. 57, 59, 62.

197. PB, Minutes, 9–10 April 1932.

198. *Daily Worker*, 20 August 1932.

199. H. Pollitt, 'The Cotton Fight To-day', *Communist Review* (May 1932), 264–8.

200. PB, Minutes, 20 February 1932.

201. Ibid., 19 March 1932.

202. *Daily Herald*, quoted in Branson, *Communist Party 1927–1941*, p. 91.

203. 'The Twelfth Party Congress of the CPGB', *Communist Review* (December 1932), 563–9.

204. J. Shields, 'Economic Struggles and the Drive into the Trade Unions', *Communist Review* (December 1932), 570–5.

205. Branson, *Communist Party 1927–1941*, pp. 93–4.

206. Ibid., pp. 58–73.

207. W. Allen, 'The NUWM and the Mobilizing of the Unemployed for Mass Struggle', *Communist Review* (1931), 486–91.

208. 'Second Five-Year Plan', *Communist Review* (April 1932), 168.

209. PB, Minutes, 7, 14 May 1932.

210. 'The Expulsion of J.T. Murphy and its Lessons' and 'The Statement of the Political Bureau on J.T. Murphy', *Communist Review* (June 1932), 298–304. For account of Murphy's expulsion see R. Darlington, *The Political Trajectory of J.T. Murphy* (Liverpool, Liverpool University Press, 1998), pp. 201–16.

211. PB, Minutes, 19 February 1931.

212. Dutt Papers, CP/IND/DUTT/06/03, Letter from D.A. Wilson to R.P. Dutt, 24 January 1931.

Chapter III The United and Popular Fronts against Fascism and the Outbreak of the Second World War, 1933–41

1. CC, Minutes, 17 February 1933.

2. Ibid., 18 February 1933.

3. ECCI Manifesto, 5 March 1933; *Inprecorr*, vol. 12, no. 11, 9 March 1933, 261–2.

4. Johnstone, 'The CPGB, the Comintern and the War, 1939-41', pp. 27–45.

5. J. Stevenson and C. Cook, *The Slump* (London, Jonathan Cape, 1977), pp. 127–44; M. Johnstone in debate with A. Rothstein in *Bulletin of the Society for the Study of Labour History*, nos 33–37 (1976–8).

6. K. Morgan, *Against Fascism and War: Ruptures and Continuities in British Communist Politics 1935–1941* (Manchester, Manchester University Press, 1989); Attfield and Williams, *1939: The Communist Party and the War*, introduction by M. Johnstone, pp. 54–5, 71.

7. Johnstone, 'The CPGB, the Comintern and the War, 1939-1941', p. 28.

8. R. Stevens, '"Disruptive Element?": The Influence of the Communist Party in Nottingham and District Trades Council, 1929–1951', *Labour History Review*, 58, 3 (1993); R. Stevens, 'Containing Radicalism: the Trades Union Congress Organisation Department and the Trades Councils, 1928–1951', *Labour History Review*, 62.1 (Spring 1997), 5–21; Fishman, *British Communist Party*.

9. R.P. Dutt, *Fascism and Social Revolution* (London, CPGB, 1934), p. xi.

10. MacDermott and Agnew, *The Comintern*, p. 122.

11. CC, Minutes, 9 March 1933. The Political Bureau meeting of 9 March 1933 suggests that this was a special enlarged meeting of the PB.

12. *Daily Worker*, 19 March 1933, quoting from *Pravda*, and further quoted in the CC, Minutes of the CPGB, 25 March 1933.

13. PB, Minutes, 6 April 1933, 4 May 1933.

14. CC, Minutes, 25 March 1933, from a speech by Comrade Mostyn (Peter Kerrigan).

15. E.H. Carr, *The Twilight of the Comintern 1930–1935* (London, Macmillan, 1983), p. 117.

16. J. Degras (ed.), *The Communist International 1919–1943*, vol. 3, *Documents 1929–1943* (London, Frank Cass, 1971), pp. 258–63.

17. PB, Minutes, 6 April 1933.

18. Ibid., 4 May 1933.

19. Ibid., 8 September 1933.

20. CC, Minutes, 17 June 1933; European Anti-Fascist Congress, 4–6 June 1933, see *Inprecorr*, vol. 13, no. 26, 16 June 1933, 573–5.

21. CC, Minutes, 19 February 1933.

22. PB, Minutes, 20 April 1933, Pollitt's report on the ILP Conference.

23. CC, Minutes, 10 September 1933.

24. Ibid., report of meeting between CPGB and ILP, 21 September 1933.

25. F. Brockway, *Inside the Left* (London, Allen & Unwin, 1942), pp. 252–3.

26. S. Bornstein and A. Richardson, *Against the Stream: A History of the Trotskyist Movement in Britain 1924–1938* (Socialist Platform, 1986), p. 175, and *Two Steps Back: Communists and the Wider Labour Movement 1935–45* (Socialist Platform, 1982), p. 16.

27. *Bradford Pioneer*, 26 October 1934.

28. CC, Minutes, 6 January 1934.

29. Ibid., 4 June 1933.

30. *Daily Worker*, 11 October 1933.

31. *Communist Review* (October 1933), 393–6.
32. N. Barratt, 'A Bright Shining Star: The CPGB and Anti-Fascist Activism in the 1930s', *Science and Society* vol. 61, no. 1, (Spring 1997), 10–26; N. Todd, *In Excited Times: The People Against the Blackshirts* (Bewick Press, 1995).
33. Barratt, 'A Bright Shining Star', p. 19, quoting the *Daily Worker*, 17 March 1933 and *Manchester Guardian*, 26 November 1934.
34. Public Record Office (PRO), HO 45/25383.
35. *Inprecorr*, vol. 14, no. 5, 30 January 1934, 130–4.
36. CC, Minutes, January 1934.
37. J. Jacobs, *Out of the Ghetto* (London, Janet Simon, 1978); *Daily Worker*, 18 May 1934; PB, Minutes, 7 June 1934.
38. CC, Minutes, 7–8 April 1934.
39. PRO, HO 45/25383 Anti-Fascist Activities 1929–1934, Special Branch Report 18 June 1934; *Daily Worker*, 18 June 1934.
40. CC, Minutes, 10 August 1934.
41. PRO, HO 45/25383, Special Branch Report 11 September 1934.
42. CC, Minutes, 15 December 1934, comments of Comrade Spence.
43. *Daily Worker*, 11, 13, 15–16, 18, 22, 29, 30 June; 3, 10, 12–13, 18, 23, 30–31 July; 2, 10, 28 August 1934.
44. Degras (ed.), *Communist International*, vol. 3, *Documents 1929–43*, p. 336.
45. *Daily Worker*, editorials 3–4 October 1934.
46. Ibid., 20 October 1934.
47. Dutt Papers, CP/IND/DUTT/31/01.
48. CC, Minutes, 14 December 1934.
49. Degras (ed.), *Communist International*, vol. 3, *Documents 1929–43*, p. 333.
50. G. Dimitrov, *Selected Speeches and Articles* (1951), pp. 53, 63, 71, 113–4; Degras (ed.), *Communist International*, vol. 3, *Documents 1929–43*, pp. 359–70, 372–8; *Inprecorr*, vol. 15, no. 34, 10 August 1935, 889–92.
51. Bornstein and Richardson, *Two Steps Back*; Pierce and Woodhouse, *Communism in Britain*.
52. PB, Minutes, 6 September 1935, Pollitt report on the Seventh Congress; PB, meeting, 20 September 1935; PB, Minutes, 6 October 1935; H. Pollitt, 'The Seventh Congress of the Communist International', *Labour Monthly* (October 1935 and November 1935).
53. *Daily Worker*, 7 October 1935.
54. Morgan, *Against Fascism and War*, pp. 51-2.
55. CC, Minutes, 9 October 1937.
56. Ibid., 4–5 January 1936; PB, Minutes, 7 February 1936.
57. CC, Minutes, 1 February 1935.
58. PRO, HW/17/18 4003/4, British Intelligence interception of messages, 24 October 1935, transcript of London to Moscow message 55, 56, 11 October 1935, Pollitt to Moscow; 4136/UK, 8 November 1935, referring to 87–9, 2 November 1935, message from Pollitt to Kerrigan.
59. The financial contributions to Moscow dominate the British Intelligence interception of messages reports from the end of 1934 to the end of 1936, PRO, HW/17/17–22.
60. PB, Minutes, 21 November 1935 and 4 January 1936; Dutt Papers, CP/IND/DUTT/18/05, Secretariat Circular 26 November 1935, 'The Lessons of the General Election and the Next Task of the Communist Party'.
61. CC, Minutes, 4–5 January 1936.

62. *Daily Worker*, 29 February 1936.

63. Branson, *Communist Party 1927–1941*, p. 152; *Daily Worker*, 16 June 1936.

64. PB, Minutes, 19 June 1936.

65. Ibid.

66. Labour Party, *Annual Conference Report, 1936*, Appendix 9, pp. 297–300.

67. J. Gollan Papers, CP/IND/GOLL/04/01.

68. B. Pimlott, *Labour and the Left in the 1930s* (London, Allen & Unwin, 1986 paperback edition), pp. 87–8.

69. Executive Committee (EC), Minutes, 16 August 1943.

70. *New Leader*, 5 March 1937, p. 2.

71. CC, Minutes, 16 April 1936.

72. Ibid., 26 August 1938.

73. Ibid., 13 November 1936.

74. Ibid., 27 November 1936 and 28 January 1937; CC, Minutes, 16 January 1937.

75. Dutt Papers, CP/IND/DUTT/06/09, 'Proposals of the CP for a National Unity Campaign', Miscellaneous papers, Unity Campaign; Dutt Papers, CP/IND/DUTT/29/10, Secretariat circulars on Unity campaign.

76. Four-page report on the negotiations to be found on the 1995 unlisted Moscow Reel, dated 20 November 1936 and presented to the PB, 28 January 1937; 1995 Moscow Reel, H. Pollitt letters to R.P. Arnot regarding Unity Negotiations, 29 October 1936, 6 November 1936; 1995 Moscow Reel, H. Pollitt's report on unity negotiations to ECCI in Moscow, 4 January 1937.

77. H. Pollitt, Report to ECCI, 4 January 1937; 1995 Moscow Reel, Letter from Pollitt to R.P. Arnot, 29 October 1936.

78. Idem.

79. *Tribune*, 1 June 1937.

80. *Daily Herald*, 25 January 1937, *Manchester Guardian*, 25 January 1937; Pimlott, *Labour and the Left*, pp. 94–106.

81. CC, Minutes, 16 January 1937; PB, Minutes, 11 February 1937.

82. Ibid., 16 August 1937; *Daily Herald*, 18, 30 January, 10 June 1937.

83. Pimlott, *Labour and the Left*, pp. 170–82.

84. 1995 Moscow Reel, unlisted, 495/100/1040.

85. CC, Minutes, 10 September 1937. Both the listed and the unlisted Moscow Reels contain a series of documents charting the CPGB's campaign against Trotsky and Trotskyism.

86. Pimlott, *Labour and the Left*, p. 88.

87. TUC, General Council, *Report 1936*, pp. 424–7; W. Citrine, *I Search for Truth in Russia* (London, TUC, 1936).

88. CC, Minutes, 16 April 1936.

89. PB, Minutes, 7 February 1936.

90. Bradford Trades Council Minutes, 19 September 1935.

91. *Daily Worker*, 17 March 1936.

92. *Discussion*, May 1936, 21–4.

93. *Daily Worker*, 22 June 1936.

94. Ibid., 27 June 1936.

95. Jacobs, *Out of the Ghetto*, pp. 204–5.

96. Ibid., p. 241.

97. PRO, HO 45/25388.

98. CC, Minutes, 24 June 1939.

99. D. Blaazer, *The Popular Front & the Progressive Tradition: Socialists, Liberals and the Quest for Unity, 1884–1939* (Cambridge, Cambridge University Press, 1992).

100. Pimlott, *Labour and the Left*, p.194.

101. *Daily Worker*, 27 July 1936.

102. PRO, HW/17/22/ 6801/UK, British Intelligence interception of messages, 31 August 1936, Moscow to London, 398–402, 19 August 1936.

103. Branson, *Communist Party, 1927–1941*, p. 230.

104. CC, Minutes, 10 October 1936.

105. Ibid., Minutes, 16 January 1937. See also B. Alexander, *British Volunteers for Liberty: Spain 1936–39* (London, Lawrence & Wishart, 1982).

106. Branson, *Communist Party 1927–1941*, p. 232.

107. Pollitt Papers, CP/IND/POLL/2/4. He first visited Spain in January 1937 after the battle of Jarama and his fifth, and last, visit occurred in September 1938.

108. CC, Minutes, 23 April 1938.

109. PB, Minutes, 16 August 1939.

110. MacDermott and Agnew, *The Comintern*, p. 142.

111. Dimitri Volkogonov, *Trotsky: The Eternal Revolutionary* (London, HarperCollins, 1996), p. 405; J. Arch Getty and R.T. Manning (eds), *Stalinist Terror: New Perspectives* (Cambridge, Cambridge University Press, 1993), pp. 266–9.

112. 1995 Moscow Reel, Letter from H. Pollitt to R.P. Arnot, 11 February 1937.

113. 1995 Moscow Reel.

114. Branson, *Communist Party 1927–1941*, pp. 245–7.

115. J. Haslam, 'The Soviet Union, the Comintern and the demise of the Popular Front 1936–1939', in H. Graham and P. Preston (eds), *The Popular Front in Europe* (London, Macmillan, 1987), p. 158.

116. PRO, HW/17/22/6787/UK, British Intelligence interception of messages, 28 August 1936, M[oscow] to L[ondon], 423–4, [about 21 August]1936 to CC of CPGB [precise date of interception not given although 6,785, reported 27 August 1936 was intercepted 20 August 1936].

117. 1995 Moscow Reel, R.P. Arnot, report for the ECCI, 9 September 1936, 'The Campaign of the CPGB in Relation to the Trotsky-Zinovievite Terrorist Trial'.

118. *Daily Worker*, 25, 26, 31 August, 1 September 1936.

119. Ibid., 2 September 1936.

120. Ibid., 17 August, 1, 4 September 1936.

121. TUC *Report 1936* (London, TUC, 1936), pp. 424–7; 1995 Moscow Reel, Letter from H. Laski to H. Pollitt, 21 August 1936 and Letter from H. Pollitt to R.P. Arnot, 11 February 1937.

122. Record of the CPGB National Conference on 11 October 1936, attached to CC Minutes of 10 October 1936.

123. Branson, *Communist Party 1927–1941*, pp 246–7.

124. MacDermott and Agnew, *The Comintern*, p. 149.

125. Record of the CPGB National Conference, 11 October 1936, attached to CC Minutes 10 October 1936.

126. PB, Minutes, 28 January 1937.

127. 1995 Moscow Reel, N. Raylock, 'Information on Trotskyism in Britain'.

128. PB, Minutes, 11 February 1937.

129. CC, Minutes, 6 August 1937.

130. Ibid., 5 March 1938.

131. Ibid., 5 June, 9 October 1938.

132. S. Bornstein and A. Richardson, '"Midnight in the Century": The Moscow Trials' in *Against the Stream: A History of the Trotskyist Movement in Britain 1924–1938*' (London, Socialist Platform, 1986), pp. 214–37; Pierce and Woodhouse, 'The British Stalinists and the Moscow Trials' in *Communism in Britain*, pp. 225–45.

133. *Daily Worker*, 23 January 1937.

134. Ibid., 16 May 1939, from the comments of Comrade Shield.

135. CC, Minutes, 1–2 July 1938.

136. Morgan, *Against Fascism and War*, p. 419.

137. Stevens, '"Disruptive Element?": The Influence of the Communist Party in Nottingham and District Trades Council, 1929–1951', pp. 22–37.

138. R. Stevens, 'Trades Councils in the East Midlands, 1929–1951: Trade Unionism and Politics in a "Traditionally Moderate Area"' (unpublished PhD dissertation, University of Nottingham, 1995), p. 93.

139. Ibid., p. 100, quoting from the Nottingham Trades Council Minutes, 3 and 17 April 1935.

140. Stevens, 'Trades Councils in the East Midlands', pp. 415–6.

141. Fishman, *British Communist Party*, p. 154.

142. Ibid., p. 154.

143. Ibid., p. 4; *Daily Worker*, 2 January 1937.

144. Fishman, *British Communist Party*, p. 154.

145. 'The Fight of the Taximen', *Communist Review* (October 1933), 392 ; J.R. Campbell, 'The Future of Rank and File Movements, *Labour Monthly* (March 1933), 189–95; T.M. Robinson, 'Lessons of the Textile Strike', *Communist Review* (February 1933), 61–7; 'The Communist Party and Strike Leadership', *Communist Review* (September 1934), 145–9; J. Shields, 'One Year of the January Resolution', *Communist Review* (March 1933), 143.

146. *Discussion* ran a series of articles on working with the existing trade unions throughout 1936. J. Mahon wrote in April 1936, 12; D. Wilson in May 1936, 16–17; Alec Brown in June 1936, 26–7; Lew Thomas in July 1936, 26–7.

147. Pierce and Woodhouse, *Communism in Britain*, pp. 140–1.

148. CP/CENT/CONG/04/02, 'Report of the Central Committee to the Sixteenth Party Congress, October 1939' (not held due to the War), pp. 3, 8; unlisted 1995 Moscow Reel, J.R. Campbell, 'Report for the ECCI of Comintern, 11 April 1938'.

149. PB, Minutes, 4 February 1933.

150. Ibid., 4 January 1933, 16 February 1933; CC, Minutes, 18 February 1933.

151. PB, Minutes, 19 May 1933.

152. CC, Minutes, 5–6 January 1934.

153. Ibid., 6–7 April 1934.

154. Ibid., 14 December 1934.

155. CP/CENT/CONG/03/04/1938, Thirteenth CPGB Congress Report, 2–5 February 1935, pp. 79–80.

156. CC, Minutes, 17 December 1937, Report on the CPGB and Trade Unions.

157. PB, Minutes, 7 May 1936.

158. Ibid., 11 February 1937.

159. Ibid., 12 November 1937.

160. Ibid., 29 October 1937.

161. Ibid., Minutes, on the 1938–1939, Political Bureau microfilm reel.

162. Ibid., 16 May 1939, see comments of Comrade Shield.

163. Ibid., 19 March 1939, in a comment made by Comrade Cornforth.

164. CC, Minutes, 21 May 1939.

165. H. Pollitt, *Can Conscription Save Peace?* (London, CPGB, May 1939). For the debate over conscription see CC, Minutes, May 1939.

166. *Daily Worker*, 23 August 1938.

167. Attfield and Williams, *1939: The Communist Party and the War*, pp. 149–52, copy of the Manifesto and report of Conference, 21 April 1979.

168. Idem.

169. MacDermott and Agnew, *The Comintern*, p. 192.

170. Morgan, *Against Fascism and War*, p. 89.

171. CC, Minutes, 24 September 1939.

172. CPGB, extra reel 6, September–December 1939; CC, Minutes, 23, 24 and 25 September 1939.

173. MacDermott and Agnew, *The Comintern*, p. 193.

174. Pollitt Papers, CP/IND/POLL/2/7, Letter to Pollitt from Salme Dutt, 1 October 1939.

175. CC, Minutes, 2 October 1939.

176. Ibid.

177. *Daily Worker*, 12 October 1939.

178. Pollitt Papers, CP/IND/POLL/2/7, Letter from Comrade Rose to Pollitt, 7 October 1939.

179. Ibid., Letter of Harry Pollitt to Central Committee, 18 November 1939.

180. *Daily Worker*, 7 October 1939.

181. Attfield and Williams, *1939: The Communist Party and the War*, p. 170.

182. Ibid., pp. 175–6.

183. Ibid., p. 54.

184. Ibid., pp. 59–60.

185. Ibid., p. 71.

186. CP/HIST/2/7, Kevin Morgan interview with Eddie Frow, 4 April 1986, p. 19.

187. Tape recorded interview with Dylan Murphy on 12 February 1996.

188. E. Benson, *To Struggle is to Live* (London, Peoples' Publications, 1980), pp. 195–6.

189. CC, Minutes, 1939.

190. Morgan, *Against Fascism and War*, p. 91.

191. Morgan, *Against Fascism and War*, p. 122.

192. PRO, HO/45/25549, Intelligence Enquiries Communist Party (IECP) Activities and Meetings, 1940.

193. Morgan, *Against Fascism and War*, p. 140.

194. PRO, HO/45/25549, IECP Activities and Meetings 1940.

195. Dutt Papers, CP/IND/DUTT/06/02, Letter from L. Strachey to R.P. Dutt, 6 May 1940.

196. Ibid.

197. Morgan, *Against Fascism and War*, pp. 140–2.

198. PRO, HO 45/25549, IECP Activities and Meetings 1940.

199. Ibid., 8 February 1940, Special Branch Report regarding a meeting on 5 February 1940.

200. Ibid., Special Branch Report, 15 February 1940.

201. Ibid., Special Branch Report, 15 March 1940.

202. Morgan, *Against Fascism and War*, p. 32.

203. PRO, FO 371/24856.

204. Attfield and Williams, *1939: The Communist Party and the War*, p. 32.

205. W. Gallacher, article in *World News and Views*, 3 August 1940 and W. Rust, 'Imperialism and Counter-Revolution', *Labour Monthly* (November 1940), 606–7.

206. PRO, HO 45/25552 1940–1, Letter from Sir Alexander Maxwell, July 1940, and letter from Lord Swindon to Dr John Anderson, 17 September 1940.

207. *Labour Monthly* (June 1940), 335. See also D.N. Pritt, *Forward to a People's Government* (London, 1940), p. 16.

208. *Daily Herald*, 14 January 1941.

209. Morgan, *Against Fascism and War*, p. 15.

210. CP/CENT/CONG/03/04, Thirteenth CPGB Congress, Manchester, 2–5 February 1935.

211. Pimlott, *Labour and the Left*, p. 80.

Chapter IV War and Peace, 1941–51

1. Pollitt's political letter to the CP Secretariat, in V. Gollancz, *Russia and Ourselves* (London, Gollancz, 1941) pp. 118-26; *Britain's Chance Has Come* (London, CPGB, 1941).

2. N. Branson, *History of the Communist Party of Great Britain 1941–1951* (London, Lawrence & Wishart, 1997), Appendix I, p. 252.

3. W. Rust, 'Speaking for the Germans', *Daily Worker*, 21 July 1944.

4. Bornstein and Richardson, Two Steps Back (London, Socialist Platform, 1982), pp. 82–3.

5. H. Pollitt, 'Speech to CPGB National Conference, May 1942', in *The Communist Party and the Way to Win* (London, CPGB, 1942), p. 34.

6. Pollitt Papers, letter of Pollitt to Nehru, 27 July 1942, quoted in Morgan, *Pollitt*, p. 130.

7. Morgan, *Pollitt*, p. 131, quoting M-O TC 8/5, Mass Observation Archive, University of Sussex.

8. D.N. Pritt Papers, British Library of Political and Economic Science, 1/3, Diary date 15 March 1942.

9. Ibid., diary 17 February 1942.

10. Ibid., diary 15 January 1942.

11. Laurence Olivier, *Confessions of an Actor* (London, Sceptre edition, 1987), p. 130.

12. Jeffrey Richards, 'National Identity in British Wartime Films', in Philip M. Taylor (ed.), *Britain and the Cinema in the Second World War* (London, Macmillan, 1988), p. 50.

13. The Fifteenth Congress was held on 18–19 September 1938 and the Sixteenth was supposed to be held between 7–9 October 1939 at Stoke Newington Town Hall but was cancelled because of the war and not held until 3–4 July 1943; Report of the Central Committee to the Sixteenth Congress, 7–9 October 1939.

14. Pollitt, *The Communist Party and the Way to Win*, pp. 12–14, 18–19, 34–7.

15. CP/CENT/CON/4/13, 1941, Sixteenth Congress material; *Unity and Victory*: Report of the Sixteenth Congress of CPGB, 3–4 July 1943, p. 4.

16. 1995 Moscow Reel, unclassified, 495/101/1042, CC statements, 13 June, 16 and 30 July 1942.

17. Ibid., CC letter, or circular, 11 September 1942.

18. *16th Congress Discussion Statement*, January 1943.

19. CPGB, EC, Minutes, 15 August 1943.

20. 1995 Moscow Reel, National Museum of Labour History, 495/100/1046.

21. Ibid., 495/100/1042, PB letter to the Comintern, 13 June 1942; CPGB, EC, Minutes, 21 November 1943.

22. EC, Minutes, 16 April 1944.

23. *The Fight for National Unity of the British-Soviet Alliance Against Trotskyist Disruption. Against Leftist Confusions*, CPGB Circular, 10 November 1941, p. 3.

24. R. Croucher, *Engineers at War* (London, Merlin Press, 1982), pp. 174–6, 193.

25. Bornstein and Richardson, *Two Steps Back*, p. 89.

26. 1995 Moscow Reel, unclassified, 'Trade Union Policy in the War Against Fascism', December 1942.

27. CPGB, EC, Minutes, 15 August 1943.

28. 1995 Moscow Reel, 'Trade Union Policy in the War Against Fascism'.

29. Croucher, *Engineers at War*, pp. 157–73.

30. Arthur L. Horner, *Coal and the Nation* (London, CPGB, 1943).

31. CPGB, EC Minutes, 17 October 1943 and 16 April 1944.

32. Fishman, *British Communist Party*, pp. 294–5.

33. Ibid., p. 296; Croucher, *Engineers at War*, pp. 218–24.

34. Fishman, *British Communist Party*, pp. 310–11.

35. M. MacEwan, *The Greening of a Red* (London, Pluto Press, 1991), pp. 93–4.

36. Huddersfield Trades and Labour Council records, Kirklees branch of West Yorkshire Archives, Huddersfield.

37. M. Heinemann, *Britain's Coal: A Study of the Mining Crisis* (London, 1944), p. 28.

38. Croucher, *Engineers at War*, pp. 311–23.

39. Labour Party, Minutes, NEC meeting, 27 January 1943.

40. Labour Party, *Annual Report, 1943*, pp. 9–16.

41. Dutt Papers, CP/IND/DUTT/31/18, Central Committee Statement, 'Affiliation – Information on the campaign' indicates that by 15 April 1943 2,071 union branches and 178 Labour Party organizations had voted for Communist affiliation and that this had reached 3,352 organizations by 2 June 1943.

42. Labour Party, *Annual Report, 1943*, pp. 162–5.

43. *Tribune*, 7 April 1944.

44. CP/CENT/EC/ 01/03, CPGB, EC, Minutes, 21 January and 18 February 1945.

45. Ibid., Draft of Political Letter on Party Discussion.

46. H. Pollitt, *Answers to Questions* (London, CPGB, May 1945), p. 45.

47. CPGB, EC, Minutes, 18 March 1945.

48. Branson, *Communist Party 1941–1951*, p. 96

49. CP/CENT/EC/01/03, Documents A and B, election results, August 1945.

50. CP/CENT/EC/01/03, Typed statement.

51. Labour Party Archives, General Secretary's Papers, Box 4, Communist Party, GS/COM/ HR.

52. Ibid., GS/Com/36ii.

53. E. Burns, 'In Perspective', *Communist Review* (July 1946), 3–4.

54. CP/CENT/EC/01/02, EC, Minutes, 16 January 1944.

55. Gallacher advocated a proportional representation system at the House of Commons Speaker's Conference on 18 February 1944.

56. *Communist Review* (March 1946), 7.

57. R.P. Arnot, 'Notes on the Communist Effort for Unity', *Communist Review* (April 1946), 18–23.

58. CP/CENT, EC/01/04, EC, Minutes, 28 April 1946.

59. W. Rust, 'The Fight for a Communist Policy in Yugoslavia', *Daily Worker*, 6 July 1948.

60. CP/CENT/EC/01/07, EC, Minutes, 10 September 1949.

61. CP/CENT/EC/01/04, EC, Minutes, 13 March 1948.

62. CP/CENT/EC/01/06, EC, Minutes, 19 October 1948; Kerrigan gained 4,223 votes compared to the 13,706 gained by the Labour candidate.

63. CP/CENT/EC/01/07, EC Minutes, 10 September 1949; draft of the Political Report to the Twenty-First Congress, 26–28 November 1949, section 6.

64. *World News and Views*, 27 August 1949; CP/CENT/PC/02/03, Four-page copy of 'The Fight for our General Election Programme'.

65. CP/CENT/EC/02/02, Letter 2 August 1950; letter making much the same point 26 July 1950.

66. CP/CENT/EC/01/07, List of candidates endorsed by PC, 14 October 1950; CP/CENT/EC/02/03, EC Minutes, 8 September 1951.

67. *World News and Views*, 13 October 1951.

68. E. Burns, 'The Meaning of the Dollar Crisis', *Communist Review* (October 1947), 291–7.

69. J. Klugmann, 'America's Plan for Britain', *Communist Review* (October 1948), 291–8.

70. H. Pollitt, 'The Trade that Britain Needs', *Communist Review* (September 1949), 675–81.

71. Branson, *Communist Party 1941–1951*, pp. 129–31.

72. Ibid., pp. 132–3.

73. Ibid., pp. 133–40.

74. E. Barnett 'Nationalization of Transport', *Communist Review* (January 1948), 3–6; M. Hudson, 'The Nationalized Miners', *Communist Review* (September 1948), 272–8.

75. CP/CENT/CONG/05/03, Britain's Problems can be solved', Pollitt Report to CPGB Nineteenth Congress, 1947, p. 17.

76. CPGB, Nineteenth Congress, 1947.

77. *Labour Monthly* (July 1949), 201.

78. For a rebuttal of these charges see A. Horner, 'Trade Unions and Communism', *Labour Monthly* (February 1948), 41–52, also *Daily Worker* (6 January 1948).

79. *Daily Worker*, 12 January 1948.

80. Ibid., 16 January 1948.

81. Ibid., 2 February 1948.

82. Ibid., 10 June 1948.

83. CP/CENT/CONG/05/08, H. Pollitt, 'For Britain Free and Independent', Pollitt's report to Twentieth Congress, p. 47.

84. *World News and Views*, 6 March 1948, p. 99.

85. *Daily Worker*, 30 June 1948.

86. TUC, *Annual Report, 1948*, pp. 78, 274–5; *Daily Worker*, 28 October 1948; H. Pollitt, 'The Margate Conference', *Labour Monthly* (October 1948), 298–303.

87. *Daily Worker*, 15 March 1949.

88. *Daily Herald*, 18 September 1950.

89. Idem.

90. CP/CENT/EC/02/03, Mollie Guiart, 'The Fight for Peace and Unity', July 1950.

91. CP/CENT/EC/01/07, EC, Minutes, 21 July 1946.

92. Ibid., Report of the Organization Commission to the Executive Committee, 10 September 1946.

93. EC, Minutes, 14 September 1947.

94. *World News and Views*, 6 March 1948.

95. EC, Minutes, 13 March 1948.

96. CP/CENT/EC/01/07, Political Report to 1949 Conference, section IX.

97. CP/CENT/PC/02/04, Minutes, 18 June 1950, report attached.

98. Ibid., enlarged EC, Minutes, 18 June 1946.

99. Ibid., EC, Minutes, 19 January 1947.

100. H. Pollitt, 'The USSR and the Communist Party', *Communist Review* (November 1948), 324.

101. J. Gollan, 'Anglo-American Relations', *Communist Review* (June 1947),163–71.

102. CP/CENT/EC/01/02, EC, Minutes 12 July 1947.

103. EC, Minutes, 10 January 1949.

104. Ibid.

105. CP/CENT/EC/01/07, EC, Minutes, 10 September 1949; CP/CENT/PC/2/03, Press Statement for release to newspapers, Saturday 17 December 1949.

106. CP/CENT/EC/O1//07, EC, Minutes, 1 April, 13 May 1950.

107. Ibid., EC, Minutes, 8–9 July 1950.

108. H. Pollitt, 'Our Tasks', *Communist Review* (September 1950), 261.

109. *Hansard*, 14 November 1950.

110. Pollitt, 'Our Task', 259–62; E. Burns, 'New Stage in the Fight for Peace', *Communist Review* (November 1950), 323–7.

111. CP/CENT/PC/02/06, PC, Minutes, 4 June 1951.

112. J. Duclos article in *Labour Monthly* (August 1945); *World News and Views*, 18 August 1945.

113. H. Pollitt, report to EC, February 1945.

114. *Daily Worker*, 26 November 1945.

115. Morgan, *Pollitt*, pp. 148–9.

116. *Communist Review* (April 1947), 113–18; J. Symons and E.B., 'Britain's Road', *Communist Review* (July 1947), 200–7.

117. H. Pollitt, *Looking Ahead* (London, CPGB, 1947), pp. 87–8.

118. H. Pollitt, *Answers to Questions*, pp. 38–42; CP/CENT/COMM/01/01, *The British Road to Socialism* (London, CPGB, January 1951).

119. H. Pollitt, 'A New Perspective for the British People' and John Mahon, 'The Fight for Unity', *Communist Review* (February 1951), pp. 35–7.

120. E. Burns, 'People's Democracy – Britain's Path to Socialism', *Communist Review* (March 1951), 67–71.

121. J. Klugmann, 'Party Education and the British Road to Socialism'; *Communist Review* (June 1951), 178–81; M. Morris, 'The Social Services and the British Road to Socialism', *Communist Review* (July 1951), 201–7.

Chapter V British Communism: 'Intellectual Immorality', Division and Decline, 1951–91

1. Thompson, *The Good Old Cause*, pp. 91–3.

2. *Communist Review* (March 1953), 79–86.

3. CP/CENT/PC/02/05, PC, Minutes, 22 May 1952.

4. CP/CENT/PC/02/34, Report to the PC, 28 June 1956.

5. CP/CENT/PC/02/32, PC, Minutes, 18 October 1956, North-East District Report.

6. CP/CENT/PC/02/33, PC, Minutes, Draft Report of the NEC, 10 and 11 November 1956.

7. Eric Hobsbawm in *Marxism Today* (November 1986), p. 16.

8. *Daily Express*, 14 May 1956.

9. Morgan, *Pollitt*, pp. 171–2.

10. *Daily Express*, 14 May 1956. For an in-depth description of the Twentieth CPSU Congress and its effect on the CPGB see J. Saville, 'The XXth Congress and the British Communist Party', *Socialist Register*, 1976, 1–23.

11. Hobsbawm in *Marxism Today* p. 19.

12. CP/CENT/ORG/18/04, contains *The Reasoner* correspondence and many of E.P. Thompson's letters.

13. CP/CENT/PC/02/28, Copy of E.P. Thompson's letter to the editor of *World News and Views* and a copy of the article 'Winter Wheat in Omsk'.

14. Ibid., Letter from E.P. Thompson to J. Klugmann, 15 March 1956.

15. Ibid., 22 March 1956.

16. Ibid., 2 May 1956.

17. Ibid., Letter from James Klugmann to E.P. Thompson, 20 March 1956.

18. Ibid., Letter from E.P. Thompson to Bert Ramelson, 28 May 1956.

19. Ibid., Letters from E.P. Thompson to editor of *World News and Views*, 31 May, 8 June 1956.

20. PC/CENT/PC/02/23, PC files, June 1956.

21. CP/CENT/ORG/18/03, Copies of the first, July, edition and the third, November, edition of *The Reasoner*.

22. CP/CENT/EC/03/26, EC, Minutes, 8–9 September 1956.

23. Resolutions of the Communist Party EC, 'Lessons of the 20th Congress of the CPSU', *Marxist Quarterly* (July 1956).

24. CP/CENT/ ORG/18/04, Letter from E.P. Thompson to Howard [Hill], 9 November 1956.

25. *Yorkshire Post*, 15 November 1956.

26. Ibid., Letter from E.P. Thompson to Howard [Hill], 9 November 1956.

27. C. Thornton and W. Thompson, 'Scottish Communists 1956–7', *Science and Society*, vol. 61. no. 1 (Spring 1997), 68–93; also letter from Geoff Hodgson to Dylan Murphy, 8 April 1998.

28. CP/CENT/EC/04/01, EC, Minutes, 10–11 November 1956.

29. CP/CENT/ORG/18/05, upwards of 100 letters from districts and branches.

30. Ibid., Letter from B. Ramelson, no date.

31. CP/ CENT/04/02, 'Resolutions of branches to EC', 15 December 1956.

32. CP/CENT/ORG/18/05, Letter from R. Cocker, Halifax branch, to EC.

33. *Yorkshire Post*, 19 November 1956.

34. CP/CENT/PC/02/01, 'Some Thought About Intellectuals' presented to the Political Committee meeting, 17 January 1957.

35. Sandor Kopacsi, *In the Name of the Working Class* (London, Fontana, 1989).

36. Gollan Papers, CP/IND/GOLL/02/06.

37. Ibid., notes to EC meeting, 3 November 1956; J. Saville, 'The XXth Congress and the British Communist Party', *Socialist Register* (1976), 1–23.

38. CP/CENT/EC/04/01, Notes for meeting 3 November 1956.

39. M. MacEwan, 'The Day the Party had to Stop', *Socialist Register* (1976), 24–42.

40. Gollan Papers, CP/IND/GOLL/02/06.

41. *Marxism Today* (November 1986), p. 21.

42. CP/CENT/EC/04/01, Draft Resolution 'Stop the War in Egypt' and 'Draft Resolution on Hungary'.

43. CP/CENT/PC/02/33, George Matthews hand written notes, PC meeting, 15 November 1956.

44. Ibid., PC, Minutes, 15 November 1956.

45. Gollan Papers, CP/IND/GOLL/02/06.

46. Gollan Papers, CP/IND/GOLL/02/06, CP/IND/GOLL/02/07, articles for *Daily Worker*, 5 and 7 November 1956; report to EC, 10 November 1956; report to PC, 8 November 1956; the Draft Resolution on Hungary; and several other items.

47. *Yorkshire Post*, 14 November 1956.

48. CP/CENT/EC/04/02, EC, Minutes, 10–11 November 1956.

49. Ibid., Letter from P.J. Wexler, secretary of the Manchester University Graduates Branch of the CPGB.

50. Ibid., 'Resolutions from Party Organizations since Last Executive Committee', to the Executive Committee 15 December 1956. Ten resolutions asked for investigation and analysis of the situation and twenty-five asked for an independent investigation. There were no resolutions positively in favour of the EC position in the list.

51. *Yorkshire Post*, 15 November 1956.

52. Saville, 'XXth Congress', 16, 23.

53. CP/CENT/PC/02/34, Letter dated 5 December 1956.

54. Thompson, *The Good Old Cause*, pp. 105–6.

55. Letter from Geoff Hodgson to Dylan Murphy, 8 April 1998.

56. Thompson, *The Good Old Cause*, pp. 106–7, quoting Twenty-Eighth Communist Party Report, 1963.

57. CP/CENT/EC/04/03, Report to the Executive Committee of the Commission on Inner Party Democracy, p. 153.

58. The KGB released this information in November 1991, indicating that the sums fell in the 1970s and disappeared in 1979. R. Falber published an unrepentant article in *Change*, 15 November 1991, indicating that this had been kept from Nina Temple, the new General Secretary. The Political Committee then condemned the action.

59. W. Lauchlan, 'The Communist Party and the Daily Worker', *Marxism Today* (June 1959).

60. Thompson, *The Good Old Cause*, pp. 126–7.

61. *Daily Worker*, 14 August 1962.

62. *Marxism Today* (September and October 1963).

63. Michael McCreery, *Destroy the Old to Build the New!* (Scarborough, Committee to Defeat Revisionism for Communist Unity, November 1963).

64. CP/CENT/EC/12/08, EC, Minutes, 11-12 May 1968, Comments on the Draft of The British Road to Socialism.

65. CP/CENT/04/04, Eighteen-paged typed Political Report, 24 November 1957, p. 13.

66. Thornton and Thompson, 'Scottish Communists, 1956–57', pp. 78–9, 90–1.

67. J. Mahon, 'The Greater London Elections', *Marxism Today* (April 1964).

68. *Comment*, 6 February 1965.

69. *Daily Mail*, 21 June 1966.

70. *Daily Telegraph*, 23 June 1966.

71. CP/CENT/PC/10/08, Political Committee, 1 August 1968, statement on Government Incomes Policy and the Prices and Incomes Act.

72. CP/CENT/PC/10/10, PC, 17 October 1968, Draft Report of the Lancashire and Cheshire District Committee.

73. CP/CENT/EC/12/07, EC, 9–10 March 1968, Report from Peter Kerrigan.

74. Ibid., Draft Report on Branch Life to the EC, 21 October 1968.

75. CP/CENT/EC/12/07, Executive Committee, 9–10 March 1968, Report on The Fight Against Racial Discrimination.

76. CP/CENT/EC/12/07, EC, 11–12 May 1968, 'Rebellion, The Left and Ultra-Left Report', 12 May 1968, Report by J. Klugmann and Betty Read, Listing of Left and ultra-left organizations. Additional information on the Trotskyist movement was supplied by Martin White.

77. The Revolutionary Socialist League fused with WIL in 1943 to form the Revolutionary Communist Party.

78. B. Reid, 'Trotskyism in Britain Today', *Marxism Today* (September 1964), 274–83.

79. CP/CENT/EC/12/07, Executive Committee, 11–12 May 1968; 'Rebellion, The Left and Ultra-Left Report', 12 May 1968; Report by J. Klugmann and the Betty Reid listing.

80. CP/CENT/PC/10/05, Report on May Day Conference, 27–8 April 1968.

81. CP/CENT/PC/10/09, PC, 12 September 1968.

82. CP/CENT/PC/10/10, London District Report, 3 October 1968.

83. Ibid., PC, 17 October 1968, Draft Report of Lancashire and Cheshire District Committee.

84. Ibid. This information was normally part of a weekly letter which began in 1968.

85. *Morning Star*, 27 July 1968.

86. CP/CENT/PC/10/07, PC, Draft Report on Eastern Europe, 11 July 1968.

87. Ibid., 25 July 1968.

88. CP/CENT/PC/10/08, PC, 8 August 1968.

89. CP/CENT/ EC/12/111, various letters to EC, CP/CENT/EC/ 12/12.

90. PC, 29 August 1968.

91. CP/CENT/PC/10/09, PC, 12 September 1968.

92. Gollan Papers, CP/IND/GOLL/02/01, CPSU statement, 13 September 1968;CP/IND/GOLL/03/07, EC Resolution, 21-22 September 1968; CP/CENT/EC/12/11, EC material.

93. Gollan Papers, CP/IND/GOLL/03/07, news cutting of PC statement. This particularly contains numerous notes, files and rafts of statements on the Czechoslovakian position as it developed throughout the summer months. It contains *Pravda* material and much from Soviet News.

94. Ibid., YCL of GB statement.

95. CP/CENT/PC/10/10, Resolution to be presented to the London District Congress, 16–17 November 1968.

96. S. Carillo (General Secretary of the Spanish Communist Party), *Eurocommunism and the State* (London, Lawrence & Wishart, 1977), chapter on 'The Historical Roots of Eurocommunism', p. 111.

97. F. Claudin, *Eurocommunism and Socialism* (London, NLB, 1978).

98. Ibid., p. 7–9.

99. W. Thompson, *The Communist Movement since 1945* (Oxford, Blackwell, 1998), pp. 166–70.

100. CP/CENT/EC/15/14.

101. CP/CENT/EC/15/16.

102. CP/CENT/EC/17/07, Details of *Morning Star*'s golden anniversary.

103. *Comment*, 2 September 1967.

104. Ibid., 13 November 1967.

105. CP/CENT/EC/15/17, Surrey District vote to leave the CPGB and form the New Communist Party, supported 21 votes for 5.

106. The Thirty-Fourth Congress occurred between 15–18 November 1975. The Thirty-Fifth Congress took place between 12–15 November 1977.

107. *Comment*, 27 May 1978.

108. Ibid., 24 June 1978.

109. CP/CENT/CONG/06/04, *The British Road to Socialism* (London, CPGB, 1978), p. 54.

110. Ibid., p. 25.

111. CP/CENT/EC/15/16, Letter from Reuben Falber to EC, 18 July 1977 EC file.

112. CP/CENT/EC/17/07, EC, 10–11 March 1979.

113. CP/CENT/EC/17/06, for EC meeting 27–28 October 1979.

114. CP/CENT/EC/17/10, EC, July 1980, 'Internal Policy Review', p. 8.

115. Ibid., p. 11.

116. CP/CENT/EC/17/07.

117. *Comment*, 27 May 1978.

118. E. and R. Frow, *The Liquidation of the Communist Party of Great Britain* (Salford, Jubilee House, 1996).

119. Ibid., p. 3.

120. T. Lane, 'The Unions caught on an Ebb Tide', *Marxism Today* (September 1982), p.13.

121. E. and R. Frow, *Liquidation*, p. 23.

122. CP/CENT/PC/14/15, Draft Report on the *Morning Star*, 1 September 1977.

123. CPGB, Statement for the Executive Committee, Sub-Committee, the *Morning Star*, 1978, p. 14.

124. T. Lane, 'The Unions: caught on the Ebb Tide', pp. 6–13; CP/CENT/EC/19/02.

125. Thompson, *The Good Old Cause*, p. 184.

126. CP/CENT/EC/19/02, Letter from Tony Lane to EC, 26 August 1982.

127. CP/CENT/EC/15/14, Martin Jacques replaced James Klugmann, who had edited *Marxism Today* for twenty years, at the Executive Committee meeting, 12–13 March 1977.

128. CP/CENT/EC/11/01, Statement of EC, 12 September 1982.

129. CP/CENT/EC/19/02, EC, 11–12 September 1982.

130. *Morning Star*, 7 October 1982.

131. E. and R. Frow, *Liquidation*, p. 14; Thompson, *The Good Old Cause*, p. 185. Of course, the *Morning Star* did not have to consult the CPGB on appointments.

132. CP/CENT/EC/19/05, EC, 12–13 March 1983.

133. CP/CENT/EC/20/06, Copy of letter from Beatrix Campbell.

134. CP/CENT/EC/19/05, 'Report to EC', *Marxism Today*, 12–13 March 1983.

135. CP/CENT/EC/1/01, 'Factional & other Unprincipled Activity at the 38th Congress'.

136. CP/CENT/EC/20/06, East Midland Report, 1984 and Carlisle branch letter 17 January 1984.

137. Jon Blomfield, 'Crossed Lines: Communists in Search of an Identity', *Marxism Today* (April 1984), 27; Dave Cook, 'No Private Drama', *Marxism Today* (February 1985), 25–9.

138. H. Francis, 'Mining: The Popular Front', *Marxism Today* (February 1985), 12–15.

139. *Morning Star*, 11 June 1985.

140. CP/CENT/EC/21/06, Report to London District Congress, 24 November 1984 by Gordon McLennan; see also E and R. Frow, *Liquidation*, pp. 21–2.

141. CP/CENT/EC/21/06, Minutes of Special Executive Committee, 30 November 1984.

142. E and. R. Frow, *Liquidation*, pp. 20–1.

143. Ibid., p. 22.

144. *Morning Star*, 12 May 1985.

145. Ibid., 20 May 1985.

146. Blomfield, 'Crossed Lines', p.27.

147. CP/CENT/PC/16/08, Report to Political Committee, 15 December 1984.

148. J. Grahl and B. Rowthorne, 'Dodging the Taxing Questions', *Marxism Today* (November 1986), 24–5; B. Rowthorne in *The Guardian*, 14 January 1987, admitted that 'I've become a left reformist. The crisis has been long and drawn out, but I can't see the agencies of change and I'm not convinced about the socialist answers any more.'

149. CP/CENT/PC/17/04, Letter from Gordon McLennan to Political Committee, 24 March 1988.

150. CP/CENT/PC/16/18, PC, 2 February 1987.

151. CP/CENT/EC/22/07, Report to EC, 11–12 January 1986.

152. Ibid., PC, 14 February 1987.

153. CP/CENT/EC/23/03, EC Meeting, 14–15 November 1987.

154. P. Taaffe, *The Rise of Militant* (London, Militant Publications, November 1995), pp. 248–50, 257–69, 298–306.

155. CP/CENT/EC/13/05, Minutes from a Special Emergency Executive Committee Meeting, 28 June 1987, 'Some points of discussion from Nina Temple'.

156. Ibid., 18 July 1985.

157. CP/CENT/PC/16/18, Letter from Graham Taylor, Secretary of Brent North branch, 8 February 1987.

158. *Morning Star*, 11 November 1985.

159. CP/CENT/EC/24/01, includes the views of Nina Temple in this respect.

160. *Daily Telegraph*, 10 January 1990.

161. CP/CENT/ EC/24/01, Tony McNally, 'In Support of a Special Congress to Transform the Communist Party into a Broad Eco-Socialist Movement'.

162. Martin Jacques found that his power base shrank as the Party withdrew its subsidy of £50,000 per year. *Marxism Today* sought finance from outside the Party.
163. CP/CENT/EC/24/01, Letter from David Green to EC, 6 January 1990.
164. Thompson, *The Good Old Cause*, p. 200.
165. CP/CENT/CONG/25/06, Draft Constitution.
166. CP/CENT/PC/17/18, PC, 23 September 1991.
167. CP/CENT/EC/24/15, Letter from Dave Priscott to EC, 26 October 1991.
168. CP/CONT/CONG/25/06, *New Times: the Journal of the Democratic Left*, no. 1, 30 November 1991, report of Forty-Third Congress debate.
169. Ibid., Nina Temple's opening speech.

Epilogue and Conclusion

1. Copy in National Museum of Labour History, Manchester.
2. The 'Lost Sheep' Files, Labour Party Archives, General Secretary, Box 4; Communist Party Archives CS/Com/HR series and GS/Com/36ii.

A Short Bibliographical Essay

All the sources used in this book, both primary and secondary, are referred to in the chapter end notes. The principal purpose of this section is not to list them but to indicate the main books, articles and, in some cases, document collections that are readily accessible and that might be consulted profitably on various aspects of the history of communism in Britain. For books, only the date of publication is given.

For the specialist, there is a wide range of primary material on the CPGB, much of which has only become available in the last few years. The National Museum of Labour History contains an extensive archive of the personal papers of prominent communists such as R.P. Dutt, Harry Pollitt and John Gollan. There are also the transcripts, as well as tapes, of interviews with leading communists conducted by Kevin Morgan, plus copies of the main communist newspapers and journals such as *Inprecorr*, the *Daily Worker*, the *Morning Star*, *7 Days*, *Communist Review*, *World News and Views*, and many others. However, the main acquisition in recent years has been the CPGB archive, much of which has come in microfilm form from Moscow. It deals with the records and minutes of the Political Committee/Bureau, the Secretariat, and the Central Committee/Executive Committee of the Party. There are subcommittee minutes and reports. There is also a random mixture of documents in both the 1995 Moscow reels. The CPGB photographic archive was also deposited in the National Museum of Labour History at the beginning of 1998 and is in the process of being catalogued. These records have added considerably to our detailed knowledge of the inner workings of the CPGB, especially for the 1930s when the Central Committee and Political Bureau minutes were verbatim, which means that there are often 200 pages of minutes for one meeting. This is a far cry from the 1940s onwards when minutes might be summarized in less than a page, or in the 1950s when hand-written notes are often all that is available. There were later attempts to provide short typed reports of the meetings. There is a wealth of material in the Party records which have just been deposited. Each subcommittee of the Party had detailed files, although in-depth studies into each file is beyond the scope of this wide-ranging study of Marxism and the CPGB in Britain. This collection also contains numerous copies of the circulars and pamphlets issued by the CPGB, and, most obviously, various versions of *The British Road to Socialism* (1951, 1957, 1977) before it gave way to *Manifesto for New Times* (1989). In effect, there are several hundred pamphlets and their drafts in the CPGB Archive – some of them listed in the notes. Lastly, one might mention that the Public Record Office contains Home Office papers relating to communism and fascism in the 1930s and during wartime, and that there are some British Intelligence records on intercepted messages between the CPGB and the Comintern/CPSU from the autumn of 1934 until the end of 1936. For the pre-CPGB days, the writings of Karl Marx and Frederick Engels are useful, most obviously *Selected Correspondence* (4th printing, 1982).

Turning to secondary sources, it is clear that the 860 or so notes in this book provide a vast range of material on Marxism and the CPGB. It is impossible to give the full flavour of the debates that have convulsed communism in Britain but some of the main secondary sources connected with them are given below.

Until recently the Social Democratic Federation has not attracted much analytical literature. C. Tsuzuki, *H.M. Hyndman and British Socialism* (1961), is a very narrative study which makes no real attempt to analyse the role and place of Marxism in Britain. However, it is more than compensated for by S. Pierson, *Marxism and the Origins of British Socialism* (1973) and by M. Crick, *The History of the Social Democratic Federation* (1994). M. Bevir has also produced two excellent studies on Hyndman and his thought in 'H. M. Hyndman: A Rereading and a Reassessment', *History of Political Thought*, XII, 1 (Spring 1991) and 'The British Social Democratic Federation 1880–1885', *International Review of Social History*, XXXVII (1992). Although now challenged because of its representation of a dominating and inflexible Hyndman, one should not ignore the article by H. Collins entitled 'The Marxism of the Social Democratic Federation', in A. Briggs and J. Saville (eds.), *Essays in Labour History, 1886–1923* (1971).

As a subsidiary to this topic there has been considerable debate on the related question of why Britain never saw the creation of an effective or representative Socialist Unity party. Apart from some of the more general books on the SDF, the ILP and the Socialist League, the four main articles on this subject are M. Crick's, '"A Call to Arms": the Struggle for Socialist Unity in Britain, 1883-1914', in D. James, T. Jowitt and K. Laybourn (eds), *The Centennial History of the Independent Labour Party* (1992); K. Laybourn, 'The failure of Socialist Unity in Britain *c.* 1893–1914', *Transactions of the Royal Historical Society*, (Sixth Series, 4, 1994); K. Laybourn, 'A Story of Buried Talents and Wasted Opportunities: The Failure of the Socialist Unity Movement in Yorkshire 1911–1949', *The Journal of Regional and Local Studies*, 7, 2 (1987) and D. Morris, 'The Origins of the British Socialist Party', *North-West Society Bulletin*, 8 (1982–3).

William Morris was prominent in this socialist unity debate. He and the Socialist League are well provided for by E.P. Thompson's *William Morris: Romantic to Revolutionary* (1977) and F. MacCarthy, *William Morris: A Life of Our Time* (1994). There must also be upwards of another 100 books dealing with Morris, most of them worth dipping into. R.P. Arnot's reprint of a book he first wrote in the 1930s, *William Morris: the man and the myth* (London, 1964) should be examined if only because of the way in which he knocked down the idea that Morris's socialism was an aberration. S. Yeo, 'A New Life: The Religion of Socialism in Britain 1883–96', *History Workshop Journal*, no. 4 (1977) also provides an excellent, and controversial, study of the impact of William Morris's commitment to 'making socialists'. One should also not forget the valuable insights on Morris and the Socialist League offered by Y. Kapp, *Eleanor Marx* (1979).

Of the broad-ranging books on the history of British Marxism/communism there are only five that have attempted to give a full history of the Party. In 1937 Tom Bell, a founding member of the Party and still a communist, produced *The British Communist Party: A Short History* (1937) which was quickly withdrawn from circulation since it attacked the Party's sectarianism. The second was Henry Pelling's *The British Communist Party: A Historical Profile* (1957) which was a vehement, though not always well-informed, attack upon the Party. In recent years there has been Willie Thompson's *The Good Old Cause: British Communism 1920–1991* (1992). This is a full account of the history of the Party by a member who joined in 1962 and attempts to assess its history, warts and all. Despite his natural interest, it often lacks detailed discussion. B. Pierce and M. Woodhouse, *A History of Communism in Britain* (1995) is a more detailed and analytical study of communism but appeared too early to include any of the recent archival material that has become available. There is also F. Beckett's *Enemy Within: the Rise and Fall of the British Communist Party* (London, John Murray, 1995), which has two particularly useful chapters on the CPGB after 1970. Although not specifically a history of Communism in Great Britain, K. Laybourn, *The Rise of Socialism 1881–1951* (1997) does provide a wide-ranging study which examines Marxism and communism in Britain against other socialist movements.

The CPGB is well served with more detailed studies. J. Klugmann, *History of the Communist Party of Great Britain*, vol. 1, 1919–1924 (1968), and vol. 2, 1924–6; N. Branson, *History of the Communist Party of Great Britain 1927–1941* (1985), and *1941–1951* (1997) provide useful, but often uncritical analyses, of the switches in party policy, the abandonment of revolutionary struggles, the Moscow Show Trials and the failure to support workers' rights during the Second World War. In addition one can usefully consult W. Kendall, *The Revolutionary Movement 1900–1921* (1969), S. Macintyre, *A Proletarian Science: Marxism in Britain 1917–1937* (1980) and S. Macintyre, *Little Moscows*, (1980). L.J. Macfarlane, *The British Communist Party: Its Origins and Development until 1929* (1966) offers a rather administrative approach to the study of the CPGB. On the communists and trade unions R. Martin, *Communism and British Trade Unions 1924–1933* (1969) examines the rise and fall of the National Minority Movement and N. Fishman, *The British Communist Party and the Trade Unions*

(1995) takes the issue further and suggests that there was little that divided Communist and Labour by the late 1930s. Indeed, she argues that the Communist Party was increasingly successful between 1933 and 1945 because it followed the Harry Pollitt and Jimmy Campbell approach of playing down the rank-and-file interests in favour of those of the official trade union movement. K. Morgan, *Against Fascism and War: Rupture and Constitution in British Communist Politics, 1935–1941* (1989) focuses upon the CPGB's attack upon fascism and the difficulties that the Russian-German pact of August 1939 created for the Party, especially in the light of the fact that there appears to have been broad support for the new Comintern-inspired anti-war line. For a more wide-ranging study of the factors that made Marxism a failure, based upon the nature and structure of British society, R. McKibbin, 'Why was there no Marxism in Britain?', *English Historical Review*, (1984) is a valuable, innovative and decidedly non-Marxist study. Also for a critical study on the formation of the CPGB one should look at R.C. Challinor, *The Origin of British Bolshevism* (1977). One should also not forget the excellent studies of the Communist leaders, most obviously K. Morgan, *Harry Pollitt* (1993).

For more recent events E. and R. Frow, *The Liquidation of the Communist Party of Great Britain* (1996) is particularly useful and contentious. It examines the way in which the Party lost support and fragmented, especially from the mid-1970s and the early 1980s with the split between the Eurocommunist-dominated Party and the Moscow-dominated *Daily Worker*.

The international context in which the CPGB operated has been vital to this book, particularly the work of the Comintern. Apart from the works already mentioned, the most useful books are K. McDermott and J. Agnew, *The Comintern: A History of International Communism from Lenin to Stalin* (1996); A. J. Sobolev, *et. al., Outline History of the Communist International* (1971); E.H. Carr, *Twilight of the Comintern*, (1982); F. Claudin, *The Communist Movement: From Comintern to Cominform* (1975) and M. Johnstone, 'The CPGB, the Comintern and the War, 1939–1941: Filling in the Black Spots', *Science and Society* (spring 1997). The last of these stresses the way in which the Comintern determined the changing position of the CPGB on the Second World War. Also useful on this issue is S. Williams, *1939: The Communist Party and the War* (1984). There is also an informative article by K. Morgan on 'The CPGB and the Comintern Archive', *The Journal of Socialist History* (1992, part 2).

Trotsky and Trotskyism have obviously shaped both international and British communism, especially since they represented a challenge to the Comintern and the CPGB for abandoning revolutionary activity in favour of the compromising policy of the Popular Front in 1935. The most useful publications on this are D. Dimitri Volkogonov, *Trotsky: The Eternal Revolutionary* (1996); L. Trotsky, *Selected Writings 1930–40*, several volumes (1970–3), and S. Bornstein and A. Richardson, *Against the Stream: A History of the Trotskyist Movement in Britain 1924–1938* (1986).

INDEX